Jane Austen

A NEW REVELATION

Jane Austen

A NEW REVELATION

Nicholas Ennos

Senesino Books Limited
31 Sackville Street
Manchester
M1 3LZ

ISBN 978-0957687-004

British Library Cataloguing in Publication Data.
A catalogue record for this book is available from the British Library.

Typeset by Troubador Publishing Ltd, Leicester, UK
Printed and bound in the UK by TJ International, Padstow, Cornwall

TO MITYA

Mindenemet magammal hordozom.
És ami enyém volt, enyém marad
Innen is, túl is a csillagokon,
Mert lélek vagyok, végtelen, szabad.
Bennem elférnek mind, kik rámhajoltak,
A fák, s a lombok – s az aluvó rét,
Bennem elférnek az élök s a holtak.

All that I have I bring with me
And all that was mine stays with me
Here on earth and beyond the stars
For my soul is free and without end
In it there is room for all who leaned on me
The leafy trees and the sleepy meadows
In it there is room for the living and the dead

(Sándor Reményik)

Acknowledgements

Firstly, I would like to thank my wife Larisa for all her help and support with this project, including her pencil illustrations.

Secondly, I would like to thank all those who gave me permission to use parts of their work in this book, and to reproduce their illustrations and paintings. In particular, I would like to thank David Gilson and Peter Jones, Librarian of King's College, Cambridge for the use of the poem by James Austen. I have used my best endeavours to contact everyone I can to obtain permissions for any quotations and would welcome any correspondence from those who I have been unable to contact.

I would like to apologise for the lack of footnote references or superscript numbers, although full references, for those who would like them, are given for all quotations in the bibliography. This is something that I feel strongly about.

I would wish to return to the former practice that read non-fiction as literature, rather than academic research. Lately literature has become increasingly corralled within that by now rather tired form, the unaptly named novel. Another consideration is that I have written my book for the intelligent reader rather than the academic. A further justification is that the presence of footnotes or reference numbers can lend a spurious air of authority to even the most outrageous falsehoods.

Apology

Tuon aber ich diu gelîche nuo
und schepfe mîniu wort dar zuo,
daz mir ir iegelîches sage
von disem maere missehage,
so wirbe ich anders, danne ich sol.
ich entuon es niht: sî sprâchen wol
und niwan ûz edelem muote
mir unde der werlt ze guote.
binamen si tâten ez in guot.
und swaz der man in guot getuot,
daz ist ouch guot und wol getân.
aber als ich gesprochen hân,
daz sî niht rehte haben gelesen,
daz ist, als ich iu sage, gewesen:

But were I now to do the same
And in this book of mine should claim
That every word of theirs they write
Is not pleasing in my sight
I would act wrongly, truth to tell
I won't do this: for they wrote well
And their intentions, as they understood
Were only for mine and for the world's good.
No doubt they wrote in good faith for us
And anything which a man does thus
Is also good, nobly done and sincere
But as I have already made it clear
What they have written is untrue
This is the case, as I have told it you.

(Gottfried von Straßburg, Tristan)

Contents

1.

Introduction

Ich hân mir eine unmüezekeit
der werlt ze liebe vür geleit
und edelen herzen z'einer hage,
den herzen, den ich herze trage,
der werlde, in die mîn herze siht.
ine meine ir aller werlde niht
als die, von der ich hoere sagen,
diu keine swaere enmüge getragen
und niwan in vröuden welle sweben.
die lâze ouch got mit vröuden leben!
Der werlde und diseme lebene
enkumt mîn rede niht ebene.

An endeavour I have undertook
Set out in this my modest book
Of the world to please the better part,
To bring solace to their noble heart
The world over which my heart has charge –
This part – but not the world at large
Like those of whom I've heard it said
Believe everything that they have read.
Their only wish in life is this:
To remain happy in their ignorant bliss.
Of their world here you will not find a trace
I gladly leave them to God's grace!

(Gottfried von Straßburg, Tristan)

1

Literary biography is the illegitimate child of biography and literary criticism. The literary biographer is faced on the one hand with the life of the writer and, on the other, their works. Literary biography is the attempt to shoehorn the one into the other. Whilst literacy criticism is an art using the highest intellectual powers to investigate the works of the author, identification of the author usually consists of nothing more than a cursory inspection of the flyleaf.

To me it is incontestable that the great works of these two authors, Fanny Burney, who has been called by Virginia Woolf "The mother of English fiction", and Jane Austen, compared by Thomas Babington Macaulay and George Henry Lewes to "a prose Shakespeare", were the work of one and the same directing mind, a woman of outstanding genius who was forced to remain anonymous during her lifetime, but whose genius and generosity were reflected in her colourful and eventful life.

This book is written for those people with enquiring minds who wish to discover the life of this woman and to look for her reflection in the great works that she left behind her, which were to revolutionise literature, create the modern novel and reward readers of future times with a legacy of literary masterpieces. Once a biographer is no longer burdened with the task of describing the inconsequential and uneventful lives of Jane Austen and Fanny Burney, he is free to open up vistas revealing the creative mind that lay behind these works of genius.

2.

The Authorship Problem

Ir ist sô vil, die des nu pflegent,
daz si daz guote z'übele wegent,
daz übel wider ze guote wegent:
die pflegent niht, si widerpflegent

So many critics now we read
That judge what's good as bad, indeed,
The bad, in turn, to good transmute
They bring critics into disrepute.

(Gottfried von Straβburg, Tristan)

Brian Dillon in his essay *Circumventing the Biographical Subject: Jane Austen and the Critics* states that the evidence on which biographers have connected the life of Jane Austen to the books which bear her name is extremely flimsy. He writes that the existing material relating to Jane Austen's biography is "relatively slight", consisting merely of "a volume of censored letters, a brief biographical statement penned by one of her brothers a year after her death, a memoir by a nephew recollected in tranquility over half a century after her death". He says that readers often "wonder how this simplified biographical subject could have authored such powerful, challenging novels". In particular he notes that "Readers are often troubled by the apparent gap between her life and her art when it comes to the issue of marriage." Could the author of *Pride and Prejudice* really be a woman with no personal experience of sex or

3

marriage? Dillon concludes that "The private Jane Austen remains far too nebulous to function as a definitive origin for her works of fiction".

The novels of the author now known as Jane Austen were all published anonymously in her lifetime and, upon her death, the majority of Jane Austen's letters were burned or heavily censored by her sister, Cassandra. Further letters that may have been kept by her brother, Henry, or other relations, have disappeared. The letters of Jane Austen that remain are long-winded, inconsequential, of little literary or artistic merit, and barely discuss the literary and philosophical themes of the books. There is no single record of Jane Austen ever meeting with any other author, or of her mixing with literary and artistic society of the time in any way. From the evidence of her own letters and the letters of her relations, we know that she occupied most of her time doing needlework and other home crafts. When she died in 1817 she was buried in Winchester Cathedral in Hampshire, where her memorial stone on the floor of the cathedral makes no mention of her being a writer. Indeed, as we shall see, the very idea of her being a writer was considered a joke by most of her close family, and astonished her acquaintances.

The first two novels now known as those of Fanny Burney were similarly published anonymously. Frances, or "Fanny" Burney was considered by her own family, however, to be of low intelligence. With no formal education, she acted for much of her life as secretary to her musician father, and spent several years working in a ceremonial position in the English court, where her duties related to the upkeep of the Queen's dresses. Thus, like Jane Austen, she was also an amateur seamstress. At the age of forty-one she married a penniless French exile and no novels appeared under her name for the last twenty-five years of her life.

The works that bear the names of Jane Austen and Fanny Burney are the product of a mind which is the complete opposite of their characters; the mind of a woman with a deep experience and understanding of love and especially of marriage, of outstanding education and a brilliant mind.

There has always been a problem in reconciling the life of Jane Austen with the works which bear her name. Jane Austen herself was a retiring spinster with only a basic primary education, who knew little of London society, remained unmarried all her life and spent most of her life in rural backwaters, sinking gradually into increasing genteel poverty. In her later years this poverty was only relieved by her brother Edward offering her, her sister and her mother a rent-free cottage to live in on his estate in Chawton in Hampshire. It was also relieved, but to a very small degree, by the income from the novels which came to bear her name.

To avoid further circumlocution, I will from now on distinguish the authors Jane Austen and Fanny Burney and the women themselves by writing the names of the authors in italics. As mentioned, one thing *Jane Austen* and *Fanny Burney* had in common is not widely known to the general reading public: they both published the novels for which they are famous anonymously (with the exception of *Fanny Burney's* last two novels, *Camilla* and *The Wanderer*). Until the publication of *Fanny Burney's* third novel, *Camilla*, in 1796, it was left to "general report" to spread the rumours of Fanny Burney being the author. It would seem paradoxical that an author who wished to remain anonymous should then proceed to spread rumours of her authorship. As Mr Darcy in *Pride and Prejudice* might have said, "Surely that would defeat the purpose." It is much more likely that such rumours would be spread to further the concealment of the true author.

All of *Jane Austen's* novels which were published in her lifetime were published anonymously. Jane Austen was only revealed as the author of these novels by her brother Henry, informally to certain friends and, in writing, in his *Biographical Notice of the Author* prefacing *Northanger Abbey*, dated 13th December 1817, the year of her death. Crucially, as we shall see, this revelation was made by the husband of the true author, presumably wishing thereby to protect the true author's identity.

We are fortunate in the solution of the authorship question for Jane Austen and Fanny Burney, in that there remain in existence many examples of the writings of both of them, which we can be certain were written by them. As we shall see, this genuine writing by the two of them is so decidedly inferior to the language of the accomplished novels which now bear their names that it greatly strengthens the case that neither of them were authors. I refer to the personal letters of Jane Austen, widely considered a great disappointment by literary critics, and to the only two books published by Fanny Burney after 1813, *The Wanderer* and *Memoirs of Doctor Burney*, both of which were considered by critics at the time to be not just bad writing, but the worst kind of writing.

At this point, the reader may be wondering "What is the link between *Jane Austen*, one of the most famous authors in the English language, and *Fanny Burney*, a fine author but one who has been relatively neglected since her death and much of whose work has not been widely read between her death and recent times?" In setting out to write this book, I at first intended only to reveal the true author of *Jane Austen's* novels but, as I researched the matter more fully, the works of *Jane Austen* became more and more interconnected with those of *Fanny Burney*, so that it became second nature to me to think of the two authors as one.

In writing this book, some readers may argue with my identification of real people and real places with places and characters in the works of *Fanny Burney* and *Jane Austen*. They will state that characters and places in fiction are creations of the imagination and do not correspond with real people or places. However, the reason I feel justified in doing this is that it has been so widely practised by previous authors who have written about *Jane Austen's* life and works. Even those biographers who deny that *Jane Austen's* works are based on real people or places later go on to identify characters and places in the books with those in the life of

Jane Austen. There is also overwhelming evidence that, in naming places and people, the author drew on real places and people in selecting such names.

3.

If Jane Austen Did Not Write The Books That Bear Her Name, Then Who Did?

Der guote man swaz der in guot
und niwan der werlt ze goute tuot,
swer daz iht anders wan in gout
vernemen wil, der missetuot

When a good man acts with good intent,
Only seeking what is good for the world,
It is wrong for anyone to misrepresent
Him and not take him at his word.

(Gottfried von Straβburg, Tristan)

The reason why I began to investigate the authorship of the works of *Jane Austen* was principally the incongruity between the life of Jane Austen and the world view portrayed in her books. There seems to be little connection between the two. I am not alone in finding this. Carol Shields has written in her biography of Jane Austen:

"The two 'accounts' – the life and the work – will always lack congruency and will appear sometimes to be in complete contradiction".

She also writes that "what is known of Jane Austen's life will never be enough to account for the greatness of her novels". The next question it was necessary to ask therefore was, if Jane Austen did not write these works, then who did? There are two ways in which to determine the identity of the author, the instinctive and the logical. I would like to claim that my approach was logical but I would have to admit that it was instinctual.

When considering who the author was, it is imperative that we do not forget the quality of *Jane Austen's* work. The writer, George Henry Lewes, and the historian, Thomas Babington Macaulay, compared her to a "prose Shakespeare". Macaulay wrote of *Jane Austen* in an article on *Fanny Burney* in *The Edinburgh Review* of 1843 that "She has given us a multitude of characters, all, in a certain sense, common-place – all such as we meet every day. Yet they are all as perfectly discriminated from each other as if they were the most eccentric of human beings." *Jane Austen* has always been widely admired by great writers. Virginia Woolf called her "the most perfect artist among women, the writer whose books are immortal". George Henry Lewes himself wrote of her in 1852: "First and foremost let Austen be named, the greatest artist that has ever written, using the term to signify the most perfect mastery over the means to her end."

Therefore one would expect the author to be a person of genius with a very high, if not exceptional, level of education. The author must indeed be considered one of the leading figures of Enlightenment Europe. Jane Austen herself plainly fails to meet any of these criteria since any claims for her genius rest solely on the works that now bear her name. Although her father was well educated, as a poorly paid clergyman with a large family, he did not have the means to provide a proper education for his two daughters, Jane and Cassandra. The education of the two girls consisted merely of two years up to 1786 (Jane Austen was born in 1775) at a basic girls' boarding school (which **were** very basic in those days). Her education was gained at the Abbey School, a girls' boarding school in Reading run by a Sarah Hackitt, who styled herself for effect "Mrs

La Tournelle". Here the main subjects learnt were spelling, needlework and French. Such a school was later to be described ironically in *Jane Austen's* novel *Emma,* in the shape of Mrs Goddard's school, to which the illegitimate Harriet Smith was sent by her unknown (but reasonably caring) father. Mrs Goddard's school was described there as a "real, honest old-fashioned Boarding-school, where a reasonable quantity of accomplishments were sold at a reasonable price, and where girls might be sent to be out of the way and scramble themselves into a little education, without any danger of coming back prodigies".

There was a painting of the Abbey School in Jane Austen's house in Chawton in Hampshire, and the caption to the painting there admitted that the Abbey School resembled Mrs Goddard's school as described above in *Emma.* The *Jane Austen* expert Deirdre Le Faye also agrees this to be the case. Those who claim Jane Austen to be the true author of the works that bear her name are therefore left with a huge educational deficit. To make up this deficit, biographers of Jane Austen often claim, without direct evidence, that she engaged in "omnivorous reading". They rely heavily on her supposed reading from the private library of five hundred books owned by her father. These "five hundred books" have become as much of a source of pride to Jane Austen biographers as her "four-and-twenty families" were to Mrs Bennet in *Pride and Prejudice.* Some biographers even claim that Jane Austen had rigorous private tuition by her father, but there is no evidence to support this either. It seems very unlikely that her father, George Austen, would have given any private tuition to his daughter if he was only willing to send her to a basic boarding school for two years. Mr Austen had a large family to support and was obliged to supplement his limited clergyman's income by teaching Latin and Greek to the sons of noblemen and rich gentry, who stayed in his house as boarders. Indeed, some biographers believe that Jane and Cassandra were only sent to the Abbey School in order to create space for these boarders, which is not an unlikely supposition. This shows that he was not in a financial position to use his time to give a free education to his own daughter, a female education which in any event would have been most unusual at the time.

David Nokes in his biography *Jane Austen – a Life*, however, attempts to make up for this deficit in Jane Austen's education as follows:

> "Jane Austen's education began the day that she left school. Unlike Mrs Cawley's school at Southampton and Madame La Tournelle's school at Reading, Mr Austen's library at Steventon opened out to her a whole world of intellectual adventures. Browsing among the several hundred volumes on her father's shelves, she fed her youthful imagination with works of history and poetry, essays, sermons, plays, and, above all, novels. The family were all 'great novel-readers & not ashamed of being so' and she readily pounced on volumes of Fielding and Richardson, Goldsmith, Swift and Defoe… *The Arabian Nights* was another early favourite, together with Johnson's *Rasselas*."

A "forensic profiler" would no doubt tell us, as does common sense, that the brilliancy of the author's works would have revealed itself in the author's life. The novels of *Jane Austen* reveal an author with a tendency to be wayward, brilliant, unconventional and unattracted to general social life, but with a preference for deeper and more intellectual study and relationships. Jane Austen herself, from what we know of her from her own letters and the events of her life, had a stolidity and love for routine. Moreover, the letters of hers which survive contain very little discussion of intellectual matters or love of wordplay. They are mostly confined to accounts of everyday events. Her relationships with others, apart from her sister Cassandra, appear to have been of a fairly superficial nature.

The logical approach to determine the true author of the novels of *Jane Austen* would be to make a list of the author's qualities based on reading her works and then to find the person in Jane Austen's life who most aptly fitted these criteria. From the evidence of the novels, I list the author's attributes as follows:

A highly educated and intelligent woman, well read in European literature of the time and especially in French literature in the original language, well acquainted with Classical Literature, with a knowledge of it in the original Latin and Greek; a "lady" of independent means, who did not need to write to earn a living, rich enough to put principle before necessity and to write at leisure; a woman who did not depend on men financially, with experience of marriage in her own life, and with a somewhat cynical view of marriage; of equivalent social standing to the men who surrounded her, of independent thought, an outsider looking in, whose social class lay somewhere between the rich gentry and the lower aristocracy but remained uncertain and shadowy; a woman able to move freely between the gentry and aristocracy but never completely at home in either class, a lover of language and languages, a lover of music and theatre, but with little interest in painting or visual art; somebody closely connected with France for whom the French language was almost a second mother tongue; a lover of London with a somewhat patronising attitude to "provincial manners" and a person who was sexually attracted to, and probably married to, the more feminine, artistic kind of man. In religion, a person belonging to the Church of England but with Catholic tendencies, but who witnessed her religion in the principles of her everyday life and the practical action of helping people, rather than by outward devotion. Above all, the author was the product of the Enlightenment Europe of the eighteenth century, the "Age of Reason", who probably grew up at a time when Enlightenment ideas held sway, but whose novels, when published, were already out of date and out of touch with the Romantic movement then sweeping Europe. This suggests that the author of the *Jane Austen* novels would have been born in the 1770s at the very latest. Lord David Cecil has written of *Jane Austen* that she "was born in the eighteenth century; and spiritually speaking, she stayed there".

I have laid out the list above and it may be possible to draw up a long list of candidates, including Jane Austen herself, to see who fits the bill most closely. However, there is one person in Jane Austen's milieu above all who clearly stands out as the most likely to be the author of *Jane Austen's* works. She could not have been more closely connected with Jane Austen. She was twice related to Jane Austen; not only was she Jane Austen's first cousin but also the wife of Jane Austen's favourite brother, Henry. We have documentary evidence that she was staying at Steventon Rectory in Hampshire, the home of Jane Austen's family, during the late 1780s and the first half of the 1790s at the time that the first works of *Jane Austen* were conceived and written. The first novels of *Jane Austen* were later published from this lady's house in London between 1811 and 1813, and this lady almost certainly acted as financial guarantor for the cost of their publication. She had also received in her youth the most advanced literary, artistic and musical education that eighteenth century London could afford.

The lady I am describing is Eliza Austen, previously Eliza de Feuillide, née Eliza Hancock. I shall refer to her throughout this book as "Eliza". The reason for this is not because I wish to show any familiarity or identify closely with her, but merely because of the different surnames she had at different times of her life. This could cause confusion to a modern reader, as indeed it did among her family and friends. They also referred to her just as "Eliza" (coincidentally, also the name by which the heroine of *Jane Austen's Pride and Prejudice* was referred to by her family and friends. Critics have often viewed Eliza Bennet as a portrait of the author).

The present biographies of Jane Austen and Fanny Burney, while very scholarly and detailed, present one with a Ptolemaic world view. While Fanny Burney and Jane Austen are the central characters in these universes, there can only be anomalies in the system of each, which every successive biographer tries to remedy by adding an extra sphere, without ever achieving harmony. By placing Eliza at the centre of my biography, I hope to replace this Ptolemaic world view with a Copernican one, in which events fall into place naturally. I cannot ascertain every fact, just as every event in the universe cannot be tested, but there is at least a satisfying coherence between what we know of Eliza's life and the works of *Jane Austen* and *Fanny Burney*.

In this book I will first briefly outline the details of Eliza's life, and I will demonstrate how the chronology of her life fits in with the authorship of the works now bearing the names of *Fanny Burney* and *Jane Austen*. I will then discuss the authors who were the greatest influences on her. Then I will detail the connections between Eliza, Jane Austen and Fanny Burney and how their lives were intertwined. This will lead on to a deeper analysis of how their lives are reflected in the novels of *Jane Austen* and *Fanny Burney*. I will also examine those works of *Jane Austen* which were only published many years after her death, such as her "Juvenilia" and Jane Austen's letters to her sister, Cassandra, and compare the literary quality of the letters of Jane Austen with those written by Eliza.

Next, I will show the means by which the Austen family in the nineteenth century attempted to cover up the evidence of Eliza's authorship, primarily through the destruction of any documentation mentioning or relating to her, but also through the publication of authorised family histories portraying Jane Austen as a reclusive author never mixing with literary society in any way. I will then go on to describe the life of Fanny Burney, which was a curious one. I will show how her famous diary was a mixture of truth and invention, and how she led a double life pretending to be a famous novelist. This was recognised subconsciously by Hester Thrale, a leading literary lady and friend of Fanny's father, who described her as an "Actress not a Woman of Fashion". After examining in more detail the novels of *Jane Austen*, I will show the importance in Eliza's life of Warren Hastings, the Governor General of India. I bring forward new information about him which has recently been published in Germany, revealing more about the personal side of Warren Hastings. Finally, I will explore the very real possibility that Eliza wrote in several different genres using a different pseudonym for each, as was the practice of the time.

Throughout the book I have tried to back up all the points I have made with relevant evidence which, I hope, will "lend credence to all my assertions".

4.

The Life Of Eliza Hancock

"Every man's work, whether it be literature or music or pictures or architecture or anything else, is always a portrait of himself, and the more he tries to conceal himself the more clearly will his character appear in spite of him."

(Samuel Butler, *The Way of All Flesh*)

The life of Eliza Hancock was far from uneventful and indeed biographers of Jane Austen often contrast the adventure and colour of Eliza's life strongly with the humdrum existence of their subject.

Elizabeth Hancock was born on 22nd December 1761 in Calcutta, in Bengal in North East India, now known as Kolkata. Her mother, Philadelphia Austen, was the sister of Jane Austen's father, George Austen, the Rector of Steventon in Hampshire. Philadelphia was born in Tonbridge in Kent. She was born in 1730 but by 1737 both her parents had died. It is not known exactly where she was brought up. There is evidence that during her youth she was helped by members of the Freeman family, who were maternal cousins who lived in Hertfordshire; Eliza's mother and father were always grateful for the generosity shown in particular by John Cope Freeman to her when she was young. It is possible, as I shall discuss later, that one of the homes of the Freeman family in Hertfordshire may have served as the model for Mr Bennet's estate of "Longbourn" in *Pride and Prejudice*.

On 9th May 1745, having few other prospects, Philadelphia was apprenticed by her family to a milliner (a cap or hat maker) in

Russell Street, Covent Garden, London by the name of Cole. Millinery and dressmaking at this time was work that was hard and also not entirely respectable, since many of these milliners shops in Covent Garden were a front for the more lucrative trade of prostitution which took place at the rear of the shop.

Philadelphia Austen's situation in life did not offer her a great future. As a young and beautiful woman, however, she was able to find a way out of these unpromising circumstances. She made up her mind to travel by ship to India aboard the *Bombay Castle* to find a husband. So on 18th January 1752 she set sail to India, where European women were in short supply, and were usually able to find a husband soon after their arrival. Such cargos of young women were known disparagingly at the time as "the fishing fleet". Such a practice was later to be lamented by *Jane Austen* in one of the first short novels attributed to her, *Catharine, or the Bower*. Philadelphia Austen's ship survived the voyage from England, which was often extremely dangerous, and arrived safely in Madras (now known as Chennai), on 4th August 1752. On 22nd February 1753 she was married to one Tysoe Saul Hancock, a surgeon belonging to the East India Company, the private company which controlled the British part of India at that time. It was this company which was eventually to develop into the British government in India. It was probably a marriage that had been arranged before her journey through Philadelphia's uncle, Francis Austen, who was Mr Hancock's lawyer and man of affairs in England. It may also have been from Francis Austen that Philadelphia had received the large sum of money needed to undertake the voyage. Mr Austen was a rich lawyer and his stern portrait by Ozias Humphrey may be viewed today in the Graves Art Gallery in Sheffield. Mr Hancock himself had studied medicine in London and travelled to India in 1745, where he became an employee of the East India Company, nominally in the position of surgeon. However, like most employees of the East India Company at the time, his main intention was to make a large sum of money through trading activities with the local population, and to return home with his profits as soon as possible before he could succumb to the risks of illness that life in India always threatened for the European. In fact he later wrote in his one of his letters to his wife that he detested the practice of surgery.

Mr Hancock and his new wife lived together at the British base of Madras until 1759, when Mr Hancock was sent north up the East Coast of India to Calcutta, the British base in Bengal, after he had been appointed as surgeon there by Lord Clive, the Governor of Bengal. It was in Calcutta that Mr and Mrs Hancock met Warren Hastings, then an employee of the East India Company but who was later to rise to the top of the administration in India as Governor General of Bengal in 1771 and later, in 1773, as Governor General of India. Warren Hastings and Mr Hancock became business partners, trading in various goods including rice and opium. Sadly, Warren Hastings' infant daughter, Elizabeth, and his wife, Mary, both died, in 1758 and 1759 respectively. After his wife's death, Warren Hastings and Philadelphia were ready to find comfort for their respective circumstances in each other's company. A love affair ensued and Philadelphia gave birth on 22nd December 1761 to a daughter, Elizabeth. The fact that Philadelphia's daughter was given the same name as Warren Hastings's dead daughter may be no coincidence (one is reminded of Thomas Hardy's novel *The Mayor of Casterbridge* in which Henchard's wife gives the daughter of her new husband, Newson, the same name (Elizabeth-Jane) as Henchard's infant daughter who had died). As we will see, there is almost indisputable evidence, from various sources, that Eliza's biological father was not Mr Hancock, but Warren Hastings.

According to biographers of Jane Austen such as Claire Tomalin, Hastings and Hancock became business partners in the trade of "salt and timber and carpets, Bihar opium, and rice for the Madras market" and this was the source of Hastings' wealth. However, this was probably not in fact the main source of it. As I shall explain later, most of Hastings' wealth was probably acquired by corrupt and secretive means.

When Elizabeth Hancock was born on 22nd December 1761, Mr and Mrs Hancock had been married for eight years without issue, reinforcing the idea that the father of the child was not Mr Hancock. At her baptism the next month Warren Hastings was present as her godfather. We have first-hand knowledge of the matter through the letters of Mr Hancock to his wife Philadelphia, written to her at a later date, at a time when he was living in India and she in England. Mr Hancock all but confirms Warren Hastings' parenthood in a letter dated 11th December 1772 in which he says that Warren Hastings had given 40,000 rupees (approximately £5,000) to him for the benefit of Eliza "under the polite Term of making his God daughter a present". In an earlier letter to his wife of 23rd September 1772 Hancock had written that "Debauchery under the polite name of Gallantry is the Reigning Vice of the Settlement". (We can therefore be sure that "polite name" was Hancock's term for a euphemism, and that the idea that Hastings was Eliza's godfather was merely a polite fiction). In the same letter of 23rd September 1772, Hancock also wrote pointedly to his wife, "You yourself know how impossible it is for a young Girl to avoid being attached to a Young Handsome Man whose address is agreeable to Her."

There had been great secrecy surrounding Warren Hastings' gift to Betsy (as Eliza was known as a child), a secrecy which would not have been necessary had Warren Hastings been merely her godfather. In his letter of 11th December 1772 Mr Hancock wrote to his wife of this gift of £5,000 to Eliza:

"Let me caution you not to acquaint even the Dearest Friend you have with this Circumstance; tell Betsy only that her Godfather has made her a great Present, but not the particulars; let Her write a proper Letter on the Occasion."

There is also in existence a letter from Lord Clive, the then Governor of Bengal, Warren Hastings' superior at this time, who wrote to his wife in the late summer of 1765, warning Lady Clive not to associate with Mrs Hancock:

"In no circumstances whatever keep company with Mrs. Hancock for it is beyond a doubt that she abandoned herself to Mr. Hastings, indeed, I would rather you had no acquaintance with the ladies who have been in India, they stand in such little esteem in England that their company cannot be of credit to Lady Clive."

Deirdre Le Faye, in her excellent biography of Eliza, *Jane Austen's Outlandish Cousin: The Life and Letters of Eliza de Feuillide* is, however, in a small minority of writers on *Jane Austen* in denying that Warren Hastings was Eliza's father. Most biographers of Jane Austen agree either expressly or tacitly that Eliza was in reality his natural daughter. Deirdre Le Faye, however, writes that this was just scurrilous gossip put about by Jenny Strachey, whose husband was Lord Clive's secretary. It seems likely that she is correct, in that the gossip was put about by Jenny Strachey. Mr Hancock wrote to his wife in November 1773: "I am much mistaken if Lady Clive's most extraordinary Coolness be not owing to the Pride of that Woman". However, Mr Hancock seems here to be criticising Jenny Strachey's indiscretion rather than her veracity.

Later in life, Eliza herself was to demonstrate in many ways, both consciously and unconsciously, that she believed herself to be Hastings' daughter. She named her son, Hastings, born on 25th June 1786, after him. After her return to England from France in 1786 she was a frequent visitor to Warren Hastings at his house in London and at his country homes of Beaumont Lodge in Old Windsor, Berkshire and, later, Daylesford in Gloucestershire. And in a letter of 19th September 1794 to Warren Hastings written from the home of her friends, the Egertons, in Washington, County Durham she signed off:

"...but if between the present period and January You will bestow a Line on me just to say how You are, it will afford me much Satisfaction, and add to the many favors You have already conferred on her **who must ever be**, Dear Sir, Your truly affectionate Goddaughter, Elizabeth de Feuillide."

This use of the words "who must ever be" [my highlighting] implies that Eliza would have wished to be known as Warren Hastings' daughter, not his goddaughter, and to use Hastings' surname, but that she knows it can never be. It reminds us of the plot of *Fanny Burney's* first novel, *Evelina*, where the heroine, Evelina, must ever be known as "Evelina Anville" and can never be recognised by her father, or use his surname and be known as "Evelina Belmont". That Eliza saw Warren Hastings as her father is also shown in her letter to him of 26th December 1797, asking for his approval to her marriage to Henry Austen, Jane Austen's brother:

"Need I say, My dear Sir, that I most earnestly wish for your approbation on this occasion, and that it is with the sincerest attachment I shall ever remain, Your much obliged and affectionate God-daughter, Elizabeth de Feuillide."

I believe that Deirdre Le Faye rather misrepresents the true character of Warren Hastings. She sees his provision of a trust fund for Eliza as being merely a sign of his generosity. To me, this is all part of the "legend" of Warren Hastings which does not really stand up to objective scrutiny. Warren Hastings was a man who made his fortune in the East India Company and was a trusted servant of the Company, where business practices were often highly unscrupulous and totally ruthless, if not completely corrupt. I will also mention later how, as well as being an opium trafficker, the true basis of his personal fortune was a corrupt payment from an Indian prince in return for restoring him to his throne. In his personal life Hastings cuckolded at least two husbands, and the grounds of his later indictment by

Parliament showed he was capable, if not of war crimes, at least of acting completely ruthlessly in the interests of the East India Company. For instance, in the spring of 1774, as Governer General of Bengal, on behalf of the East India Company he made war on the Rohilla Afghans merely for the sake of a £400,000 payment that the Company received from the Nawab of Awadh, Shuja-ud-Daula. The enormous fortune Hastings returned with to England from India in 1785 on his retirement as Governor General, with which he was able to buy back his family estates at twice their market value and build on them a lavish new residence, hardly squares with him being over-generous to anyone except his immediate family. The great trust placed in him by the Directors of the East India Company must in any case have been due to his willingness to place their interests well above those of the native population of India.

It is of course of crucial importance in Eliza's history that she was the daughter of a man of genius like Warren Hastings, as this helps us to explain the genetic component of her own extraordinary talents. Hastings, as a pupil of Westminster School in London, had been an exceptional scholar of Latin and Ancient Greek, and in later years he taught himself Persian. While in India he conversed with Indian princes in their own languages. Some of Hastings' translations of Latin and Greek were used as a model by Jane Austen's father when teaching the Classics to his son, Henry. In a letter to Warren Hastings of 5th June 1802 Henry wrote:

"Your works of taste, both of the pencil & the pen were continually offered to my notice as objects of imitation & spurs to exertion. I shall never forget the delight which I experienced when on producing a translation of a well-known ode of Horace to my father's criticism, he favored me with a perusal of your manuscript and as a high mark of commendation said that he was sure Mr Hastings would have been pleased with the perusal of my humble essay."

Eliza's admiration for her father is reflected in the dedication to *Fanny Burney's Evelina* in which the author credits her father with passing on to her many admirable traits such as the "Love of Virtue". As we shall see later in this book, however, Hastings' personal life was not so exemplary. His treatment of Mr Hancock was not to be the only time in his life that he would cuckold a friend.

Some biographers have exaggerated the age difference between Mr Hancock and his wife, partly because the age shown on Hancock's tombstone in Calcutta was greater than his real age. In fact, as Deirdre Le Faye confirms, Hancock was only seven years older than his wife, an age difference which at the time would have been completely unworthy of note. It seems this age difference has been exaggerated by some biographers to make Warren Hastings' behaviour towards Hancock's wife seem more respectable and understandable. However, as I will attempt to show later in this book, Warren Hastings in his private life could be a cold, cruel and selfish man and he unfortunately left a trail of broken lives in the wake of his ambition. I will also show that he was amongst the most corrupt and venal of the employees of the East India Company at the time. Looking at the bare historical details, I am at a loss to understand where the sympathetic portrayal arose of Warren Hastings as a kindly man who cared nothing for material rewards and rooted out corruption fearlessly. It is hard to imagine in any case how such a man would have risen to the top of such a ruthless money making organisation as the East India Company of the eighteenth century, whose closest equivalent today in terms of organisation and ethical business standards would be the Mafia.

Elizabeth Hancock, or Betsy as she was then known, returned to London from Calcutta with Warren Hastings and the Hancocks at the age of three in 1765. On his arrival in London, Warren Hastings learnt of the sad death from a "putrid sore throat" of his only son, George, who had previously been sent to England to be in the care of George Austen, Jane Austen's father. It seems that Mr

Hancock was intending to retire from the East India Company but Warren Hastings' motivation for returning to England is less clear. It may be that in coming to London he wished to continue his relationship with Mrs Hancock, which Mrs Hancock seems to have wished for as well, as they continued to live close to each other in London. On the other hand, Warren Hastings may have had no intention of staying permanently in England. The East India Company did not usually give any financial support to those that returned, but they accorded great support to Warren Hastings on his return to India in 1769. Also, Warren Hastings had retained the valuable real estate he owned in Alipur in Calcutta and had let it out rather than sold it before he left India. This is an indication that he had always had the intention to return. He in fact returned to India with a strong written recommendation from the Directorate of the East India Company in London, given by them on 26th January 1769 to their Presidency in Madras:

> "Mr. Warren Hastings, a Gentleman who has served Us many Years upon the Bengal Establishment with great Ability and unblemished Character offering himself to be employed again in our Service, We have from a Consideration of his just Merits and general Knowledge of the Company's Affairs been induced to appoint him one of the Members of our Council at your Presidency, and to station him next below Mr. du Pré. – He will proceed on one of the Coast and Bay Ships by which you will be advised of such further Directions as may be necessary concerning this Appointment."

There still exists from around this time a portrait miniature of Eliza's mother, Philadelpia Hancock, painted by John Smart, one of the most accomplished miniature painters of the time, which is on display in Jane Austen's house in Chawton. On his death this was the only item left to Eliza by Mr Hancock "to remind her of her Mother's Virtues as well as of her person". It is useful to look at this portrait to compare it with those of Eliza and Warren Hastings as a family group. It is not stretching the imagination too far to see how the delicate facial features of Warren Hastings are reflected in his daughter. As far as I am aware, however, there is no surviving portrait of Mr Hancock.

Soon after his return to England, Mr Hancock himself was forced to return to India in 1768, as the money he had earned in India before his return proved insufficient to support the lifestyle to which his wife had now become accustomed. His wife and daughter remained in London. Mr Hancock often lamented in his letters from India his wife's lack of economy and her extravagance, which had necessitated his return there. He also expressed in his letters to his wife his determination that Eliza should have a proper education in bookkeeping, in order that this extravagance would be avoided in her own life. Perhaps it was this strict education in bookkeeping which gives to the *Jane Austen* novels the acute awareness of the value of money, which is such a feature of them. Warren Hastings wrote to Mr Hancock on this subject in his letter of 5th November 1769:

"A frugal Style of, & an early Practice in Economy will be a sufficient Precaution. – I cannot say all I will upon this Subject."

London at this time was the most expensive city in the world in which to live. The German miniature painter, Christoph Adam Carl von Imhoff, reported that it was necessary to bring back a very large fortune from India in order to be able to afford to live there comfortably on the income alone. Fortunately for their financial hopes, however, in 1771 the Hancocks received news that Warren Hastings was to be appointed Governor of Bengal. This was fortunate, as Hancock had started to suffer from ill health and it looked like he would never be able to earn enough to support his family by his own efforts.

During her childhood in London, Mr Hancock and Mr Hastings

had devised a plan for Eliza's education. They paid for her to study with the best masters in London in music, languages, arithmetic, bookkeeping and writing. We have evidence that the education of Eliza was planned jointly between them. In a letter from Warren Hastings to Mr Hancock of 5th November 1769 he wrote:

"Make no Change in the Plan you have already laid down. Neither French nor Dancing will disqualify a Woman for filling the Duties of any Sphere in Life. Her own Natural Understanding & gentle Disposition improved by the Precepts of such a Mother as few Children are blest with will fit her Mind to be satisfied with any Lot that she may meet with & to become it… My own Prospects and my Life are precarious, and it will require some years for me to get much above the world, but if I live & meet with the success which I have a Right to hope for, she shall not be under the Necessity of marrying a Tradesman, or any Man for her Support. I would not say thus much, but that I wish in every respect to dispell your Apprehensions."

Hancock confirmed this in a letter to his wife of 17th January 1770:

"In a former Letter I mentioned that I would write about Betsy's Education; at that Time it occurred to me that there was a very little Chance of her having a Fortune which might entitle Her to a Station in Life Suitable to the Education We give her, and that therefore it might conduce to her happiness to be Educated in such a Manner that She might enjoy a more humble Lot should she be Obliged to Submit to it. After long revolving every thing I could possibly recollect on a Subject of such Importance, I am resolved that the same Plan of Education as We formerly agreed on shall be pursued. In this Resolution I am confirmed by Mr. Hastings to whom I wrote on the Subject. Many Reasons might be given why Betsy's Studies should not be interrupted, but I shall only Mention two. It is very certain that neither Languages nor Exercises can be attained to any Degree of Perfection but in the earlier Years of Life, therefore Time now lost will be hereafter."

Eliza was, from all the evidence of the correspondence between her mother and Mr Hancock, a model student, and she astonished those around her with her progress. Mr Hancock wrote to Eliza (or Betsy, as she was known as a child) on 20th December 1770 "My Pleasure is greatly increased by the improvement, I understand, you make under your Masters. Your Mama writes me of your diligence and that she is well pleased with you". On 13th March 1771 he again stressed to his wife the importance of Eliza's education:

"Let your own & Betsy's Health be your first and great care; in the Second Place Betsy's Education. I have a right to insist upon this as it is so material to my happiness and the only reward I can hope for my Labours."

In order for her to learn French perfectly, Eliza's mother had found a French speaking companion for Eliza, and Mr Hancock wrote to his wife on 28th August 1771:

"I am convinced that you have taken a right Method in making Betsy speak French, for if she be not well accustomed to speak the Language now, she will never Attain it in more Advanced Years… The Improvement of Betsy gives me great Pleasure."

Those who can speak French fluently, like myself, can appreciate from the writings of *Jane Austen* and *Fanny Burney* that French was almost a second language to the authors, sometimes from expressions that are used in English that can be seen to be direct translations from French, sometimes by the easy and accurate use of French phrases. For example, in *Fanny Burney's* novel *Cecilia* there is one character, Captain Aresby, who is always using French expressions inappropriately.

Mr Hancock continued to be pleased with Eliza's progress in her education and wrote to his wife on 23rd September 1772 "You say She will be so well accomplished at twelve as many are at fifteenYears of age; I believe she will". He also wrote, "Let me repeat a former request, that you will put her under the Tuition of the best Writing Master and Accomptant you can procure; if you have any regard to me, Value not the Expense." On 7th November 1772 Hancock wrote again to Betsy directly, "I was sorry to hear that you had not begun to learn Arithmetick when your last Letter was written; I request you will apply to it with as much diligence as you do to your other Studies and you will make me very happy."

From the above, we can see that Eliza was one of the most educated women of her age and that she was of outstanding intelligence. What is more, her education was supervised by Warren Hastings, who was a friend of many of the literary and artistic elite in London, including the writer Samuel Johnson. As we shall see later, Hastings himself was also one of the leaders of intellectual life in London. In comparison with the sophisticated Eliza, Jane Austen and Fanny Burney were almost completely uneducated.

As I have already mentioned, a Respondentia Bond of 40,000 rupees, worth approximately £5,000, had been paid to Mr Hancock by Hastings in 1772 for the benefit of his "goddaughter", and there were strict instructions that its origin was to be kept secret by the Hancocks. A lump sum of £10,000 was later given by Hastings to Hancock in 1775 to be invested in trust, with the interest paid to Mr Hancock and his wife during their lifetimes, and the principal to go to Eliza after both her parents had died. However, in a letter to his wife of 25th March 1775, this sum of £10,000 is described by Hancock as being "in Lieu of what the Donor gave to me in the

Name of Betsy". It seems therefore that the total sum Hastings gave to Eliza was only this trust fund of £10,000. Mr Hancock wrote to his wife in the same letter that "The Interest of this Money will produce to you while you shall live nearly four hundred Pounds p. Annum, and the whole, should She Marry, be a large Fortune to Betsy after your Death." The two trustees of the fund were Warren Hastings' brother-in-law and lawyer, John Woodman, and Jane Austen's father, George Austen. It is notable that these two trustees were both close personal friends of Hastings, rather than just business connections. This suggests that there was something extremely secretive and personal about the trust. This was confirmed later in life, when Eliza applied for the capital sum of the trust after the death of both her parents. Hastings refused to take legal advice on the trust himself, maybe fearing his secret might be exposed. He wrote to John Woodman on 6th July 1797: "nor can I with propriety take the opinion of Counsel upon it, or take any other steps regarding it."

The reason for the creation of the trust fund for Eliza has been put down by Deirdre Le Faye to Hastings' generosity but, as will be seen when examining the character of Warren Hastings, selfless generosity was not one of his major traits. It is more likely that the trust fund was intended as a final pay-off to Eliza's mother, since Hastings by now had no intention of seeing her again. His attentions by this time had turned to another "married" woman, Anna Maria Apollonia Chapuset, the common law wife of the German portrait and miniature painter, Christoph Adam Carl von Imhoff, who I mentioned earlier. Imhoff and Anna Maria were unable to be formally married due to the conditions of Imhoff's service as an officer in the army of the Duke of Württemburg in Germany. Anna Maria had travelled out to India with her "husband" and young son Carl on the *Duke of Grafton*, the same ship as Warren Hastings, in 1769. During the trip a love affair had developed between the two of them, according to tradition while she was nursing Hastings through an illness. This news was reported with relish by Mr Hancock to his wife in a letter from Calcutta of 19th April 1772:

> "In a former letter I promised to give You some Account of Mr. Hastings… There is a Lady by name Mrs. Imhoff who is his principal favorite among the Ladies… She is about twenty six Years old has a good person & has been very Pretty, is sensible, lively, and wants only to be a greater Misstress of the English Language to prove she has a great share of Wit."

The story of Mr Imhoff and his wife is recorded in Imhoff's surviving journal, written in the form of letters, which has recently been published in Germany and which I shall discuss later.

I have mentioned above the plan of education Mr Hastings and Mr Hancock conceived for Eliza. From the letters that survive, we know that this was to include French, dancing, horse riding, languages, music, handwriting and arithmetic. We do not know exactly what was meant by "languages". From several different arguments later in this book, I have presumed that Eliza was acquainted with Latin, if not Ancient Greek as well. It was unusual, though not unheard of, to teach classical languages to women at this time. Warren Hastings, however, was a great scholar of Latin and Greek and as a boy had been the top scholar of his year at Westminster School in London. I have already mentioned how George Austen, Jane Austen's father, used Hastings' Latin translations as a model when teaching his own son, Henry. Therefore it seems likely that Warren Hastings would have considered a knowledge of Latin and Greek to be essential for Eliza's education. The easiest way for Eliza to have learnt Latin and Greek would have been to have taken lessons from her uncle, George Austen, Jane Austen's father, at their house in Steventon. He taught private pupils in these subjects in order to support his large family on his modest clergyman's income; it was a necessary supplement for a clergyman with an ever increasing family. We know that, since the social season in London in the eighteenth century did not continue into the summer, Eliza and her mother often visited George Austen at Steventon in Hampshire during the summer months. They also visited Steventon on other occasions, in particular to help Mrs Austen after the birth of her children. George Austen was a close friend of Hastings; he had had the care of his young son, George, who sadly died in his care, and also acted as trustee for Eliza's secret trust fund. George Austen would have welcomed the extra income no doubt provided by his friend Hastings through Eliza's mother for instructing Eliza. Mary DeForest, who has a doctorate in Classics and teaches Latin at the University of Colorado at Denver, USA, has been researching the influence of Greek and Latin on the novels of *Jane Austen*; it is her opinion also that the author was probably taught these subjects by George Austen, though of course she identifies the author as Jane Austen.

We have written evidence that Eliza was staying with her uncle, George Austen, at Steventon during this period. In June 1771, Henry Austen was born, and his mother, Mrs Austen, wrote on 8th November 1772 to Susanna Walter, the mother of Eliza's cousin, Philadelphia Walter, that she was expecting that Eliza and her mother would visit them again:

> "My little boy is come home from nurse, and a fine, stout little fellow he is, and can run anywhere, so now I have all four at home, and some time in January I expect a fifth, so you see it will not be in my power to take any journeys for one while… I believe my sister Hancock will be so good as to come and nurse me again."

Thus it seems Eliza and her mother spent a large part of the years 1771 to 1773 at the Austens' house in Steventon, where Eliza would have had the chance to broaden her education with tuition in Latin and Greek from George Austen. A portrait miniature of Eliza as a very young lady can be found in the biographies written by Claire Tomalin and Jon Spence, although unfortunately I have not been able to reproduce it here for copyright reasons, as the whereabouts of the original are unknown. Another clue we have that Eliza may have been a student at the home of her uncle, George Austen, is in a much later letter, from George Austen's wife, Cassandra, (Jane Austen's mother) to Phylly Walter on 31st December 1786, commenting on Eliza that she had "grown quite lively, when a child we used to think her too grave".

Mr Hancock was also pleased to hear that Betsy had an ear for music, and he wrote on 31st January 1772 to her mother, "I am pleased to hear that she likes Musick. When you buy an Harpsichord, let it be the best, mind not the Price. Kirkman is the best Maker…" The novels of both *Jane Austen* and *Fanny Burney* reveal their authors to have been lovers of music. This discernment in music is shown by Eliza in the *Jane Austen* novels, for instance in *Emma*, where Frank Churchill travels to London seemingly to get a haircut, but in reality to order a piano for his secret fiancée, Jane Fairfax, from Broadwood, the best piano maker in London at the time. There is still in existence a Broadwood square piano such as Eliza would have used, which was made for a Ms Northey, a neighbour of Eliza in Orchard Street, London. We know that Eliza was very keen on music in later life also. In her letter of 31st December 1786 to Philadelphia Walter, Jane Austen's mother remarks of Eliza that, "We have borrowed a Piano-Forte, and she plays to us every day". Later, in a letter of 25th April 1811, Jane Austen describes a musical party organised by Eliza at her home in Sloane Street in London, in which professional musicians performed to a large party of invited friends.

It appears from his letters to his wife in England that Mr Hancock had suffered very badly from illness during his life in India. Warren Hastings in his letters refers to Mr Hancock suffering badly from gout, and it is likely that he also suffered from malaria, which was endemic in Calcutta. Hancock blamed these illnesses for his not being able to earn enough to support his family, although he may not have been much of a businessman in any case. In November 1773 he wrote to his wife "I am now too Old and too infirm to Struggle with the World again, and can only hope to spend the Dregs of Life in saving what may enable my Family to subsist comfortably". The letters of Hancock at this time are full of melancholy and bitterness, and there is an undercurrent in them that it was his wife's former extravagance which had ruined his life by making it necessary for him to return to India.

Elizabeth Hancock, who had now decided to style herself the more sophisticated "Eliza" instead of "Betsy", as she had been known as a child, remained in London and continued her studies. Mr Hancock did not wish her or her mother to return to India. She lived with her mother at various addresses in the fashionable West End of London. A letter to Warren Hastings from his brother-in-law, John Woodman, of December 1773 confirms the progress Eliza continued to make in her education. He wrote to him "Mrs. & Miss Hancock, I need not mention, only that Miss grows a fine Girl, very accomplished, & perfectly agreeable in her behaviour."

Mr Hancock died in Calcutta on 5th November 1775, aged fifty-one, leaving little money after his debts had been paid, worn out by his exertions, illness and probably his unhappy relationship with his absent wife. However, Mrs Hancock received payment directly to her of £3,500 from John Woodman, and £4,800 was deposited in her account in the form of a bill on the East India Company to settle her husband's estate in India. Since it appeared that Hancock's finances on his death were considerably embarrassed, it is probable that this money came from Hastings as a final "pay off" to Eliza's mother, as Hastings had by this time been living with his beloved Anna Maria Chapuset (whom he always called "Marian") for six years, and he was to marry her two years later. There is certainly no doubt that Hastings was by this time in a financial position to help Eliza's mother, as he was now Governor General of India. On

Hancock's death, Philadelphia Hancock and Eliza had little else to live on than the income from Eliza's trust fund, which amounted to about £400 per year when invested in government bonds. So they left England, probably in late 1777, in order to save money, as London was then, as it is has been up until recently, the most expensive city in the world in which to live. It seems they first visited Germany and Belgium, reaching Brussels in 1778, and then arrived in Paris in 1779.

At about the time that Eliza left for the continent, on 29th January 1778, Eliza's first novel, *Evelina, or the History of a Young Lady's Entrance into the World* (conventionally attributed to Fanny Burney) was published anonymously, leading to furious speculation as to the identity of the author. It was rumoured that its author was very young, maybe just seventeen years old. Eliza herself became seventeen years old in the year in which *Evelina* was published, whereas Fanny Burney was twenty-five years old.

According to Fanny Burney herself, the novel had been written between 1776 and 1777. However, according to her biographer Claire Harman, Fanny Burney burnt all of her diary and most of her correspondence for both of these years. Fanny Burney was not able to give any explanation for this highly suspicious behaviour, but it is readily explicable if we assume that during this time she had been collaborating as secretary to Eliza in the writing of *Evelina*. *Evelina* was published from a manuscript which was not in Fanny Burney's handwriting. Her own handwriting would have been recognised by publishers, as she acted for her musician father, Charles Burney, as his secretary. Rather the manuscript was, according to Burney, in a "disguised hand". The proofs of the novel had been sent to Fanny Burney for correction in the middle of January 1778 by the publisher, Thomas Lowndes, but it must be remembered that proofreading at this time, as now, was usually done by someone other than the author. In a later letter to the publisher, Fanny Burney mentions that she has carried out the proofreading herself. She wrote "I should not have taken the pains to copy & correct it for the Press, had I imagined that 10 guineas a volume would have been more than its worth." This is a strange view for a new author to take, who I would presume would be very happy to see their first book appear in print.

Evelina was a novel about the entry of a seventeen-year-old girl into London society, and was widely believed by readers at the time to be by an author who was also seventeen years old. It is about a heroine whose father, like Eliza's, is an important man who refuses to recognise her publicly as his daughter. As we shall see, the plot of the novel and especially the poem addressed to the author's father at the beginning of the novel, represented a plea for recognition by Eliza from own natural father, Warren Hastings. Eliza was able to use the common convention of the ingénu, as used previously by the French novelist Voltaire in *Candide*, to comment on and satirise London society of the time. Shortly after completing the novel, due no doubt to the extremely high cost of living in London, Eliza had travelled with her mother, as previously mentioned, to Belgium and Germany, and then to Paris.

The choice of Fanny Burney as Eliza's secretary, proofreader and agent would not have been unlikely, since Fanny Burney acted as secretary and copyist to her father, the musician Charles Burney, and would have been one of the few women at the time in London who carried out this role. Eliza may also have had connections with Fanny Burney, as I shall show later, through the London literary society of the time in which Fanny Burney's father was a well known figure. He was a close friend of Mrs Hester Thrale, the famous London literary hostess who was in turn a close friend of Dr Samuel Johnson. It seems that the relation of Eliza to Fanny Burney was that, in return for acting as secretary, copyist and proofreader, the profits from the novels and the credit of their authorship were to go entirely to Fanny Burney. This is exactly the same relationship that Eliza was to have later with Jane Austen. As a lady of means, Eliza herself did not need the relatively small amount of extra money she would have received from publication of the novels. Like many literary figures of the time, Eliza was a wealthy amateur, not a professional writer. In Jane Austen's house at Chawton are preserved some of the accounts showing how the proceeds of the *Jane Austen* novels accrued to Jane Austen herself. The connection between Fanny Burney and Jane Austen was that they were both single and beyond marrying age for the time (as mentioned, Fanny Burney was twenty-five at the time of publication of *Evelina*) and therefore not likely to marry. As single women of the middle class, they would be unlikely to be able to support themselves in any way and, had they not acted as secretary and proofreader for Eliza, they would have no other way to earn money to relieve the burden on their families. In contrast to Jane Austen, her elder sister Cassandra Austen was not in need of such financial help as, although she was unmarried, she had received the sum of £1,000 in the will of her fiancé, Tom Fowle, after he died of yellow fever at St Domingo in the West Indies in February 1797.

As we shall see later, the same need for financial support applied to Elizabeth Hamilton, another author whose name was to be used by Eliza. Eliza's epitaph on her grave supports this, as it describes her as "just disinterested and charitable". The words "disinterested" and "charitable" suggest that Eliza was not only charitable in providing the income of her works to penniless women, but also disinterested, in that she allowed them to take the credit of their authorship.

In the novel *Evelina*, which is written in the form of letters, the heroine, Evelina, is the daughter of an Englishman living in Paris, Sir John Belmont, but he refuses to acknowledge her as his daughter or to acknowledge his marriage to her mother, who died in childbirth. Evelina is brought up in the country by her guardian, the Reverend Villars, and at the beginning of the novel she makes her first entrance into London society at the age of seventeen. Her naivety enables the author to comment ironically on the fashionable London society of the time. The novel also introduces various characters for comic effect, such as the coarse sea captain, Captain

Mirvan, and Evelina's bourgeois relatives, the Branghtons, who live in the then unfashionable area to the East of London known as "the City", where the trade of London was carried on. The Branghtons also have a friend, Mr Smith, "the Holborn beau", a young man from this unfashionable district of London who apes the manners of a gentleman to comic effect, and who was an especial favourite of the author Samuel Johnson. As well as dealing with the question of Evelina's father, the main plot of the novel concerns the love affair of Evelina with the hero, Lord Orville, and her dealing with the unwanted affections of a scheming baronet, Sir Clement Willoughby. This anonymously published novel met with a huge success, in fact it was the talk of fashionable London society of the time, and further editions of it were soon printed. There was much speculation as to the identity of its anonymous author who was rumoured to be only seventeen years old.

It is in 1780 from Paris that Eliza wrote, aged eighteen, the first of her letters that we are so fortunate to have still in existence. It is absolutely essential to bear in mind that these letters, written to her distant cousin Philadelphia Walter, have only survived by accident. Philadelphia Walter was a step-cousin who shared a grandmother, Rebecca Hampson. Had these letters of Eliza been written to a member of the immediate family of Jane Austen, they would no doubt have been destroyed by them in the nineteenth century, to further the pretence of Jane Austen's authorship. These letters of Eliza, such precious literary treasures, have only survived because Eliza wrote them to a distant cousin belonging to a branch of the family outside the control of Jane Austen's family at this time. The letters were passed down through the Walter family and so did not come into the hands of the Austen family early enough for them to be destroyed. A few short letters also remain written by Eliza to Warren Hastings and a few to her trustee, Mr Woodman. Every single other letter that Eliza ever wrote or received in her life, including those to or from any members of the Austen family, has disappeared, no doubt deliberately destroyed by the Austen family in the nineteenth century. The most glaring omission is that there are no letters remaining between Eliza and Jane Austen. This is despite Eliza's second husband, Henry Austen, being the brother with whom Jane Austen was on the closest terms, and with whom she corresponded most often. Had Eliza's letters to Philadelphia Walter not have survived by the luckiest of chances, the family of Jane Austen would have succeeded in the nineteenth century in their aim of obliterating almost every trace of Eliza from history.

In her letters from Paris from 1780 onwards, Eliza describes in great detail and with some humour the French court at Versailles and its fashions, and what is especially interesting is how she describes the appearance and dress of Louis XVI, his queen, Marie Antoinette, and the rest of the royal family:

"The Queen is a very fine Woman, She has a most beautiful complexion, & is indeed exceedingly handsome; She was most elegantly dressed, She had on a corset & Petticoat of pale green Lutestring, covered with a transparent silver gauze, The petticoat & sleeves puckered & confined in different places with large bunches of roses an amazing large bouquet of White Lilac, The same flower, together with gauze, Feathers, ribbon & diamonds intermixed with her hair. Her neck was entirely uncovered & ornamented by a most beautiful chain of diamonds, of which She had likewise very fine bracelets; She was without gloves, I suppose to shew her hands, & arms, which are without exception the whitest & most beautiful I ever beheld. The King was plainly dressed, he had however likewise some fine diamonds. The rest of the royal family were very elegant, & indeed I may say The court of France I believe upon the whole one of the most magnificent in all Europe."

Eliza also became close friends with various members of the French aristocracy, including the Comtesse de Tournon. In addition, she writes interestingly in her letters about the early balloon flights which were being carried out in Paris at the time.

During her stay in Paris, it seems she had been persuaded by her mother in 1781 to get married when she was just nineteen or twenty. Her husband to be was a French captain of dragoons, Jean-François Capot de Feuillide, ten years her senior, who styled himself as a Comte, or Count, but there is no evidence that he had a right to this title. He was the son of the mayor of Nérac, a beautiful small old town, sixteen miles south-west of Agen in the South of France, containing a castle in which King Henry IV of France once held court as King of Navarre. The delightful town of Agen is nowadays famous both for rugby and the production of very tasty prunes (the town boasts a Prune Museum). No doubt Eliza's mother, who had married for material reasons herself, was seeking in a similar way through Eliza's marriage to ensure the future prosperity of her daughter and herself. Eliza wrote to her cousin, Philadelphia Walter, on 27th March 1782 of the marriage, in a tone reminiscent of Charlotte Lucas in *Jane Austen's Pride and Prejudice*, when talking of her impending marriage to Mr Collins:

"This event, the most important one of my life, was you may imagine the effect of a mature deliberation, & as it was a step I took much less from my own judgment than that of those whose councils & opinions I am the most bound to follow, I trust I shall never have any reason to repent it; on the contrary, if I may be allowed to judge of the future from the past & present I must esteem myself the most fortunate of my sex. The man to whom I have given my hand is everyways amiable both in mind & person. It is too little to say he loves, since he literally adores me; entirely devoted to me, & making my inclinations the guide of all his actions, the whole study of his life seems to be to contribute to the happiness of mine.

My situation is everyways agreeable, certain of never

being separated from my dear Mama whose presence enhances every other blessing I enjoy, equally sure of my husband's affections, mistress of an easy fortune with the prospect of a very ample one, add to these the advantages of rank & title, & a numerous & brilliant acquaintance, amongst whom I can flatter myself I have some sincere friends, & you will unite with me in saying I have reason to be thankful to Providence for the lot fallen to my share; the only thing which can make me uneasy is the distance I am from my relations."

It was certainly no love match, in spite of her writing that her new husband was "reckoned handsome". In a letter to her brother, James Walter, of 19th September 1787 Eliza's cousin, Philadelphia Walter, ("Phylly") wrote of Eliza "for her husband she professes a large share of respect, esteem and the highest opinion of his merits, but confesses that Love is not of the number on her side, tho' still very violent on his". Eliza was also later to confide to Phylly, in *Austenesque* mode "I never was but at one Wedding in my Life & that appeared a very stupid Business to me." There seemed to be little affection in the marriage between her and the Count, and in her letters Eliza was never to refer to the Count by his first name. The Comte's family were, on the face of it, prosperous gentry with an estate in the South of France in Nérac, near Agen, not far from Toulouse. His father had been the Mayor of Nérac, and there were expectations that on his father's death valuable family estates would pass into the hands of the Comte, but when his father died in 1779 he did not receive as much land or money as he expected. It seems fairly unlikely that he was in fact a genuine Comte as he claimed, but perhaps the English viewed foreign titles at that time with as much suspicion as they do nowadays. The marriage was probably arranged through a Paris friend of Eliza's mother, Sir John Lambert, whom we have mentioned previously as a model for Sir John Belmont in *Fanny Burney's Evelina*. On her marriage, Eliza thus became at least nominally a Comtesse, or Countess, as she liked others to call her in London. This later entitled Eliza, or so she believed, to ride around London in a coach with a coronet on the side, a fact mentioned in one of her cousin Phylly's letters. As I have stated, Eliza admitted in the letter to her cousin that the marriage was not a love marriage, but one she undertook to please her mother and her mother's friends ("persons close to me"). Her mother's purpose in the marriage was possibly to increase the family's fortunes. As will be seen, her husband's motives for the marriage were somewhat unusual, but equally unromantic.

Eliza's second novel, *Cecilia, Or Memoirs of an Heiress* (also published anonymously but now attributed to Fanny Burney) was more deep and reflective. It was published in June 1782 in London, at a time when Eliza was in Paris. It may have been completed before Eliza left England but if it was composed while Eliza was abroad, it would have been necessary for Eliza to communicate by post with Fanny Burney. However, there are indications in Eliza's letters to her cousin, Philadelphia, that she may not have spent all her time in Paris, but may have returned to London secretly from time to time. In a letter to Philadelphia Walter of 7th May 1784 from Paris she describes the severity of the previous winter in England, but then seems to remember herself, and writes that no doubt the winter was the same in England as it was on the continent. Like *Evelina*, *Cecilia* was also to a large degree an autobiographical novel. It told the story of a twenty-one-year-old heroine and heiress of £10,000. Eliza was herself twenty-one in the year of its publication and an heiress of £10,000. This novel is generally regarded by biographers of Jane Austen as being the prototype for *Pride and Prejudice*, since the plot of the book is rather similar and the title of the latter novel comes from the last chapter of *Cecilia*, in which the phrase "Pride and Prejudice" is repeated several times, and is the theme of the book. As in *Pride and Prejudice*, the hero makes an initial clumsy proposal to the heroine, which is rejected. There is of course a reconciliation and a passage in the final chapter reads as follows:

"'The whole of this unfortunate business' said Dr. Lyster, 'has been the result of PRIDE and PREJUDICE. Your uncle, the Dean, began it, by his arbitrary will, as if an ordinance of his own could arrest the course of nature! And as if *he* had power to keep alive, by the loan of a name, a family in the male branch already extinct. Your father, Mr. Mortimer, continued it with the same self-partiality, preferring the wretched gratification of tickling his ear with a favourite sound, to the solid happiness of his son with a rich and deserving wife. Yet this, however, remember; if to PRIDE and PREJUDICE you owe your miseries, so wonderfully is good and evil balanced, that to PRIDE and PREJUDICE you will also owe their termination.'"

The final sentence sums up the theme that runs though the whole of the novel *Pride and Prejudice*. It is astonishing, therefore, that Jane Austen, who supposedly based *Pride and Prejudice* on *Fanny Burney's Cecilia*, made no attempt in her life to meet Fanny Burney and indeed actively avoided her, as we shall see later. What is more, Fanny Burney also made no attempt to contact Jane Austen or any of her family, and never in her life, as far as we know, did she mention Jane Austen or her books in writing.

The heroine's name had originally been Albina, who was an Etruscan goddess of the dawn and, more relevantly, the protector of ill-fated lovers. The Etruscans were the civilisation in Italy which predated the Romans and it is likely that the relevance of the name would be well known to the classically educated Eliza. The heroine's eventual name of Cecilia, the patron saint of music, perhaps reflects Eliza's love of music. This novel, like *Evelina*, was very successful and the first edition of 2,000 copies sold out by October 1782. Like Evelina, Cecilia is a young heiress from the country who arrives in London. When her parents die she lives with her uncle, the Dean of ——. Upon his death she is entrusted to three guardians: Mr Delville, who is not particularly rich but has an inordinate pride in his ancient family; Mr Briggs, a rich but rather common London merchant and confirmed miser; and Mr Harrel, an unprincipled spendthrift, who is the husband of Cecilia's childhood friend. As she is unable to put up with the spartan conditions at Mr Briggs' house, Cecilia lives instead with the spendthrift Harrels at their house in the fashionable West End of London, where she is introduced to the pleasures of London society, such as masquerades, the opera and the theatre.

The plot deals with her love affair with the hero, the young Mortimer Delville. However, their marriage is impeded by a clause in the will of the Dean that, in order for Cecilia to inherit, her husband must give up his family name and take her surname of Beverley. Because of the pride of the Delvilles in their old family and the objections of both of Mortimer Delville's parents, at first he is not willing to give up his family name in order to marry her. Another obstacle to their union is Mr Monckton, a family friend of Cecilia's, who has married a rich and bad tempered old widow, Lady Margaret, who refuses to die. Mr Monckton's object in persuading her against Mortimer Delville is to marry Cecilia himself. Other characters in the novel include the cynical lawyer, Morrice, and a rather silly but amusing young woman, Lady Honoria Pemberton, who does not mind to say what she thinks and who mocks Mortimer Delville's father's pride in his old castle and old family. It has been remarked how Lady Honoria Pemberton greatly resembles the character of Camilla Stanley in *Jane Austen's Catharine, or the Bower*, written only six years later. Another character in *Cecilia* is an eccentric London moralist known as Albany, who warns Cecilia to use her inheritance to help the poor as much as possible.

One of Eliza's first duties after her marriage was to visit her new mother-in-law in Nérac in the South of France. Thus she travelled south from Paris in 1784 to meet her new mother-in-law and to see the lands belonging to her husband. This somewhat bizarre journey led her from the excitement of London and Paris to a very different world, the Landes in the south west of France, an isolated part of the country covered in malarial marshland and forest and inhabited by what Claire Tomalin calls "a sparse population of peasants speaking an unintelligible patois and living in conditions so primitive they seemed almost another species." To prepare a reception for his new bride, her new husband had rented a beautiful French chateau, the Château de Jourdan, an idyllic retreat on the edge of the region of Les Landes in the hamlet of Sainte Meille, near the small village of Gabarret. This beautiful country house still survives. I paid an impromptu visit to the house during the writing of this book, where I was shown round by a member of the charming family who now own it, for whom it has been a holiday home for more than 150 years. It stands on top of a hill in an idyllic position amid woodland and looks down on its lake below. I was informed that the towers on both sides of it only had crenellations added at a later date and, at the period Eliza lived there, they were tiled and pointed. Reaching this area by taxi was an unusual experience, as I believe no one else at the tourist office had ever requested a taxi to go to this town. It is certainly an isolated spot.

The Comte de Feuillide was staying at this isolated village while he built himself a chateau to live in nearby, since he had acquired 5,000 acres of undrained marshland next to the village of Gabarret known as "*le Marais*" (the marsh). He had been able to obtain this land as his father had been the head of the forestry and marshland department for the area. He was in the process of draining the land to turn it into farmland and it seems likely his main motive for marrying Eliza was to try to finance this project by tapping in to her fortune. Unfortunately for him, the money was still in trust for Eliza and, under the terms of the trust, the capital of it was not to be in Eliza's hands until the death of both her parents. However, he was able to circumvent the terms of the trust by obtaining a large amount of money from Eliza's mother in the form of a loan for £6,000 which in the event was never repaid. The future marriage had not been met with any enthusiasm by the trustees of Eliza's trust fund, one of whom, Mr Woodman, the brother-in-law of Warren Hastings, reported as such to Warren Hastings. He reported he feared that the trust fund would, like the marsh itself, also be "drained" and as a result he and the other trustee, Jane Austen's father George Austen, refused to allow the money from the trust fund to be released to either Eliza or her new husband.

It was here in these idyllic surroundings that Eliza spent two quiet years between 1784 and 1786; two letters of hers survive which were addressed from this beautiful chateau and one addressed from this region in France, Guyenne. Her husband was not in good health at this time and to help cure him they travelled together to the lovely spa town of Bagnères in the Pyrenees (Eliza's friend Lady Sophia Burrell refers to the Pyrenees in the poem below). Eliza, in her letter of 17th January 1786, describes the beauty of the landscape in Bagnères to which she travelled through the foothills of the Pyrenees. Her husband's cure was effective and it was on her return to the Château de Jourdan at Sainte Meille that Eliza became pregnant. No doubt because he wished to exploit the family connection with Warren Hastings, the Comte had put pressure on her to travel back to England to have the child there. However, as it turned out, the child, a son they named Hastings, was actually born on her way back to England in Calais on 25th June 1786. It had been an uncomfortable journey for Eliza to undertake when pregnant and indeed it seems she had done so somewhat unwillingly. She wrote to her cousin Phylly Walter on 17th January 1786, "I own I have some repugnance to undertaking so long a journey in a situation so unfit for travelling". It could have been the stress of travelling that contributed to the fact that her son never developed properly and was to die in childhood.

Eliza finally reached London in July 1786. Deirdre Le Faye states that it was at this time that she became reacquainted with Warren Hastings and met his new wife; Hastings had returned from India in 1785 following his wife's return due to ill health a year earlier. Eliza also met once more Sir William Burrell and his wife, the poet and playwright Lady Sophia Burrell, who lived near Dorking in Surrey, whom I will describe more of later. The literary Lady Sophia

Burrell was one of Eliza's closest friends. It is to her that we owe the scant information on Eliza's life which supplements Eliza's letters. Lady Sophia Burrell wrote a poem to her at this time:

To Eliza –
When you no more have power to please
By artless elegance and ease;
When that dear guileless heart shall grow
Cold as the Pyrenean snow;
Light and inconstant as the wind,
Artful, capricious, and unkind,
Devoid of honour, virtue, sense,
And ev'ry claim to excellence,
Then will Eliza cease to be
Thus tenderly esteem'd by me;
(Whose friendship ev'rything defies,
But cold neglect – and mean disguise.)

The "artless elegance and ease" described by Lady Sophia Burrell could equally refer to Eliza's literary accomplishments as well as her social nature, especially as the compliment came from a writer, and it is an apt description of the style of *Fanny Burney* and *Jane Austen*. There is one other reason why Lady Sophia Burrell in using the phrase "artless elegance and ease" is describing Eliza as a novelist. This is because, in using this phrase, Lady Sophia Burrell is quoting directly from William Mason's *Epistle to Sir Joshua Reynolds* published on 10th October 1782. In this poem Mason uses the phrase "artless elegance and ease" to describe the writer John Dryden's prose style, a prose style that was an important influence on all eighteenth century writers:

"Yet still he pleas'd; for *Dryden* still must please,
Whether with artless elegance and ease
He glides in prose, or from its tinkling chime,
By varied pauses, purifies his rhyme,

And mounts on Maro's plumes, and soars his heights sublime."

I will discuss later in the book in detail the evidence showing Lady Sophia's high regard for Eliza as an author.

In 1785, Warren Hastings had finally returned for good to England, having retired from the post of Governor General of India. He had been in continuous dispute with the other members of his government at home and in India over policy. This had even led to a duel with pistols in 1780 between Hastings and his main rival, Sir Philip Francis, in which Francis was wounded but not killed. However, the main reason for Hastings' return was that his wife, Marian, whom he adored, had been forced to return to England the previous year because of her serious ill health. Shortly before leaving India a painting was made of the two of them by the famous artist, Zoffany, standing in front of their house and garden at Alipur in Calcutta. This painting can be seen in the Victoria Memorial Museum in Calcutta and also on the website of this museum. On his return to England, Hastings formally retired from government and devoted the rest of his life to literary pursuits, and especially to studying and translating works of literature from the languages of India. Warren Hastings' view of himself was often that of a literary figure. In the famous portrait of him by Sir Joshua Reynolds which hangs in the National Portrait Gallery in London, painted in 1768 before his return to India, he is shown with quill in hand, rather than with any symbol of power or administration. Under the artistic conventions of the time, this pointed him out as a writer. He was painted in a similar pose in his old age by Sir William Beechey. Reynolds' portrait of Samuel Johnson also shows Johnson in a similar pose with quill pen in hand. In the admirable and beautifully illustrated book *Indian Renaissance: British Romantic Art and the Prospect of India* by Hermione De Alemeida and George H Gilpin it states:

"Reynolds painted Hastings' portrait in 1768, and the pose

and details of the painting offer explicit recognition by the London artistic circle that Hastings was a fellow intellectual. Hastings is in the pose of an antiquarian scholar: he is seated at a reading table, with Persian documents at hand."

We know that Hastings had taught himself the Persian language, which was at that time the language of the ruling class in Northern India. The above book also outlines in detail how Hastings created an intellectual culture in India, and promoted the understanding and translation of the Indian languages. Eliza's friend, Lady Sophia Burrell, also acknowledged Warren Hastings as a writer when she referred to his "skilful pen" in her poem "On perusing an Ode written by Warren Hastings, Esq. on his return to England":

No wonder that the skilful pen,
Of one among the best of men,
His noble soul displays;
He in whose bosom virtue dwells,
Can best describe the thoughts he feels,
When virtue claims his praise.

Hastings! to thee applause is due –
Whose anxious care, whose utmost view,
Was still the public good;
Wealth, power, and all their tempting train,
Strove to engage thy mind in vain,
Thy mind with worth endu'd.
No thorns shall from thy pillow spring,
Nor conscience feel a poignant sting,
From retrospective scenes;
Thy memory, when she backward treads,
From thy disinterested deeds,
A secret pleasure gleans.

Thou ne'er hast with tyrannic hand
Spread desolation o'er the land,
Or taught the poor to weep;
Thy breast no keen remorse can know,
Nor pangs that from dishonour flow,
Nor care "that murders sleep."

To bless has been thy glorious aim –
The worthy, (not the great,) cou'd claim
A patronage from thee;
No ostentatious love of power
Cou'd ever gain dominion o'er
A mind from error free.

Those who amass unbounded store,
May in their prosperous state be poor
In virtue, and in fame;
But thou, of higher wealth possest,
Hast brought this treasure from the east,
An uncorrupted name.

Lady Sophia Burrell added the following note to her poem:

"This Ode was written previous to the Prosecution of Mr.
Hastings, and was founded upon the testimony given by
many of Sir Charles Raymond's friends in India, of Mr.
Hastings's exemplary conduct."

This poem of Lady Sophia Burrell's is placed in her book of
collected poems directly after her poem to Eliza above, perhaps
hinting at their relationship of father and daughter. John H Farrant,
in his article *The Family Circle and Career of William Burrell, antiquary*
states of Lady Sophia Burrell that "She was also writing poetry from
at least 1773 and indeed in 1786 exchanged verses with Warren

Hastings, an exact contemporary of her husband's at Westminster School, lately Governor-General of India and now a neighbour". The Hastings and the Burrells both had their London houses in Harley Street. John Farrant writes of the exchange of verses above: "Hastings' verse referred to Lord Mansfield, of whom Sophia had written in the previous October." Lady Sophia Burrell had dedicated her book of poems to Lord Mansfield, the Lord Chief Justice of England, and it is possible to identify a close knit literary circle, which consisted of Warren Hastings, Lady Sophia Burrell, Lord Mansfield and Eliza de Feuillide.

On her return to England in 1786, Eliza called on both Warren Hastings and the Burrells, who, as I mentioned, were neighbours in Harley Street in London. Harley Street, now famous mainly as a street for medical practitioners, must in the eighteenth century have been an extremely high class area. Both Warren Hastings and Lady Sophia Burrell were extremely wealthy, with fortunes of over £100,000 each. In *Sense and Sensibility*, *Jane Austen* places Mr and Mrs John Dashwood as renting a house in this street. John Dashwood is the son of Elinor Dashwood's father's first marriage and therefore he inherits the entire estate of Norland on his father's death. By placing John Dashwood as living in Harley Street, this accentuates how rich he is, how he does not need the inheritance of the Norland estate, and therefore how mean he and his wife are in making no financial provision for Elinor Dashwood, her sisters and her mother. I have already mentioned that in the same novel the less affluent Mrs Jennings, a "widow with an ample jointure", lives at Berkeley Street, while Eliza herself lived at one period at No. 24 Upper Berkeley Street, near Portman Square, so we can presume that they had a similar level of income. In the novels of *Jane Austen* and *Fanny Burney*, street names are never merely geographical locations. The name of the street a character lives in is as much an indicator of their social class as is their fortune or income. Eliza, as an inhabitant of London, would have known of the nuances of addresses and the class profile of each street in London, and this would have helped her to place particular characters in particular streets and areas of London. As an inhabitant of a small village in Hampshire, Jane Austen would have been completely unable to do this.

Eliza at this time also visited Steventon Rectory, the Hampshire home of Jane Austen and her brothers, Henry and James, and she was to spend further time there and also with her cousin Philadelphia Walter in Kent. At Steventon Eliza played the piano, danced and took the female lead in amateur theatricals with her cousins, James and Henry, Jane Austen's brothers. Earlier in the same year of 1786 she had taken part in amateur dramatics in France and she returned to England with an enthusiasm for this form of entertainment, just as Mr Yates comes back from Ecclesford to Mansfield Park with his head full of acting. It was soon after Eliza's return to England that the first works now known as those of *Jane Austen* began to appear, the dates of which coincide with Eliza's numerous stays at Steventon at this period.

In April 1787 Henry Austen went to visit Eliza at her home in Orchard Street in London. In London, Eliza also attended the court at St James's Palace and visited Almacks assembly rooms, the most exclusive venue for balls in London. This indicates that Eliza moved in the highest social circles. Later in 1787 she visited Tunbridge Wells in Kent, then an important spa town, with her mother and her cousin, Philadelphia Walter. Tunbridge Wells was later to be the scene of much of the action in *Fanny Burney's Camilla*, published in 1796. In a letter to her brother, James Walter, of 19th September 1787, Philadelphia Walter describes how she and Eliza visited the theatre there and how Eliza bespoke the plays *Which is the Man?* and *Bon Ton*. She then describes how Eliza was intending to act in the same plays at Christmas at Steventon. Jon Spence in *Becoming Jane Austen* points out the resemblance of the roles Eliza was intending to act in these plays, to her own character. He describes Miss Tittup in *Bon Ton* as "a wily flirt with a cynical view of love and marriage" and Lady Bell Bloomer in *Which is the Man?* as "a widow who has lived in France and professes to hold the cynical French view of love and marriage." Eliza wished her cousin, Philadelphia Walter, to take part in these plays and wrote to her, requesting that she come to Steventon for this purpose but, like Fanny Price in *Jane Austen's Mansfield Park*, as well as being shy, she had moral objections to acting, and refused to do so. In the end Philadelphia did not come to Steventon, and two different plays, *The Wonder* and *The Chances*, were performed instead. Most biographers of Jane Austen agree that the acting of these plays, in which Eliza took the leading female roles, provided her with chances for flirtation with her cousins, Jane Austen's brothers Henry and James, which are reminiscent of the acting scenes in *Jane Austen's Mansfield Park* between Henry Crawford and Maria Bertram, and Edmund Bertram and Mary Crawford. *Mansfield Park* is also a novel about a romance between cousins.

Although Eliza probably took the opportunity of these amateur theatricals to flirt with both James and Henry Austen, it should be remembered that at this time she was still a married woman. In any case, Henry was ten years younger than Eliza and still in his teens, and any possible romance between Eliza and Henry was suspended when a founder's kin scholarship place became vacant for Henry to go to St John's College, Oxford. Eliza's cousin, Philadelphia Walter, must have known of Henry's love for Eliza, for she remarked wryly in a letter to her brother of 23rd July 1788 that "Henry Austen is sadly mortified at one of the Fellows of St John's choosing to marry or die, which vacancy he is obliged to fill up, and wd. totally prevent his accompanying his cousin to France, wh. was particularly harped upon on both sides." In spite of his youth, Eliza seems even at this time to have felt something for Henry, for she visited him at Oxford when he went up in 1788.

Earlier in 1788 Philadelphia Walter visited Eliza in London. During this time they attended the trial of Warren Hastings for corruption in India, in the Houses of Parliament, which began on 13th February 1788 and dragged on until his final acquittal in April 1795. In 1788 Eliza also visited Warren Hastings at his home in

Beaumont Lodge in Old Windsor in Berkshire, a large imposing house fronting the River Thames, which he had bought in May 1786 shortly after his return from India, and which still stands to this day. She later visited her two cousins, James and Henry, at Oxford University, spending a day viewing Blenheim Palace nearby. Elizabeth Bennet passed the same way in *Jane Austen's Pride and Prejudice* en route to Derbyshire.

In Oxford, as she wrote to her cousin Philadelphia Walter on 22nd August 1788:

> "We visited several of the Colleges, the Museum &cc & were very elegantly entertained by our gallant relations at St. John's, where I was mightily taken with the Garden & longed to be a <u>Fellow</u> that I might walk in it every Day, besides I was delighted with the Black Gown & thought the Square Cap mighty becoming".

Later in 1788, after visiting Tunbridge Wells once again, she and her mother once more set off for Paris, but they returned to London on 7th July 1789. It seems that they then went to stay at Jane Austen's father's home in Steventon in Hampshire because one of the pieces of so-called *Jane Austen* "Juvenilia", *Love and Freindship*, is dated from this period as 13th June 1790. This story was dedicated to Eliza herself by "The Author".

Along with the growing realisation that her son, Hastings, would never develop properly mentally, there came a far worse blow for Eliza, when her mother fell ill with breast cancer in 1791. Eliza's letters of this time are especially touching as she devoted herself to caring for her mother at their home in Orchard Street in the West End of London. Eliza's cousin, Phylly Walter, wrote to her brother James on 4th September 1791, "Poor Eliza is compleatly miserable and has the hard task of being forced to appear cheerful when her heart is ready to burst with grief & vexation. My aunt privately exprest to me how much she felt for her, & that she endeavoured to stifle her pains to avoid her the concern of seeing her mother's sufferings". Eliza's mother suffered a long decline and, in the end, she died on 26th February 1792 at Hampstead in North London, where Eliza had taken her in final hopes of a cure. It was for this reason that Eliza was later buried alongside her son and mother in the churchyard at St John's Church in Hampstead. Her mother's gravestone was inscribed:

"In Memory of Philadelphia Wife of Tysoe Saul Hancock Esqr Whose Moral Excellence united the Practice of every Christian Virtue She bore with pious resignation the severest trials of a tedious and painful Malady and expired on the 26th day of February 1792 Aged 61."

It is very interesting to contrast this memorial inscription with the later one for her daughter. This inscription is a conventional one for a woman of the time, talking of her mother's "Moral Excellence", "Christian Virtue" and "pious resignation". As we shall see later, the memorial inscription of her daughter was to refer to Eliza in complete contrast, as an inspired authoress of outstanding intelligence.

Eliza's mother's competence where financial matters were concerned had not improved after her husband's death, and on her own death it was revealed she had lent all her money (£6,500) to the Comte de Feuillide, but she asked the executors of her will not to force him to honour this debt. In the same year the Comte returned to England, where he and Eliza undertook a short journey together to the spa town of Bath, but Eliza was in low spirits after her mother's death and they soon returned to London. Shortly afterwards the Comte, who at this time was on leave from the French Army, was forced to return to France to avoid his property there being forfeited to the state. It was as a result of this meeting in Bath that Eliza was later to become pregnant and suffer a miscarriage. Bath is famously the setting for part of the action of

Jane Austen's novels *Northanger Abbey*, begun in 1798, and *Persuasion*.

In France, meanwhile, the monarchy had been abolished on 21st September 1792 and Louis XVI was guillotined on 21st January 1793. These events were to have severe consequences for Eliza's husband, as he considered himself a member of the French aristocracy. It seems, however, that the flirtation between Eliza and Henry, Jane Austen's brother, was continuing in spite of her being married. She described Henry Austen in a letter of 26th October 1792 as:

> "much improved, and is certainly endowed with uncommon Abilities, which indeed seem to have been bestowed, tho' in a different way, upon each Member of this Family. As to the Coolness which You know had taken place between H. and myself, it has now ceased, in consequence of due acknowledgments on his part, and we are at present on very proper relationlike terms. You know that his Family design him for the Church."

Due to all the events described above, there seems to have been a long creative gap in the literary career of Eliza between 1782, the date of publication of *Fanny Burney's Cecilia*, and the appearance of *Jane Austen's* first writings, known as her "Juvenilia", from the late 1780s onwards. *Jane Austen's* so-called "Juvenilia" were short stories and short parodies written during the period coinciding with Eliza's visits to Jane Austen's home in Steventon in Hampshire in the late 1780s and the first half of the 1790s. One of Eliza's surviving letters, of 26th October 1792, was written from Steventon, where she had gone to stay for some time after her mother's death. Some of the Juvenilia are specifically dated for 1792, a time at which we know for sure that Eliza was staying with Jane Austen. It would have been remarkable for the barely educated Jane Austen to have written these while Eliza was staying with her, without the educated and literary

Eliza contributing to them in any way and without Eliza mentioning Jane Austen's writing ability to Philadelphia Walter in her letter of 1792. *Jane Austen's* so-called "Juvenilia" must have been written by Eliza herself as short pieces for the amusement of the family, rather than for publication, with Jane Austen acting as her secretary and her sister Cassandra as illustrator. These short pieces are the sophisticated parodies of a mature writer, which show a wide knowledge of both English and French literature of the period. However, because of them being conventionally attributed to Jane Austen, and since Jane Austen was born in 1775, they have been erroneously represented as being childhood works of Jane Austen or "Juvenilia".

Certain elements of what they parody have been identified: for instance *The History of England* is a parody of Oliver Goldsmith's *History of England*, a popularised work of history which had no pretensions to accuracy, let alone scholarship. As a well educated historian, educated by the best Masters in London, paid for by Warren Hastings, Eliza felt obliged to produce an accurate and cutting parody on this book, showing she knew the difference between such popularisations and the work of true historians. Jane Austen at the time this parody was written was only fifteen years old and had received no formal education in history; indeed it is likely that Goldsmith's *History of England* itself was the only history book she knew, and a family copy of this book still exists; it would therefore have been impossible for her to write a satire upon it.

Even the preface to the 1823 edition of Goldsmith's work describes Goldsmith as "a better poet than historian." It also says of his book "Omissions and errors will, therefore, be more readily excused by the candid reader. The author has endeavoured to unite propriety of remark, purity and force of language, with authenticity and correctness of statement; but he cannot boast of complete success. Every one is not a LIVY or a TACITUS, a DAVILA or a GUICCIARDINI, a HUME or a GIBBON."

I will discuss later on how Eliza demonstrates her deep knowledge of scholarly history in a passage from *Jane Austen's Northanger Abbey*, in which she also mentions the above Scottish historian, David Hume, and refers to the work of the Roman historian, Publius Cornelius Tacitus.

Eliza at this time was also finding that her son, Hastings, was not developing normally and was subject to fits, and she made attempts to cure him, especially by taking him sea bathing, which was a fashionable cure at the time. She also bathed in the sea herself, even in the winter, and found the experience beneficial for both of them. Her experience of these trips to the sea for such cures was later to be made use of in *Jane Austen's* final unfinished novel, *Sanditon*, which describes the fortunes of Mr Parker, a speculator in a small bathing resort he has set up in his home town.

Unfortunately, at this time Eliza's husband was in Paris at the height of the Terror of the French Revolution, where he was involved in running a casino in the Palais Royal, a sort of eighteenth century shopping centre, according to Olivier Blanc in *Last Letters: Prisons and Prisoners of the French Revolution 1793-94*. At this time the Marquise de Marboeuf, the widow of one of his friends, was accused of conspiring against the Republic; her crime was said to be causing famine by laying down arable land in her estates for pasture. The Count attempted to bribe a certain Morel, one of the secretaries of the Committee of Public Safety, in order to get her released, but unfortunately he was betrayed by him to the Committee. As a result he was tried and executed by guillotine on 22nd February 1794. Witnesses at his trial included his housekeeper "la citoyenne Joubert" and "la citoyenne Grandville", who is described as his former mistress. It is notable how the Comte's fate is shared by the "hero" of *Elizabeth Hamilton's Memoirs of Modern Philosophers*, the hairdresser Vallaton, who is innocent but is betrayed to the guillotine by his mistress, Emmeline. Eliza's marriage to the Comte had never been a happy one and she had soon come to realise what a mistake it had been. At the time of her marriage she had said that she did not love the Comte and she referred to the marriage in later life as though it had never been a proper marriage. She later wrote in a letter to Phylly Walter dated 16th February 1798, "I have an aversion to the word <u>Husband</u> & never make use of it". She also referred in a letter of 13th December 1796, prior to her second marriage, to "The last day of my Liberty, mind I do not say my Widowhood."

After the death of her husband, it was not long before Eliza's thoughts turned to re-marriage and in particular to her cousin Henry Austen, ten years her junior. Although intended by his family to be a clergyman, he joined the Oxfordshire Militia in 1793 as a lieutenant. The militia was an irregular army which had been raised due to threats to the country from revolutionary France. It is believed that Henry proposed to Eliza in 1795 and after she refused him gently he became engaged to a Mary Pearson, but this engagement was later broken off. On 7th November 1796 Eliza wrote about this Miss Pearson to her cousin Phylly Walter: "Our Cousin Henry Austen has been in Town he looks thin & ill – I hear his late intended is a most intolerable Flirt, and reckoned to give herself great Airs – The person who mentioned this to me says She is a pretty wicked looking Girl with bright Black Eyes which pierce thro' & thro'. No wonder the poor young Man's heart could not withstand them".

Eliza's main objection to marrying her cousin Henry Austen was that he was intended by his family to be a clergyman, as she mentioned in her letter quoted previously. She must have discussed the matter with her friend, Lady Sophia Burrell, who satirised Eliza's situation in a poem addressed to her: "To Eliza a Dialogue between Inclination and Prudence". This included the lines:

"Or if your fancy is not set
On scarlet coat and epaulet,
Suppose you chuse a graver line,
And file in love with a DIVINE!
…

The parsonage by yew trees bounded,
And with infernal roads surrounded,
Appears in sight – your reverend mate
There sees the whole of his estate,
And with his sermons and his wife,
Prepares to be a drone for life."

In this, Eliza's relationship to Henry Austen resembles that of Mary Crawford and Edmund Bertram in *Jane Austen's Mansfield Park*. In this novel Mary Crawford, who wishes to marry Edmund Bertram, is surprised to learn that he is to be a clergyman. However, there is no true equivalence in the characters of Mary Crawford and Eliza. Mary Crawford objects to religion in principle, as her morals are drawn from what is acceptable to the fashionable world, which she has learned from living in the household of her uncle, the Admiral, and his mistress. Eliza's objections were completely different; although she accepted the principles of religion in her private behaviour and, like her mother, always tried to live by the principles of Christian charity and forgiveness, she saw the Church itself as a somewhat ridiculous institution. At the time she was writing, the Church of England suffered from many abuses. Positions for clergymen had become mainly a source of income providing a living for the younger sons of the gentry; this was fortunate since, under the English system of inheritance, estates generally passed to the eldest son only. *Jane Austen* makes fun of this in her novels, where she cynically describes positions in the Church of England in relation to the income that they provide rather than their potential for evangelical work. It is hard to imagine Jane Austen herself, as the daughter of a country clergyman, having such disdain for the Church of England and its clergy. Eliza also loved the fashionable entertainments of London, such as the theatre and the opera, and did not wish to live away from them, stuck out in the country. Her contemporary, the Reverend Sydney Smith, once described one of his parishes as being "twelve miles from a lemon". She seems to have shared the opinion of Mr Darcy in *Pride and Prejudice* that society in the country tends to be confined and unvarying.

On 13th December 1796 Eliza wrote to Phylly Walter of the chance of her marrying Henry:

"I am glad to find you have made up your mind to visiting the <u>Rectory</u>, but at the same time, and in spite of all your <u>conjectures and belief</u>, I do assert that Preliminaries are so far from settled that I do not believe <u>the parties</u> ever will come together, not however that they have quarrelled, but one of them cannot bring her mind to give up dear Liberty, and yet dearer flirtation – After <u>a few months</u> stay in the Country She sometimes thinks it possible to undertake sober Matrimony, but a few weeks stay in London convinces her how little the state suits her taste –"

Eliza had by now also acquired her wished for pet pug dog and wrote to Phylly:

"I once more thank you for your <u>puggish</u> intentions in my favor, and wish that you may be able to realize them, tho' to say the truth I am already possessed of one of these bewitching animals, but as he is yet in a state of infancy, and has something like a weakness in one of his hind legs, it is uncertain whether his future accomplishments may answer my fond expectations, and I consequently shall joyfully receive as many more Pugs as you can procure for me – you would laugh to see me consulting my Doctor about my Dog, and administering Vapour Baths which he has prescribed for him."

In a letter of 3rd May 1797, however, Eliza relates to Phylly Walter some very important developments, which were to lead to her marriage to Henry. Henry Austen had managed to involve himself with the financing of the militia and had been promoted from lieutenant to captain. She wrote to her cousin:

> "Captn. Austen has just spent a few days in Town; I suppose you know that our Cousin Henry is now Captain, Pay Master & Adjudant, He is a very lucky young Man and bids fair to possess a considerable Share of Riches & Honours; I believe he has now given up all thoughts of the Church, and he is right for he certainly is not so fit for a Parson as a Soldier."

In April 1795 Warren Hastings, who had been on trial since 1788 in Parliament for alleged crimes committed during his governance of India, was finally cleared of all charges against him. Eliza had supported him throughout the trial and had attended the trial, and no doubt this news was a great relief to her. In 1796 Eliza had spent more time at the spa town of Tunbridge Wells in Kent. The same year she was to have one more novel published in London, which was the first to be published openly under the name of *Fanny Burney*, *Camilla; or a Picture of Youth*. Part of this novel was set in Tunbridge Wells to which Eliza had been a frequent visitor, although in her letters she tells her cousin Phylly how she enjoyed criticising the dullness of The Pantiles, the main shopping street of Tunbridge Wells, to her friends. The income of the novel was given to Fanny Burney, who had few means of support other than a small private pension of £100, given to her personally by Queen Charlotte on her retirement from her position at court as Second Keeper of the Robes.

Fanny Burney was the daughter of Charles Burney, a musician of some talent, who had worked as an assistant for the composers George Frideric Handel and Thomas Arne, and who was well known to London society as a keyboard teacher to the daughters of well-to-do inhabitants of the West End. In 1793 Fanny Burney married a penniless French exile, General d'Arblay. Later, however, with the proceeds from *Camilla*, published in 1796, she and her husband built themselves a house, Camilla Cottage, on the Norbury Park estate of the Lock family in West Humble, near Dorking in Surrey. She had received the lease of the land on which it was built from her friends, William and Frederica Lock.

Camilla is the story of three young sisters, Camilla, Eugenia and Lavinia Tyrold, and their beautiful young cousin, Indiana Lynmere. Camilla is at first the heir to her uncle, the baronet Sir Hugh Tyrold, because she is his favourite. He is a simple minded but kindly man who, through injury, is now physically unable to pursue his outdoor hobbies such as hunting, and so he tries unsuccessfully to educate himself in later life by bringing in a pedantic Greek and Latin tutor, Dr Orkborne. Because of his foolishness in not taking care of his young niece, Eugenia, and taking her to a country fair before she has been vaccinated, she contracts smallpox and is terribly disfigured by it. Eaten up by guilt and taking pity on her, he makes Eugenia his heiress instead of his previous favourite, Camilla. He also gives up his plan of learning Greek and Latin and instead Dr Orkborne becomes Eugenia's tutor. The novel is lengthy, prolonged rather artificially by the love affair of Camilla with the moralistic Edgar Mandlebert and by the caution of Edgar Mandlebert's overprotective tutor, Dr Marchmont. Camilla's cousin, Indiana, though a beauty, has little else to offer, and she is encouraged in her vanity by her fashionable but uneducated governess, Miss Margland. The story also deals with the fate of Eugenia and the courage she needs to face the world with the disfigurement caused by her smallpox. Other characters in the novel include a witty and fashionable middle-aged lady, Mrs Arlbery, who befriends Camilla, and who is the character who most resembles Eliza. She is paid court to by Sir Sedley Clarendel, who is seemingly an indolent fop, but is revealed to have sterling qualities underneath his affectations of nonchalance. The novel includes two of *Fanny Burney's* funniest characters, Mr Dubster, a tinker with ambitions to be a gentleman, and Mrs Mittin, a hanger-on and parasite, living off selling small items of clothing to the 'genteel'.

There are two interesting connections in the book with Eliza. Firstly, the character of Mrs Mittin has a similar name to Margaret Mitten, a fictional character in *The Loiterer*, the magazine published at Oxford University by James and Henry Austen when they were studying there between 1789 and 1790. Secondly, the theme of smallpox vaccination was one in which Warren Hastings seemed to take a keen interest. He had been in communication with the famous pioneer of vaccination, Dr Edward Jenner, about a supposed case where a tenant had contracted cowpox but this had not protected him, as Dr Jenner had asserted it would have, from later contracting smallpox.

Eliza's association with Fanny Burney seems to have come to an end at this time as far as novels were concerned, although Eliza did write in 1799 and shortly afterwards the plays *Love and Fashion, A Busy Day* and *The Woman Hater*, all presently attributed to Fanny Burney. During the time from 1799 to 1800, Eliza was living in close proximity to Fanny Burney, who presumably acted as secretary and copyist for these plays as she had done for the novels. Eliza was staying in Dorking in Surrey, while Fanny Burney was living in Camilla Cottage in West Humble, the closest village to Dorking and less than a mile and a half away. In a letter of the time to her cousin Philadelphia Walter, Eliza states that she had not been receiving any visitors and had been staying at home with her books for the previous six months.

Fanny Burney's third novel, *Camilla*, had been published by subscription in 1796 and had raised a very large amount of money for Fanny Burney, about £1,000 from subscription and an additional £1,000 from the sale of the copyright, and so it seems Fanny Burney was no longer in need of financial support from Eliza's novels. It was at this time that Eliza began her major novels in association with Jane Austen. *Fanny Burney's Camilla* is referred to in the novels of *Jane Austen* more than any other novel and, from this, it appears that Eliza regarded it as her finest novel prior to the publication of the *Jane Austen* novels.

5.

Eliza and Jane Austen

Eliza's close association with Jane Austen would probably not have arisen had it not been for the outbreak of the French Revolution in 1789. Since Eliza's husband was, in title at least, an aristocrat, she and her husband were both in danger of execution whilst they were living in France. The Comte returned from France to England in 1792, when they visited Bath together. However, the count, as an officer in the French Army, returned to France the same year, to avoid his estates in France being confiscated. In England during this period, Eliza stayed temporarily with Jane Austen and her family at their home in Steventon Rectory, Hampshire. She found a renewed mutual attraction between herself and the two sons of the family, James and Henry, who were Oxford students and also keen writers; together they published a literary magazine in Oxford called *The Loiterer*, to which it is possible Eliza contributed anonymously. In particular there is one article written by a "Sophia Sentiment" which is attributed by many biographers to Jane Austen. In edition number 9 of *The Loiterer* of 28th March 1789 a purported letter sent to the author states:

"As for your last paper, the story was good enough, but there was no love, and no lady in it, at least no young lady; and I wonder how you could be guilty of such an omission, especially when it could have been so easily avoided. Instead of retiring to Yorkshire, he might have fled into France, and there, you know, you might have made him fall in love with a French Paysanne, who might have turned out to be some great person."

The name of "Sophia Sentiment" is the name of a character in William Hayley's comedy *The Mausoleum*. But perhaps it also parodied Sophie Streatfeild, an acquaintance of Fanny Burney who was well known for her over-demonstrative displays of emotion and her ability to produce tears at will. Sophie Streatfeild was the lover of the literary hostess Hester Thrale's husband, Henry Thrale, and after Mr Thrale's death Charles Burney, Fanny Burney's father, was also in love with her. Sophie Streatfeild would have been well known to Eliza through her association with the Burneys but would have been unknown to Jane Austen. The "French Paysanne, who might have turned out to be some great person" could well be Eliza herself. Jon Spence opines that this article may have been written by "the thirteen-year-old Jane Austen" but in truth the style reflects a rather older and more cynical woman, namely Eliza. There is strong literary evidence that this letter from "Sophia Sentiment" is in fact written by Eliza. The previous year, 1788, Eliza had visited Henry Austen at St John's College in Oxford and it must have been this visit which inspired her to write this letter to the magazine. She says of *The Loiterer* in the "Sophia Sentiment" letter:

"I am sorry, however, to say it, but really, Sir, I think it the stupidest work of the kind I ever saw: but not that some of the papers are well written; but then your subjects are so badly chosen, that they never interest one. – Only conceive, in eight papers, not one sentimental story about love and honour, and all that. – Not one Eastern Tale full of Bashas and Hermits, Pyramids and Mosques – no, not even an allegory or dream have yet made their appearance in the Loiterer. Why, my dear Sir – what do you think we care about the way in which Oxford men spend their time and money – we, who have enough to do to spend our own. For my part, I never, but once, was at Oxford in my life, and I am sure I never wish to go there again – They dragged me through so many dismal chapels, dusty libraries, and greasy halls, that it gave me the vapours for two days afterwards. As for your last paper, indeed, the story was good enough, but there was no love, and no lady in it, at least no young lady; and I wonder how you could be guilty of such an omission, especially when it could have been so easily avoided."

The author, "Sophia Sentiment", says that she, like Eliza, has only visited Oxford once. Her description of its "dismal chapels, dusty libraries, and greasy halls" is how we would imagine that Eliza would describe it to Henry in jest. When the author of the article writes "For my part, I never, but once, was at Oxford in my life, and I am sure I never wish to go there again" this sentence is very similar in style to the quotation from a letter of Eliza's of 26th October 1792 when she wrote of her own marriage "I never was but at one Wedding in my Life and that appeared a very stupid Business to me." Eliza's letter also reflects the sentence in the Sophia Sentiment letter above "I think it the stupidest work of the kind I ever saw". The word "stupid" at this time had the modern meaning of "dull". This is illustrated by the following passage from Chapter 7 of *Jane Austen's Emma*:

> "At first it was downright dulness to Emma. She had never seen Frank Churchill so silent and stupid. He said nothing worth hearing – looked without seeing – admired without intelligence – listened without knowing what she said. While he was so dull, it was no wonder that Harriet should be dull likewise; and they were both insufferable. When they all sat down it was better; to her taste a great deal better, for Frank Churchill grew talkative and gay, making her his first object."

Emily Auerbach in *Searching for Jane Austen* also believes that another letter published in *The Loiterer* was written by Jane Austen. This is a letter in edition number 43 of 21st November 1790 from a gossipy lady called "Margaret Mitten". Readers of *Fanny Burney* will instantly recognise the name of Mrs Mittin, one of the funniest characters of *Fanny Burney*, from her *Camilla* of 1796. In this novel Mrs Mittin is a gossip and a hanger on to rich people. It is highly unlikely that Fanny Burney ever read *The Loiterer*, which although distributed in London would have mainly been read within the close circle of family and friends of the authors, and the name of Mrs Mittin would be a very rare surname to choose. Therefore this is evidence that Eliza was the author of *Camilla*. One or two phrases in this letter remind us of the humour of *Jane Austen*, especially the humour in the Juvenilia, written around the same time. The author of the "Margaret Mitten" letter is a man-chasing spinster in her late thirties who writes that "I have few failings, and am wanting in no virtue except Candour, Generosity, and Truth."

In a later article in edition number 32 of *The Loiterer* of 5th September 1789 Jon Spence believes that it is Henry Austen who is writing as "Rusticus", a young man in love with an older, more sophisticated cousin. He writes about her flirtation with him that, "Such civilities… could not fail of pleasing me, the more particularly as I had been but little used to the attractions of unreserved, yet delicate freedom". However, it could also have been written by James Austen who, it seems, was equally smitten with Eliza. A later story in a letter in *The Loiterer*, in editions number 47 and 48 of 19th and 26th December 1789 concerns the seduction of a young man called Aurelius by the Marquise de la V_ in Paris. Jon Spence believes this also to be written by Henry Austen, and it is not difficult to see how this would have related to his own feelings for his cousin, the Comtesse Eliza de Feuillide.

At Steventon in Hampshire, Eliza also became close friends with the two unmarried daughters of the family, Jane and Cassandra. In her letters to her cousin, Phylly Walter, Eliza describes the two girls with her customary generosity and hyperbole as "perfect Beauties and of course gain 'hearts by dozens'", and states that "They are I think equally sensible, and both so to a degree seldom met with, but still My Heart gives the preference to Jane, whose kind partiality to me, indeed requires a return of the same nature".

In spite of Eliza's own literary interests, nowhere in her surviving letters does Eliza write of Jane Austen being in any way a writer or gifted in this area, as we would expect if Jane Austen were the true author. She only compliments her on her looks and describes her character merely as "sensible". This is in spite of the fact that, according to the conventional biography of Jane Austen, Jane Austen was at this time writing her first literary pieces whilst Eliza was living with her at her house. Eliza was a woman of great literary interests, who read many novels both in English and French, visited the London theatre regularly and liked to act the main parts in family theatricals. She had an extensive and sophisticated literary acquaintance. If Jane Austen had been the author of the short pieces written at this period that are now attributed to her, Eliza would surely have contributed herself to these Juvenilia. Eliza would also have visited Jane Austen often in later years when Jane Austen was living in Bath, Southampton and Chawton, and there would have been an extensive correspondence and cooperation between them about literary matters. In fact Eliza rarely visited Jane Austen after Jane moved to Bath in 1801, and not a single letter survives between the two of them.

Had Jane Austen really been such a talented author herself, Eliza would have introduced her to her own literary circle, including Warren Hastings, Lord Mansfield and Lady Sophia Burrell. No such introductions were ever made. Though we know that Warren Hastings was a great admirer of the novels of *Fanny Burney* and *Jane Austen*, Hastings never made any attempt to meet either of them, not even Jane Austen, the cousin of Eliza who visited him frequently. When Jane Austen visited her relations, the Leigh family, at Adlestrop in 1806, it seems Jane Austen did not even pay a visit on Warren Hastings, who lived on the neighbouring estate of Daylesford only half a mile away, and who was a long standing friend of the Leighs.

It was at Steventon from 1795 to 1796, that Eliza began writing the first of the novels which are now world famous under the name of *Jane Austen*, to whom in fact the financial proceeds of the novels were eventually donated, as can be seen by the accounts in the Jane Austen museum at Jane Austen's house in Chawton, Hampshire. In 1795 and 1796 respectively, Eliza began the works *Elinor and Marianne* and *First Impressions* which later bore the respective names of *Sense and Sensibility* and *Pride and Prejudice* when they were later revised and abridged (or, as Jane Austen described, "lop't and crop't") and published in 1811 and 1813 respectively.

On 1st November 1797 George Austen, Jane Austen's father, wrote to the publisher, Thomas Cadell, offering him the manuscript of *First Impressions*, saying he had "in my possession a Manuscript Novel, comprised in three Vols. about the length of Miss Burney's *Evelina*". This is useful information as it tells us how long the original version of *Pride and Prejudice* was. It cannot have been much longer than the final version, since *Evelina* was itself not a very long book. Although George Austen mentioned Fanny Burney in his letter, he made no explicit link between her and the new novel, perhaps believing the publisher would notice it was by the same author as *Evelina*. If this was his intention he was unsuccessful, because the manuscript was declined by return of post. This was in spite of the fact that the author was offering to publish it at her own expense. It is notable that the publisher chosen by George Austen was the same publisher by whom *Fanny Burney's* last two novels, *Cecilia* and *Camilla*, had been published (*Cecilia* was published by T. Payne and Son and T. Cadell. *Camilla* was published by Payne, Cadell & Davies). It would seem certain that, had George Austen mentioned the manuscript as being by Fanny Burney, it would have been published without hesitation, but for some reason Eliza did not wish him to do this.

Incidentally, the title of the first version of *Pride and Prejudice*, *First Impressions*, seems to refer to an article published some years before in the magazine published in Oxford by James and Henry

Austen, *The Loiterer*. The full quotation from this was "First Impressions are seldom affected by subsequent alteration", which is also the theme for *Pride and Prejudice*. (This quote originally comes from the novelist Samuel Richardson's *Sir Charles Grandison*.)

After her husband's death, Eliza was courted by both of the Austen brothers. It is, I believe, a tradition in the Austen family that James may have proposed to her but she was later to marry the younger of the two of them, Henry, who was ten years her junior. A very long on-off courtship between Eliza and Henry culminated in Eliza visiting her cousin in 1797 when he was stationed with the Oxfordshire Militia in Great Yarmouth in Norfolk. She spent the whole autumn nearby at Lowestoft, ostensibly so that her sickly son could take the cure of sea bathing. She even wrote to her cousin Philadelphia that she drove occasionally to Yarmouth "with which I am delighted". It is noticeable in *Jane Austen's* novels how meetings in seaside resorts are a thinly veiled shorthand for illicit sexual relations. For instance, in *Emma*, it is at Weymouth that Frank Churchill becomes secretly engaged to Jane Fairfax. In *Pride and Prejudice* Mr Wickham and Georgiana Darcy nearly elope to Ramsgate and Mr Wickham and Lydia Bennett meet in Brighton. By the early 1800s seaside resorts had replaced spa towns such as Bath as the fashionable place for young people to meet. Eliza was a frequent visitor to them herself and we have documentary evidence that Eliza visited all of the above resorts.

Eliza and Henry were married in London in St. Marylebone Church on 31ST December 1797 rather than at Steventon, in a ceremony reminiscent of the shameful marriage of Wickham and Lydia in *Pride and Prejudice*, which also took place in London away from the family home of Longbourn. The fact that the marriage of Henry and Eliza took place away from the Austen family home may imply some disapproval on their part of the marriage, especially from Henry's mother. Mrs Austen was known to disapprove of Eliza and especially did not wish her for a daughter-in-law. Whilst Eliza was rich, there was the obscurity of her birth, and her beauty and flirtatious, irreverent character did little to endear her to the other female members of the Austen family. In 1798 Henry and Eliza were living in Ipswich but they were to spend most of their marriage living together in London. Henry was still in the Oxfordshire Militia at this time, however, and after the Irish Rebellion broke out in 1798 the militia were sent to Ireland in 1799, and so Eliza and Henry were separated for some time. It was at this time that Henry became further involved in the financing of the army. After returning to England he was able to use his military connections, including Lord Charles Spencer, a son of the Duke of Marlborough, to continue this work in civilian life. He set himself up as a banker and army agent in partnership with a fellow officer, Henry Maunde. Although he wrote to Warren Hastings to request financial help for this venture, it was politely turned down.

On 29th October 1799 Eliza writes in a letter from Dorking in Surrey that her health has been bad and that she has moved there to try to recuperate with the country air, but without much success. She retreated there with her books, piano and harp. Patrick Piggott states in *The Innocent Diversion: A Study of Music in the Life and Writings of Jane Austen* that there survives a printed volume of "*Feuilles de Terpsichore*", pieces to be sung at the harp and a volume of hand-copied songs by Purcell, Handel, Haydn and Mozart, which bear the names "Mrs Henry Austen" and "Eliza Austen, 19th August 1799". From Eliza's choice of music, there can be no doubt she was a musician of taste, as she has chosen songs by the four greatest composers up to that time.

It was no doubt this time spent in Dorking that Eliza was able to use as a background for two of the *Jane Austen* novels. In *The Watsons*, a short unfinished novel by *Jane Austen*, it is generally agreed by scholars that the town of D_ in Surrey in which this book is set represents Dorking, whilst the nearby town of R_ represents Reigate. (Furthermore, in the original manuscript the town of D_ was corrected by hand from the town of L_, obviously representing Leatherhead). Dorking also lies just below Box Hill, to which the expedition in *Jane Austen's Emma* takes place. Another reference in *The Watsons* to the county of Surrey is the name of the family, Lord Osborne and the Osbornes, who are the main aristocratic family in the area. To anybody with any acquaintance with Surrey either then or now, the Osbornes can only be a thin disguise for the main aristocratic family of this area, the Onslows. At the time that *The Watsons* was written, Thomas Onslow, Second Earl of Onslow, was the Member of Parliament for Guildford and lived at Clandon Park near Guildford. I have suggested later in this book how "Donwell Abbey" in *Jane Austen's Emma* may have taken part of its name from Clandon. I also mention later in the book how this part of Surrey was an area very well known to Eliza de Feuillide, but not to Jane Austen.

The time of writing of *The Watsons* has been dated to between 1801 and 1804. A calendar of 1801 has been suggested for it. Other biographies of *Jane Austen* state that *The Watsons* was written while Jane Austen was living in Bath during this period. Why should Jane Austen have set the novel in Dorking, a small insignificant town in Surrey we have no evidence that she ever visited, when she was living at the time in the exciting and famous town of Bath? Why did she not set the book in or near Bath? Surely it is much more likely that Eliza began this book set in Dorking shortly after living in Dorking herself. It is likely, however, that Jane Austen acted as secretary in writing out this book when she met Eliza in Bath in 1804.

At around this time, Eliza's son, Hastings, had been suffering very badly with fits and eventually, on 9th October 1801, he died, aged fifteen. Eliza wrote of this event to her cousin Phylly on 29th October 1801:

"So awful a dissolution of a near & tender tie must ever be a severe shock, and my mind was already weakened by witnessing the sad variety and long series of pain which the dear sufferer underwent – but deeply impressed as I am with the heart rending scenes I have beheld I am most thankful for their termination, and the exchange which I humbly hope my dear Child has made of a most painful existence for a blissful immortality".

As mentioned previously, her husband had given up the army, and he set up as a banker in Cleveland Row, near St James's Palace in London; he requested financial assistance from Warren Hastings, but was turned down. That there were ostensibly no hard feelings on the subject seems to have been confirmed by Warren Hastings and his wife calling upon Henry and Eliza Austen in London on 1st March 1802. The Austens also moved house to No. 24 Upper Berkeley Street, near Portman Square. As I have previously remarked, it is notable that Mrs Jennings' London house in *Sense and Sensibility* is also situated in Berkeley Street, near Portman Square. The address of Cleveland Row may have suggested the name of Cleveland, the hero of *Fanny Burney's* play *A Busy Day*, written at that time.

In July or August 1802, Eliza and Henry returned to France, probably in an attempt to recover some of the estates of the late Count. However, the peace in force at the time was revoked by Napoleon on 16th May 1803 and on 22nd May 1803 the order was given for all foreigners to be detained. Fortunately, Henry had returned to England earlier in the year. However, Eliza was forced to escape to England immediately but, according to Austen family tradition, she had no difficulty in disguising herself as a French woman, such was her perfect command of the language. After her return to London, in the spring of 1803 Henry arranged for a manuscript under the name of *Susan*, later to be published as *Northanger Abbey*, to be sold by his man of business in London, Mr Seymour. It was sold to Crosby & Co for £10. However, although the book was advertised in the same year, it was never published and the manuscript was later to be bought back by Henry.

In the spring of 1804, Henry and Eliza moved in London from

Upper Berkeley Street to Brompton. Henry also moved his office to No 1 The Courtyard, Albany, Piccadilly. In the same year Eliza and Henry visited Lyme Regis in Dorset with Eliza's cousin, Jane Austen. Presumably they met up with the Austens first at their home in Bath. Bath and Lyme Regis were to become the principal settings for *Jane Austen's* novel *Persuasion*. At the same time they also visited Weymouth, but Jane Austen did not accompany them there. Weymouth is mentioned in *Jane Austen's Emma* as the place where Frank Churchill and Jane Fairfax became secretly engaged.

In April 1805, as we know from a later letter from Jane Austen to her sister Cassandra, Jane Austen had sent a screen and a brooch to Henry and Eliza. This is proof that there was an ongoing correspondence between Jane Austen and Henry and Eliza, which must have been later destroyed by the Austen family in the nineteenth century to conceal Eliza's authorship.

In March and May 1806, Warren Hastings noted in his diary that he called on Henry and Eliza when they were in London. This proves that, contrary to what is written in some books, Eliza was still on good terms with him. In August 1808, Henry and Eliza visited Warren Hastings at the magnificent new mansion he had built and furnished lavishly, on his old family estate in Daylesford, Gloucestershire. After his return from India in 1785 he had been able to fulfil a lifelong ambition by buying back this estate, after his family had been forced to sell it many years earlier. In 1809 Henry and Eliza moved house again from Brompton to 64 Sloane Street in the West End of London

Jane Austen's first two novels, *Sense and Sensibility* and *Pride and Prejudice*, were published in 1811 and 1813 respectively from Eliza and Henry's house at 64 Sloane Street. The novels were published anonymously, although the title page of *Sense and Sensibility* described it as being "by a Lady". The advertisement of its publication in *The Morning Chronicle* of 1811 said it was "by Lady — —", laying even more stress on the author being a titled woman (Eliza being a Countess). *Sense and Sensibility* was published by

Thomas Egerton of the Military Library, Whitehall. It is possible that this Thomas Egerton may have been a relation of the Egertons who were Eliza's friends in Washington, County Durham. It was hardly a risky venture for the publisher as, according to Claire Tomalin, the risk of the cost of printing was undertaken by Henry and Eliza. Thus the first novel of *Jane Austen* was, in effect, self-published by Eliza. Ms Tomalin also mentions that Jane Austen appeared at this time at Henry and Eliza's house in Sloane Street, to correct the proofs of *Sense and Sensibility*. Letters from Jane Austen to her sister Cassandra of the time remain, confirming this. Jon Spence in *Becoming Jane Austen* at this point credits Eliza with the only literary achievement that any Jane Austen biographer has ever credited her with, when he suggests that Eliza may have done some of the proofreading herself. Perhaps this is how he reads the following passage in the letter of Jane Austen to her sister from Eliza's house of 25th April 1811:

"I have had two sheets to correct, but the last only brings us to Willoughby's first appearance. Mrs. K. regrets in the most flattering manner that she must wait *till* May, but I have scarcely a hope of its being out in June. Henry does not neglect it; he *has* hurried the Printer, and says he will see him again to-day. It will not stand still during his absence, it will be sent to Eliza."

It seems to me quite clear, however, that Eliza in this letter is not to do the proofreading but to take the place of Henry in dealing with the printer and publisher. It is quite clear that the proofreader is Jane Austen, as Jane Austen writes "I have had two sheets to correct". The reason for this is that it was not customary at the time for the author to proofread her own works. I quote later in this book from King George III, who confirms this, in a passage from Fanny Burney's diary. Even today it is inadvisable for an author to proofread their own work, as the author is far more likely to miss any mistakes than an outsider. In any event, an author of the calibre of *Jane Austen* would be far better employed writing a new novel than undertaking the tedious process of proofreading, a job better left to a needy relative. Far from being evidence of Jane Austen being the writer, the fact that she was proofreading the novel indicates on the contrary that this was most unlikely.

Strangely, it seems that Henry Austen and Eliza had little doubt that the novels would be successful, which was very surprising if the author had been a first time author. As a banker who knew about risk, it was unlikely that Henry Austen would risk so much of his own money publishing the works of an untested author. Similarly, Eliza, although generous, had always been careful with money throughout her life. Henry Austen stated in his *Biographical Notice of the Author* prefacing *Northanger Abbey* when it was published in December 1817, that the risk of publication of the book was undertaken by Jane Austen herself from money she set aside from her own meagre allowance. He wrote:

> "Nay, so persuaded was she that its sale would not repay the expense of publication, that she actually made a reserve from her very moderate income to meet the expected loss."

Henry must here be deliberately misleading us, however; a hard-headed businessman such as the publisher Egerton would never have accepted a financial guarantee from such a poor woman as Jane Austen. This deception therefore casts doubt on the truth of other parts of Henry Austen's *Biographical Notice of the Author*.

Another strange thing about the publication of *Sense and Sensibility* and *Pride and Prejudice* was that they were published by Thomas Egerton at the Military Library in Whitehall, whose other publications mostly related to military campaigns and famous military figures. No doubt they were published by this firm either because of a connection with Eliza's friend Catherine Egerton, or owing to the military connections of Henry Austen; another connection is that the magazine *The Loiterer* written by James and Henry Austen as students at Oxford in 1789 and 1790 had been sold by Thomas Egerton in London. It is much more likely that the impetus and financing for the publication of two romantic novels came from Henry or Eliza than from a military publisher!

Tragically, just at this time of her greatest literary success, Eliza contracted a severe illness during the winter of 1811-1812, most likely the same breast cancer that her mother suffered from, and she eventually died on 25th April 1813, aged fifty-one, after a long and painful illness, unable to enjoy her greatest success. Her death was a lingering and harrowing affair, not least because she had earlier cared for her mother while she died of the same disease, and so she was only too well aware of the suffering in store for her. Her death finally came as a release as much as a tragedy to her husband. Jane Austen wrote on 3rd July 1813 to her brother Francis "Sincerely as he was attached to poor Eliza moreover, & excellently as he behaved to her, he was always so used to be away from her at times, that her Loss is not felt as that of many a beloved wife might be, especially when all the circumstances of her long and dreadful Illness are taken into the account. – He very long knew that she must die, & it was indeed a release at last."

Thus, sadly, Eliza was not able to enjoy the success of the novels later to achieve worldwide fame under the name of her cousin Jane Austen, many of which were only published after her death.

The fact must be faced that, as some of the *Jane Austen* books were published after Eliza's death, this may be used as a strong argument against her authorship. However, this should not be so. It is very common for the works of authors to be published after their death. Probably the majority of authors have had novels published after their death. When illness and death strikes unexpectedly, as it did for Eliza, it is likely that there would have been several manuscripts in draft, novels that she had finished but which needed revising, editing, updating and proofreading before they could be published. In addition, even if they were all ready to be published at the time of her death, they could not be published all at once, rather their publication would be spaced out to appear not more frequently than one a year.

Jane Austen's sister, Cassandra, was responsible for drawing up a schedule of when the novels were written. However, this is the same sister who admitted destroying the largest part of Jane Austen's letters, in particular it seems destroying any which contained references to Eliza. Therefore, if we cannot find a legitimate reason why she destroyed Jane Austen's correspondence and why all the correspondence of Eliza was destroyed by the Austen family in the nineteenth century, we should be wary of placing any trust in her schedule of when the novels were written. However, it is conceded that Jane Austen, with Henry Austen, was responsible for the editing and proofreading of the drafts that Eliza had left after her death, and their preparation for publication. We know from her surviving letters that Jane Austen stayed in London with Henry Austen for much of the time during the years after Eliza's death, no doubt to carry out this task. If she had been the author herself it would have been unnecessary for her to go to London and she would not have needed Henry's assistance. It is likely that Henry Austen would have played a large part in amending the final versions of the novels as he was much better acquainted with Eliza and, unlike Jane Austen, he had the benefits of a university education and some literary ability.

Jane Austen's Mansfield Park was published on 9th May 1814 by Egerton. Deirdre Le Faye writes, following Cassandra Austen's schedule, that *Mansfield Park* was started about February 1811 and finished late in 1813, *Emma* was started on 21st January 1814 and finished on 29th March 1815, and *Persuasion* was started on 8th August 1815 and finished on 6th August 1816. She writes that Jane Austen's final, unfinished novel, *Sanditon*, was started on 27th January 1817 and its 24,000 words were written in a few weeks. For such a careful writer, who must have revised her novels several times before a final version was reached, this seems an extremely tight timescale. We are asked to imagine that the author knocked out one a year in the manner of a Regency Dick Francis. We know, however, that *Sense and Sensibility* and *Pride and Prejudice* were written over a time scale of ten to fifteen years. It seems likely that the above dates of Cassandra are accurate, but that they record the beginning and completion of the final versions of the novels, as they were written out by Jane Austen, adapted from the drafts and papers left over after Eliza's death. It is not unreasonable to suppose that it would have taken a year to prepare the final manuscripts from draft, especially given the technology of a time when writing was done with a quill pen. It is much more likely, given the quality of the later novels, that they were written over a period of years, perhaps during the "empty" years between 1799 and 1811, when we have no record of any of the *Jane Austen* books being written. When Jane Austen finalised the manuscripts for publication no doubt she and her brother Henry also amended the calendar of the novels and included recent events, to bring them up-to-date for publication. We know in fact that this is what happened, as Deirdre Le Faye writes that the calendar of dates used in *Pride and Prejudice*, originally 1794-1795, was updated to 1811-1812, the time of its final revision prior to being published in 1813. We can infer therefore that the same was done for the other novels and that any dates or calendar for novels dating after Eliza's death do not necessarily indicate that the novels were written at this period, but that this was the period prior to publication. No doubt at the time it was necessary to use an updated calendar when publishing novels, to prevent them from having a dated feel.

One other indication that Cassandra's schedule for when the novels were written is not true is in the *Biographical Notice of the Author*, written as a preface to *Northanger Abbey* in 1817 by Henry Austen. Eliza's husband wrote of the author of the *Jane Austen* novels "Most of her works, as before observed, were composed many years previous to their publication." At the time he wrote this there were six published novels of *Jane Austen*: *Northanger Abbey*, *Sense and Sensibility*, *Pride and Prejudice*, *Mansfield Park*, *Emma* and *Persuasion*.

Therefore, according to Henry, **at least** four of the six had been composed many years prior to their publication. According to Cassandra's chronology, however, at least three of the six novels, *Mansfield Park*, *Emma* and *Persuasion*, were written shortly before their publication. We can therefore deduce that Cassandra's schedule is not to be relied on as a true indication of when the novels were actually written, but rather as an indication of the dates of their final revision.

There are other reasons to believe that all the novels were finished before Eliza's death in 1813. Once we show that any of them were begun earlier than Cassandra states, we can prove that Cassandra's schedule is fabricated. *Persuasion* is set mainly in Lyme Regis and Bath; in 1804 Eliza and Henry met with Jane Austen and her family at Bath and together made a trip to Lyme Regis, and it is therefore likely that *Persuasion* was written shortly after this time; it has never been regarded as one of the best works of *Jane Austen*; its style does not have the perfection and maturity of the last novels of *Jane Austen*: *Mansfield Park*, *Emma* and *Sanditon*. The dates given by Cassandra Austen of 1815-1816 for the composition of *Persuasion* do not fit in with the style of the novel at all, and must therefore represent only the date of preparation of the final manuscript. The published novels of *Jane Austen* had all shown a gradual development of *Jane Austen's* style to reach the pinnacle of novel writing in *Emma*. Claire Tomalin describes *Emma* thus: "generally hailed as Austen's most perfect book, flawlessly carried out from conception to finish, without a rough patch or a loose end." However, in *Persuasion*, supposedly written after *Emma,* the author suddenly returns to the less accomplished style of such novels as *The Watsons* written between 1800 and 1805. Although *Persuasion* mentions dates after Eliza's death, these were no doubt inserted by Henry and Jane Austen when they came to preparing the draft manuscripts for publication, in order to make the novel up-to-date for the reader, as was the usual practice. Any dates on the final manuscripts prepared by Jane Austen, which are dates after Eliza's death, were also no doubt the dates that these final manuscripts were prepared, not the dates when the books were actually written.

It is extremely hard to believe, in particular, that *Emma*, considered by some to be the greatest novel in the English language, was not only written, but also prepared for publication, in a mere fourteen months. If we allow twelve months to prepare the manuscript for publication, which is a realistic timescale given the technology of the age and in accordance with the time it took to prepare *Sense and Sensibility* and *Pride and Prejudice* for publication, this leaves the author just two months in which to write one of the most admired novels ever. Jan Fergus in her article *The Professional Woman Writer* explains this exceptional speed by saying that Jane Austen "was clearly at the height of her genius". She must indeed have been at the top of her game for, according to Jan Fergus, "During this time, she also saw *Mansfield Park* through the press, made three visits to Henry in London, and three more to other friends." But, truth to tell, the flawlessness of *Emma* as described by Claire Tomalin above, can only have been arrived at by continuous amendment and re-drafting over a number of years, as Henry Austen hints at above. I will describe later how *Emma* originated in a novel of 1796 and was developed by the author in an unpublished novel of 1803/4.

Incidentally, Jan Fergus's proposition in the same article that *Jane Austen* was "a professional author who is acutely conscious of her sales (as well as the possible future value of her copyright) and eager to increase her profits" cannot be reasonably upheld, given the many years it took to write most of the novels and the comparatively meagre financial return received from them.

Henry Austen in his *Biographical Notice of the Author*, although he identifies the author as Jane Austen, seems to me to be describing Eliza. Sentences such as "her temper was as polished as her wit" bring to mind the descriptions of Eliza in the poems written to her by Lady Sophia Burrell. In a similar way to how Lady Sophia Burrell describes Eliza, Henry Austen says of the author that "she was formed for elegant and rational society, excelling in conversation as much as in composition". Other aspects of the author's character he describes accord with contemporary descriptions of Eliza and he mentions that "Her own works, probably, were never heard to so much advantage as from her own mouth; for she partook largely in all the best gifts of the comic muse". This would ring true with what we know of Eliza successfully playing the lead roles in the comedies staged at Jane Austen's house at Steventon. These descriptions by Henry Austen of the authoress are, by contrast, in contradiction to contemporary descriptions we have of Jane Austen. In this notice Henry also confirms of the writer that "She became an authoress entirely from taste and inclination. Neither the hope of fame nor profit mixed with her early motives." So Jan Fergus's view of the author as a professional writer is without foundation.

There is also a clue in its text that the final, unfinished novel, *Sanditon*, was written before 1815 and not in 1817, as Cassandra asserts. In the novel Mr Parker, the developer of the seaside resort of Sanditon, remarks:

> "You will not think I have made a bad exchange, when we reach Trafalgar House – which by the bye, I almost wish I had not named Trafalgar – for Waterloo is more the thing now. However, Waterloo is in reserve."

According to Cassandra's schedule, this novel was written in 1817. However, if the novel had been written after 1815, the date of the Battle of Waterloo, the house would without doubt have been named "Waterloo House". However, the house is named after the Battle of Trafalgar, which took place in 1805. It seems as if the manuscript was therefore first written between 1805 and 1815 and has been updated after Eliza's death, by the insertion of an extra sentence and a half. The expression above:

> "Trafalgar House – which by the bye, I almost wish I had not named Trafalgar"

is echoed in a letter of Jane Austen of 15th June 1808:

> "we drove away from the Bath Hotel; which, by-the-bye, had been found most uncomfortable quarters".

If this is an alteration by Jane Austen, it avoids the necessity of amending "Trafalgar House" throughout the novel, although this insertion does make Mr Parker look rather stupid in naming a new house after an old battle. If, as we have shown, the novel was written before 1815, this means that Cassandra's schedule, according to which *Sanditon* was begun in 1817, is misleading.

There is an interesting article by Lindsay Fleming in the *Jane Austen Society Report for the Year 1960*. There has been some debate as to the original of "Sanditon" and once again it is possible to identify. As a child brought up in what is now Greater London, it is no mystery to me. Trips to the seaside were a memorable event and the only resort with a sandy beach ("sandy town") readily accessible from London at that time was Bognor. It has certainly left me with more pleasant memories than the pain of walking barefoot over the pebbly beaches of Eastbourne and Brighton, or sitting in the depressing worm cast mud of Littlehampton. In Lindsay Fleming's article *Sanditon and Bognor* she presents compelling evidence, from a number of different sources, that *Jane Austen* based Sanditon on Bognor.

The fact that most of the novels were only published after Eliza's death appears to be evidence against her being the author, and no doubt will be used as such. However, in fact it is the opposite. Naturally, due to the sudden and unexpected illness of Eliza, some of her manuscripts were not fully revised, edited and proofed, and therefore they had not been published before Eliza's death. Presumably this is the job that Henry and Jane Austen undertook together in London, and the reason for Jane Austen's visits to Henry in London at this time. To piece together the drafts and produce a final version would probably have taken about a year for each novel. What is strange about the conventional history of Jane Austen is that, on Jane Austen's death on

18th July 1817, all of "her" books had been fully revised, proofed and edited, and there was no proofing and editing to be done, as one would normally expect after the death of an author. The last two of "her" books to be published, *Persuasion* and *Northanger Abbey*, were published in late December 1817, a mere five months after Jane Austen's death. Because we know *Northanger Abbey* had been written much earlier and it was published together with *Persuasion*, this suggests that the two of them were written at a similar period and the publication of both of them together, as the last two of *Jane Austen's* novels, was a "clearing up" exercise. This opinion is reinforced by the fact that both novels are centred on the city of Bath, visited by Eliza in 1804. It is incredible that all the books of Jane Austen had been fully prepared, proofed and published such a short time after her death. This is especially strange, since Jane Austen's death was not expected and so she would not have had time to get all her manuscripts into order. Assuming, as I have done, that it took one year to compile a novel from draft to a state ready for publishing, a not unreasonable time scale, Jane Austen would have had to have had a premonition in 1813 that she was going to die four years later, and then decided to write no more novels but only prepare the existing ones for publication. This is obviously a ridiculous supposition.

Since writing the above, it has come to my attention that there is in fact conclusive written evidence that all of the novels of *Jane Austen* had been completed by 29th January 1813, three months before Eliza's death. It is hard to understand how this has been overlooked previously. In a letter of 29th January 1813 to her sister Cassandra, quoted in James Edward Austen-Leigh's *A Memoir of Jane Austen* of 1870, Jane Austen writes of *Pride and Prejudice*, published that year:

"The advertisement is in our paper to-day for the first time: 18s. He shall ask 1l. 1s. for my two next, and 1l. 8s. for my stupidest of all."

She is writing about the publisher Thomas Egerton, who published *Pride and Prejudice* in 1813 and sold it, as above stated, for 18 shillings

(90p). Jane Austen states that Egerton will price her next two novels at £1 1 shilling (£1.05) and her final novel will be priced at £1 8 shillings (£1.40). We can be certain that the novels had already been written at this time for the following reasons. Firstly, Jane Austen already knew at this time that only three more novels of *Jane Austen* remained to be published. These were *Mansfield Park*, *Emma* and *Persuasion*, which were in the event published respectively in May 1814, December 1815 and December 1817 (although in the event *Mansfield Park* was priced at 18 shillings (90p) and *Emma* and *Persuasion* were published by the more prestigious publishing house of John Murray. The copyright of *Jane Austen's* other novel, then known as *Susan* but published in 1817 as *Northanger Abbey*, was not available to Jane Austen in 1813 as it had been sold to Crosby & Co in 1803 and was probably not bought back from them by Henry Austen until 1815 or 1816). Secondly, we know that Jane Austen is referring to specific completed novels and not proposed novels, as she specifically describes the final novel as "my stupidest of all". As I have explained previously, the word "stupid" at this time meant the equivalent of the modern word "dull". It is not hard to guess which novel Jane Austen is describing as "my stupidest of all" – it is *Persuasion*. Jane Austen seems to agree with me that it is the dullest and least accomplished of the novels of *Jane Austen* – perhaps this is why the ending of it was rewritten – this is the probable reason why *Persuasion* was to be published as the last of the three, as Jane Austen must have thought it would be better to publish it last of all to avoid readers being dissuaded from buying the next novel.

Thomas Egerton's plans for the publication of the last three novels as outlined above in Jane Austen's letter of 29th January 1813 also confirm my earlier supposition that it was for commercial reasons that the novels were not published together after Eliza's death, but spaced out to appear not more frequently than one a year.

Since Jane Austen's letter of 29th January 1813 confirms that all of the novels of *Jane Austen* were written by this date, what are we to make of Cassandra Austen's schedule of when the novels were written? It is disingenuous to believe that Cassandra Austen only wished to record the date of completion of the final versions of these novels ready for publication; we are therefore left with the inescapable conclusion that Cassandra Austen's schedule was written deliberately for the purpose of deception. The main deception that she was trying to practise was obviously to show that many of the novels were written after Eliza's death, in order to disprove anybody who might claim that Eliza was the true author of these novels. We have established, therefore, that Cassandra Austen was involved in a deception in drawing up this schedule, and this makes it very hard to rely on any written evidence provided by her, or on any information provided by her to other members of her family. In addition, it shows us that Cassandra's reasons for destroying and editing many of Jane Austen's letters must have been to disguise Eliza's authorship of *Jane Austen's* novels.

It was only on Jane Austen's death in 1817 that Eliza's husband, Henry, then "revealed" to the world that his sister Jane Austen was the author of these anonymously published novels, in his *Biographical Notice of the Author*, in the introduction to *Northanger Abbey*. Obviously it would have been impossible for him to reveal the true author, as this would have brought shame on Warren Hastings, who was still living, and on the Austen family. Thus, surprisingly to the modern reader, before Jane Austen's death in 1817 there was no association in the mind of the reading public between the famous novels and Jane Austen.

The reader may wonder what other evidence the authorship of Jane Austen relies on. In particular, of the six *Jane Austen* novels published up to and shortly after Jane Austen's death, how many original handwritten manuscripts remain? Four or five final manuscripts, perhaps? Or perhaps just the drafts of two or three novels? The answer is none. All the final manuscripts and all the drafts of all six novels have mysteriously disappeared. How can this be? To lose one or two manuscripts might be considered a misfortune, but to lose all six looks like carelessness. Proponents of Jane Austen's authorship offer no explanation as to where all these final manuscripts and drafts have gone. If we surmise that Eliza de Feuillide was the author, however, we can readily understand why they have all "been disappeared". No doubt they would have offered clues as to the identity of the true author. All that survives in manuscript of all six novels is two cancelled chapters of *Persuasion*.

James Edward Austen-Leigh, the son of Jane Austen's brother, James, summed up Eliza's life as follows in *A Memoir of Jane Austen* of 17 November 1870. This was the first biography of Jane Austen to appear in print, almost fifty years after Jane Austen's death:

> "There was another cousin closely associated with them at Steventon, who must have introduced greater variety into the family circle. This was the daughter of Mr. Austen's only sister, Mrs. Hancock. This cousin had been educated in Paris, and married to a Count de Feuillade, of whom I know little more than that he perished by the guillotine during the French Revolution. Perhaps his chief offence was his rank; but it was said that the charge of 'incivism', under which he suffered, rested on the fact of his having laid down some arable land into pasture – a sure sign of his intention to embarrass the Republican Government by producing a famine! His wife escaped through dangers and difficulties to England, was received for some time into her uncle's family, and finally married her cousin Henry Austen. During the short peace of Amiens, she and her second husband went to France, in the hope of recovering some of the Count's property, and there narrowly escaped being included amongst the *détenus*. Orders had been given by Buonaparte's government to detain all English travellers, but at the post-houses Mrs. Henry Austen gave the necessary orders herself, and her French was so perfect that she passed everywhere for a native, and her husband escaped under this protection.
>
> She was a clever woman, and highly accomplished, after the French rather than the English mode; and in those days,

when intercourse with the Continent was long interrupted by war, such an element in the society of a country parsonage must have been a rare acquisition. The sisters may have been more indebted to this cousin than to Mrs. La Tournelle's teaching for the considerable knowledge of French which they possessed. She also took the principal parts in the private theatricals in which the family several times indulged, having their summer theatre in the barn, and their winter one within the narrow limits of the dining-room, where the number of the audience must have been very limited. On these occasions, the prologues and epilogues were written by Jane's eldest brother [James], and some of them are very vigorous and amusing. Jane was only twelve years old at the time of the earliest of these representations, and not more than fifteen when the last took place. She was, however, an early observer, and it may be reasonably supposed that some of the incidents and feelings which are so vividly painted in the Mansfield Park theatricals are due to her recollections of these entertainments."

In recent years, as biographers of Jane Austen have found so little extra to add to our portrait of Jane Austen, attention has gradually shifted away from her to pay more attention to the life of those around her, and especially to the life of Eliza de Feuillide. Indeed, David Nokes in his biography of Jane Austen, devotes a large part of his biography to her, although he does not allude to her as the author. He does rather tellingly, however, quote from a letter from Jane Austen to her sister Cassandra of January 1807: "I have… endeavoured to give something like the truth with as little incivility as I could". He also refers to the Austen family tradition during the nineteenth century of producing censored versions of Jane Austen's life and works. Other biographers, such as Claire Tomalin and Jon Spence, have also devoted a large segment of their biographies to Eliza, in an attempt to flesh out the bare bones of Jane Austen's life. In some biographies of Jane Austen, to make up for the lack of documentary evidence linking Jane Austen to the works which now bear her name, there is a great deal of padding and irrelevant information about the most distant relations and acquaintances of Jane Austen. By such alchemy the slim volume of Jane Austen's life is transmuted into the weighty tome of the modern Jane Austen biography, the base metal of the life into the gold of the novels.

The most important source of information for those studying Eliza's life, however, is the book by Deirdre Le Faye, *Jane Austen's Outlandish Cousin: The Life and Letters of Eliza de Feuillide*, which examines Eliza's life in detail, and publishes all of her letters which remain, as well as most of the letters of her friends and relations which refer to her. Ms Le Faye is a wonderful researcher and it is a marvellous book for those studying the little that remains of the evidence of Eliza's life. I would strongly recommend that the reader buy this book, as through her letters it gives a far more complete picture of the life of Eliza de Feuillide than I am able to do. The reader will especially find much to amuse and delight them in the letters of Eliza de Feuillide, which contain many passages bringing to mind the humour and stylish writing of the novels of *Jane Austen*. The book also displays on its cover a portrait miniature of Eliza de Feuillide as a young woman, which may also be examined on the internet sites where the book is sold.

Ms Le Faye's wonderful biography is only marred, of course, by her seeing Eliza de Feuillide as a person peripheral to *Jane Austen's* novels. Accepting Jane Austen as the author of the novels, Ms Le Faye is forced to talk of Eliza only as the person whose colourful life influenced *Jane Austen's* novels. (Similarly, according to other biographers, much of Jane Austen's knowledge of English and French literature was passed on from Eliza. It is very strange how, according to these biographers, Eliza passed on so much literary information to Jane Austen, but chose to write nothing herself.)

Ms Le Faye also, in contrast to most other biographers, does not accept that Eliza was the natural daughter of Warren Hastings, blaming the rumour solely on the ill report of Jenny Strachey, Lord

Clive's secretary. She does not take into account the covert admission of Mr Hancock in his letter to his wife that Warren Hastings was her father. She also does not take into account Warren Hastings' later track record in this regard, in relation to his later "purchase" of his second wife from the German portrait miniature painter, Christoph Adam Carl von Imhoff, which seems to confirm Hastings' character as a man not to be trusted with friends' wives.

We can see from the originals of some of Eliza's letters, available in microfiche from the Hampshire Records Office in Winchester, that she wrote in a very neat and well educated hand and her style of writing was exemplary. It is in fact very hard to distinguish the writing style of Eliza from that of Jane Austen, which may suggest that Eliza instructed Jane Austen in handwriting while she was staying with her at Steventon. From the maturity and wit of the letter that survives, which Eliza wrote aged eighteen, we can see that she was more than capable of writing *Fanny Burney's Evelina* two years earlier. Indeed, just one paragraph of her letter of 16th May 1780, written at the age of eighteen, describing the fashions of Paris, is enough to show in Eliza's letters the elegant style and humour of the author of *Evelina*:

"There is perhaps no place in the world where dress is so well understood & carried to so great a perfection as in Paris & no wonder it should be so since people make it the chief business & study of their Lives. Powder is universally worn, & in very large quantities, no one would dare to appear in public without it, The Heads in general look as if they had been dipped in a meal tub; Hats likewise (which are called English but which do not bear the least resemblance to those of our nation) are much the fashion. The hair is cut in shades, not worn high at all. It was with reluctance, I conformed to the mode in this article, as my hair was very long on my arrival, & I was obliged to have it cut to half its length; but what will not All powerful Fashion effect & so much for the modes let us now speak of something more interesting."

6.

Literary Influences on "Jane Austen"

When writing a literary biography, it is customary for the author to assume a mantle of omniscience. At least this is what I have found on reading some biographies of Jane Austen. The author has read every major work he or she quotes and has thoroughly researched all relevant articles on the subject. Perhaps the author is an academic or a professional writer, and their reading will be wide ranging and in depth. More likely the author is a "celebrity biographer" who is writing "on commission". The author has "done" other major historical and literary figures, and has even perhaps been rewarded with one of the awards frequently bestowed on celebrity biographers, and now it is the turn of Jane Austen to receive the same treatment. Copious footnotes bear witness to sterling service in academic libraries, if not to the same effort to interpret the information so obtained.

While I have attempted to research this book as thoroughly as possible, I hope that any shortcomings in this field have been more than compensated for by the use of intelligence and reason, qualities sometimes rare in the study of Jane Austen's life as it relates to *Jane Austen's* novels. Research, in literature as in science, should not be just the collection of evidence, however diligently this is done. True research is not the evidence itself, but how it is interpreted. I have noted in my reading various faults in research in the field of *Jane Austen* studies. One major fault is the assumption that Jane Austen wrote the novels; biographers feel no need to provide any evidence for this whatsoever. The burden of proof is assumed to be on others to disprove it. This leads to the second fault, the circular argument, for example in the form of such sentences as "We know that Jane Austen had this opinion from such and such a passage in *Emma*." The third major fault, perhaps the most important, is the absence of an understanding of logic. Arguments are not followed through logically in several steps, and evidence which is inconvenient is not addressed and argued against, it is simply ignored.

In this respect it is notable to me the marked difference between scientific and literary (or even historical) research. Coming from a family of scientists (my father was a research physicist and my brothers are both university professors and researchers in natural science) makes me keenly aware of this. Scientific research is carried out according to the scientific method. Data is not just collected but is used to create theories, which are then subjected to testing and challenge. Contrary to what non-scientists believe, scientists do not prove facts, they merely create theories to explain natural phenomena. They welcome opposing views and challenges to their theories, which are necessary in order to move science forward. A theory is a system they devise to explain natural phenomena. It is not, as many non-scientists believe, a guess which may be true or untrue – scientists call this a hypothesis.

Literary research is carried out in a quite different manner, which I would describe as pre-scientific. It owes more to the mediaeval mind than the Enlightenment. Just as the mediaevals revered authority figures such as the natural philosopher Aristotle and the physician Galen, and did not attempt to disprove their theories by experiment, the views of literary critics are given weight according to their standing in the hierarchy of the academic or literary world. Many literary critics and historians have not studied mathematics or any of the natural sciences in any depth and are therefore not well qualified to apply scientific logic to their research. Often their research resembles "story-telling" or "stamp collecting" rather than logical thought. Whereas scientists test theories by thinking in logical steps, there is a tendency for literary critics to weigh heaps of evidence and authority on one side of an argument against heaps on the other, as on a weighing scale, and whichever is heavier is true. Unlike in science, in literary criticism opposing hypotheses or theories are not welcome and there is generally an orthodoxy based on the beliefs of those with high positions in the academic and literary world. Literary criticism is therefore not able to move forward, in the way that science does, but becomes mired in accepted "truths". To challenge such orthodoxies is likely to bring condemnation rather than the congratulation it would receive in the scientific world.

Some literary critics may challenge me to prove that Eliza de Feuillide wrote *Jane Austen's* novels. Because of their lack of scientific understanding, they believe that if I cannot prove that Eliza de Feuillide wrote *Jane Austen's* novels, then Jane Austen wrote them. This is like those who say that the Theory of Evolution (more properly, Darwin's Theory of Natural Selection) cannot be proved, it is only a theory, therefore it is untrue. In science it is impossible to prove anything is true. In the pre-scientific way in which literary critics think, however, it is possible to prove things. You do this by providing a large heap of evidence or the authority and support of critics of high academic standing. In their illogical and unscientific way, some literary critics believe that Jane Austen's authorship is proved: A. because her name is written on the title page of her novels (which it was not during her lifetime) and B. because all the Professors of English say that she wrote them.

Regrettably, the field of Jane Austen studies is one in which there is little scope to obtain further information about Jane Austen's life. The well is all but dry. As for the life of Eliza de Feuillide, the chief problem faced by her biographer is that nearly all of the letters she wrote, and all of the letters she received, were destroyed during the nineteenth century.

Like many people, I quickly read the whole of *Jane Austen's* main works in a flurry of enthusiasm when I was young. It is only on writing this book that I have read all of them again in more detail and have read for the first time the works of *Fanny Burney*. I would like to say that I am very glad I have had the opportunity to read *Fanny Burney's* novels (apart, of course, from her ridiculously badly written last novel *The Wanderer* which I would far rather have never set eyes upon (more of this later)). I have also read various eighteenth century English novels such as those of Fielding, Smollett, Sterne, Samuel Johnson and Ann Radcliffe, and several French eighteenth century novels in the original French. (I am fluent in French and German, and I also have a basic knowledge of Latin).

As a biographer, I have posed myself the question, "Who are the main literary influences on the writings of *Jane Austen* (and *Fanny Burney*)?" My conclusion may be surprising to some. It strikes me as obvious that there is one writer above all others who stands out as the greatest stylistic influence on *Jane Austen*. It is somebody who I have not seen mentioned in this connection, yet whose style runs unmistakeably through the works of *Jane Austen* and *Fanny Burney*. He is commonly acknowledged as the greatest classical prose stylist of them all, perhaps the greatest genius of Latin literature: I refer of course to Publius Cornelius Tacitus, the celebrated Roman historian.

In the works of *Jane Austen* and *Fanny Burney* we see again and again the hallmarks of his style: the balanced antithesis of the two halves of the sentence; the conciseness of style; the economy of expression; and the cynicism, irony and double-edged meaning. Like a sentence of Tacitus, a sentence by *Fanny Burney* or *Jane Austen* is above all remarkable for its balance. This is perhaps not surprising, as historians and other writers of the eighteenth and early nineteenth century used Tacitus as their model. This was especially true of Samuel Johnson, who was something of an imitator, both of Latin authors and of French authors such as Voltaire (Johnson's *Rasselas* owed a large debt to Voltaire's *Candide*). We often read in criticism of *Fanny Burney* of her Johnsonian style, but we need to go back further to Johnson's use of Tacitus and other Latin authors as his model.

We can see from *Jane Austen's* satirical *The History of England*, written in November 1791, and from her satire on history in *Northanger Abbey* (discussed in more detail further on) that the author was very interested in history, with a deep knowledge of the subject. Only somebody well educated in English history could have written such intelligent satires. In 1791 Jane Austen was only fifteen years old and had no formal tuition in history at all that we are aware of. Eliza, on the other hand, was twenty-nine years old and no doubt had been well educated by her London masters in this subject as a girl.

The strong influence of Tacitus is something I sensed initially without any confirmation, solely through being acquainted with the styles of Tacitus, *Jane Austen* and *Fanny Burney*. Imagine my surprise, therefore, when I found it confirmed in *Jane Austen's Northanger Abbey*, when Miss Tilney, sister of the hero Henry Tilney, discusses history and its worth with the heroine, Catherine Morland. The author uses all her irony here to disguise her own deep love of history. The dialogue is as follows:

> "'You are fond of that kind of reading?'
> 'To say the truth, I do not much like any other.'
> 'Indeed!'
> 'That is, I can read poetry and plays, and things of that sort, and do not dislike travels. But history, real solemn history, I cannot be interested in. Can you?'
> 'Yes, I am fond of history.'
> 'I wish I were too. I read it a little as a duty, but it tells me nothing that does not either vex or weary me. The quarrels of popes and kings, with wars or pestilences, in every page; the men all so good for nothing, and hardly any women at all – it is very tiresome: and yet I often think it odd that it should be so dull, for a great deal of it must be invention. The speeches that are put into the heroes' mouths, their thoughts and designs – the chief of all this

must be invention, and invention is what delights me in other books.'

'Historians, you think,' said Miss Tilney, 'are not happy in their flights of fancy. They display imagination without raising interest. I am fond of history – and am very well contented to take the false with the true. In the principal facts they have sources of intelligence in former histories and records, which may be as much depended on, I conclude, as anything that does not actually pass under one's own observation; and as for the little embellishments you speak of, they are embellishments, and I like them as such. If a speech be well drawn up, I read it with pleasure, by whomsoever it may be made – and probably with much greater, if the production of Mr. Hume or Mr. Robertson, than if the genuine words of Caractacus, Agricola, or Alfred the Great.'"

The author is here satirising two works of Tacitus: his *Annals,* Book XII, which is our chief source of information about Caractacus, the Chief of the Catuvellauni tribe at the time of the Roman invasion of Britain under the Commander Aulus Plautius in 50 AD; and Tacitus's *Agricola*, his biography of the Roman Commander Gnaeus Julius Agricola, who oversaw the final conquest of Britain from AD 78 to AD 84. Agricola was Tacitus's father-in-law.

Miss Tilney's remarks are written with acute irony. Tacitus was thus one of Miss Tilney's "sources of intelligence in former histories and records, which may be as much depended on, I conclude, as anything that does not actually pass under one's own observation." But Eliza was well aware that Tacitus was far from being able to be depended on and that the "genuine words" of Caractacus and Agricola were more likely to be the opinions of Tacitus himself. Indeed, it was well known to Latin scholars that Tacitus liked to invent speeches for the leaders of the Britons which reflected his own critical views of the Roman Empire, which *Jane Austen* here refers to ironically as their "genuine words". It is possible that Tacitus himself may have been from a Celtic family and, in any event, he had sympathies for the "barbarians" conquered by Rome, whose masculine qualities and love of freedom he often admired above the character of the "effete" Romans and their capitulation to the Empire. Tacitus used his characters as mouthpieces for his own cynical and reactionary views on Rome at the time of the Empire and especially during the rule of the Emperor Domitian, whom Tacitus served but hated intensely. The most celebrated line he gave to a British leader was that in the speech of the Caledonian leader Calgacus, on the eve of the battle between the Romans and Britons at Mons Graupius in Scotland, when he stated of the Romans *"solitudinem faciunt, pacem appellant"* (they create a desert and call it peace). However, the author of *Northanger Abbey* knew that Tacitus also gave a less well known speech to Caractacus, the leader of the Britons, where he says, after being captured by the Romans and led to Rome:

"'Si quanta nobilitas et fortuna mihi fuit, tanta rerum prosperarum moderatio fuisset, amicus potius in hanc urbem quam captus venissem, neque dedignatus esses claris maioribus ortum, plurimis gentibus imperitantem foedere [in] pacem accipere. praesens sors mea ut mihi informis, sic tibi magnifica est. habui equos viros, arma opes: quid mirum si haec invitus amisi? nam si vos omnibus imperitare vultis, sequitur ut omnes servitutem accipiant? si statim deditus traderet, neque mea fortuna neque tua gloria inclaruisset; et supplicium mei oblivio sequeretur: at si incolumem servaveris, aeternum exemplar clementiae ero.' ad ea Caesar veniam ipsique et coniugi et fratribus tribuit."

This is translated by Alfred John Church and William Jackson Brodribb as follows:

"'Had my moderation in prosperity been equal to my noble

birth and fortune, I should have entered this city as your friend rather than as your captive; and you would not have disdained to receive, under a treaty of peace, a king descended from illustrious ancestors and ruling many nations. My present lot is as glorious to you as it is degrading to myself. I had men and horses, arms and wealth.

What wonder if I parted with them reluctantly? If you Romans choose to lord it over the world, does it follow that the world is to accept slavery? Were I to have been at once delivered up as a prisoner, neither my fall nor your triumph would have become famous. My punishment would be followed by oblivion, whereas, if you save my life, I shall be an everlasting memorial of your clemency.' Upon this the emperor granted pardon to Caractacus, to his wife, and to his brothers."

We can be sure that the author of *Northanger Abbey* is referring to Tacitus, as Tacitus was the only contemporary historical source for Miss Tilney's "genuine words" of Caractacus and Agricola. Indeed, in referring to Agricola, she makes it beyond a doubt that she is referring to Tacitus, since Tacitus was the only Roman historian who recorded in detail the deeds of his father-in-law Agricola, the Governor of Britain.

It seems highly likely that Eliza read Tacitus in the original Latin, since her natural father, Warren Hastings, was the leading scholar of his year in Greek and Latin at Westminster School in London, and it was Warren Hastings, along with Tysoe Saul Hancock, who had devised the programme of education that Eliza went through as a child. It would have been anomolous to Warren Hastings for Eliza to have the best tutors in writing, music and other subjects, and a comprehensive all round education, but not to learn Latin. In any case, a woman of the intellectual curiosity of Eliza would have wanted to take advantage of the possibility of learning the classics.

She could have learnt this from her masters in London but it is perhaps more likely she learnt Latin and Ancient Greek from her uncle, George Austen, Jane Austen's father, when she and her mother stayed for long periods at his house in Steventon. George Austen was a gifted scholar of Latin and Greek, and the trust fund provided by Warren Hastings would have been sufficient to pay for these studies; no doubt George Austen, with a growing family, would have greatly appreciated the extra income. Hastings had previously no doubt paid George Austen when he had taken on the care of Warren Hastings' young son, George, who unfortunately died as a child. Hastings also trusted George Austen enough to name him as one of the trustees of the secret trust fund he set up for Eliza.

From the above excerpt from *Northanger Abbey* I draw one example to show *Jane Austen's* influence from Tacitus. Miss Tilney states about historians that "They display imagination without raising interest". This is very reflective of the style of Tacitus in its use of antithesis (contrast). It reminds me especially of Tacitus's ironic comment about the Emperor Galba: "*magis extra vitia quam cum virtutibus*" (he was without faults rather than being blessed with qualities). Indeed, the text from which the above quotation is taken from Tacitus's *Histories*, Book 1, 49-50, in the translation by Church and Brodribb, for its style could almost be from a *Jane Austen* novel. It describes the life and death of the Emperor Galba, who ruled from AD 68 to AD 69:

> "*hunc exitum habuit Servius Galba, tribus et septuaginta annis quinque principes prospera fortuna emensus et alieno imperio felicior quam suo. vetus in familia nobilitas, magnae opes: ipsi medium ingenium, magis extra vitia quam cum virtutibus. famae nec incuriosus nec venditator; pecuniae alienae non adpetens, suae parcus, publicae avarus; amicorum libertorumque, ubi in bonos incidisset, sine reprehensione patiens, si mali forent, usque ad culpam ignarus. sed claritas natalium et metus temporum obtentui, ut, quod segnitia erat, sapientia vocaretur. dum vigebat aetas militari*

laude apud Germanas floruit. pro consule Africam moderate, iam senior citeriorem Hispaniam pari iustitia continuit, maior privato visus dum privatus fuit, et omnium consensu capax imperii nisi imperasset."

"Such was the end of Servius Galba, who in his seventy-three years had lived prosperously through the reigns of five Emperors, and had been more fortunate under the rule of others than he was in his own. His family could boast an ancient nobility, his wealth was great. His character was of an average kind, rather free from vices, than distinguished by virtues. He was not regardless of fame, nor yet vainly fond of it. Other men's money he did not covet, with his own he was parsimonious, with that of the State avaricious. To his freedmen and friends he shewed a forbearance, which, when he had fallen into worthy hands, could not be blamed; when, however, these persons were worthless, he was even culpably blind. The nobility of his birth and the perils of the times made what was really indolence pass for wisdom. While in the vigour of life, he enjoyed a high military reputation in Germany; as proconsul he ruled Africa with moderation, and when advanced in years shewed the same integrity in Eastern Spain. He seemed greater than a subject while he was yet in a subject's rank, and by common consent would have been pronounced equal to empire, had he never been emperor."

"The nobility of his birth and the perils of the times made what was really indolence pass for wisdom", is a sentence worthy of *Jane Austen* in its irony. Its ironic description of laziness also reminds me of the quotation from *Fanny Burney's Cecilia* mentioned below: "her father, in whom a spirit of elegance had supplanted the rapacity of wealth, had spent his time as a private country gentleman, satisfied, without increasing his store, to live upon what he inherited from the labours of his predecessors".

The true style and irony of Tacitus can only be appreciated properly by those who understand Latin, which I believe Eliza did, as she could not have otherwise imitated it so beautifully. The reason for this is that Latin, as a language without articles and prepositions, can be more concise than English and, as it has cases, it is more flexible in its word order, and English can only attempt to imitate this concision and variation in word order. However, this is what the author succeeds in doing to great effect in the novels of *Fanny Burney* and *Jane Austen*.

We can compare the above extract from Tacitus with the introduction to *Fanny Burney's Camilla*:

> "In the bosom of her respectable family resided Camilla. Nature, with a bounty the most profuse, had been lavish to her of attractions; Fortune, with a moderation yet kinder, had placed her between luxury and indigence. Her abode was in the parsonage-house of Etherington, beautifully situated in the unequal county of Hampshire, and in the vicinity of the varied landscapes of the New Forest. Her father, the rector, was the younger son of the house of Tyrold. The living, though not considerable, enabled its incumbent to attain every rational object of his modest and circumscribed wishes; to bestow upon a deserving wife whatever her own forbearance declined not; and to educate a lovely race of one son and three daughters, with that expansive propriety, which unites improvement for the future with present enjoyment."

This is only one of many similar introductions to the works of *Jane Austen* and *Fanny Burney* which display this faux-Latin summarising style compounding concision with antithesis, exemplified in the phrase "that expansive propriety, which unites improvement for the future with present enjoyment". Another example is in the first chapter of *Fanny Burney's Cecilia*:

"Cecilia, this fair traveller, had lately entered into the one-and-twentieth year of her age. Her ancestors had been rich farmers in the county of Suffolk, though her father, in whom a spirit of elegance had supplanted the rapacity of wealth, had spent his time as a private country gentleman, satisfied, without increasing his store, to live upon what he inherited from the labours of his predecessors. She had lost him in her early youth, and her mother had not long survived him. They had bequeathed to her £10,000, and consigned her to the care of the Dean of ——, her uncle. With this gentleman, in whom, by various contingencies, the accumulated possessions of a rising and prosperous family were centred, she had passed the last four years of her life; and a few weeks only had yet elapsed since his death, which, by depriving her of her last relation, made her heiress to an estate of £3,000 per annum; with no other restriction than that of annexing her name, if she married, to the disposal of her hand and her riches."

The Latin style of concision and antithesis can be seen most clearly in the phrase "her father, in whom a spirit of elegance had supplanted the rapacity of wealth".

Similarly, in the works of *Jane Austen* we find the same style, for example in the first chapter of *Emma*:

"Emma Woodhouse, handsome, clever, and rich, with a comfortable home and happy disposition, seemed to unite some of the best blessings of existence; and had lived nearly twenty-one years in the world with very little to distress or vex her.

She was the youngest of the two daughters of a most affectionate, indulgent father, and had, in consequence of her sister's marriage, been mistress of his house from a very early period. Her mother had died too long ago for her to have more than an indistinct remembrance of her caresses, and her place had been supplied by an excellent woman as governess, who had fallen little short of a mother in affection.

Sixteen years had Miss Taylor been in Mr Woodhouse's family, less as a governess than a friend, very fond of both daughters, but particularly of Emma. Between them it was more the intimacy of sisters. Even before Miss Taylor had ceased to hold the nominal office of governess, the mildness of her temper had hardly allowed her to impose any restraint; and the shadow of authority being now long passed away, they had been living together as friend and friend very mutually attached, and Emma doing just what she liked; highly esteeming Miss Taylor's judgment, but directed chiefly by her own.

The real evils indeed of Emma's situation were the power of having rather too much her own way, and a disposition to think a little too well of herself; these were the disadvantages which threatened alloy to her many enjoyments. The danger, however, was at present so unperceived, that they did not by any means rank as misfortunes with her."

The phrase most reminiscent of the ironic antithetical style of Tacitus here is "highly esteeming Miss Taylor's judgment, but directed chiefly by her own". The opening paragraphs of most of the novels of *Fanny Burney* and *Jane Austen* are written in a similar faux-Latin style. The passage I have found most reminiscent of the style of Tacitus, however, comes from Chapter 33 of *Jane Austen's Emma* where the author describes Mr Elton's satisfaction with his new wife:

"He had the air of congratulating himself on having brought such a woman to Highbury, as not even Miss Woodhouse could equal; and the greater part of her new acquaintance, disposed to commend, or not in the habit of judging, following the lead of Miss Bates's good-will or taking it for granted that the bride must be as clever and as agreeable as she professed herself, were very well satisfied."

As the author's imitation of this Latin style was so beautiful and accurate, I believe that the author of *Fanny Burney* and *Jane Austen's* works must have been very well acquainted with Tacitus in the original Latin.

There is further evidence that Eliza was learned in the Latin language, which is also drawn from *Fanny Burney's Camilla*. There is little evidence that Fanny Burney ever learned Latin and indeed it seems she never had the opportunity to do so. However, it seems that the author of *Camilla* was learned in the Latin language. Why is this? Firstly, the author makes a joke about Latin when she says the uneducated baronet, Sir Hugh Tyrold, was totally ignorant of *hic, haec, hoc* (the paradigm for the relative pronoun in Latin). More importantly, the author stresses the importance of learning Latin to the education of a woman. Camilla's cousin, Indiana, in *Camilla* has been thoroughly spoilt and even the thought of study causes her to burst into tears. Sir Hugh Tyrold makes plans for her to be educated in Latin by his own Latin tutor, Dr Orkborne, which the author approves of, but Sir Hugh is persuaded against this by the influence of his family governess, Miss Margland. The author describes the spirit of Miss Margland as being "as haughty as her intellects were weak". The author continues:

"She seized with pleasure the opportunity offered her by Indiana, of remonstrating against this new system of education; readily allowing, that any accomplishment beyond what she had herself acquired, would be completely a work of supererogation. She represented dictatorily her objections to the baronet. Miss Lynmere, she said, though both beautiful and well brought up, could never cope with so great a disadvantage as the knowledge of Latin: 'Consider, Sir,' she cried, 'what an obstacle it will prove to her making her way in the great world, when she comes to be of a proper age for thinking of an establishment. What gentleman will you ever find that will bear with a learned wife? except some mere downright fogrum, that no young lady of fashion could endure.'

The author then goes on in *Camilla* to approve the learning of Latin and Ancient Greek by Camilla's sister, Eugenia, though she contrasts the good use of classical learning made by the clergyman, Dr Marchmont, with the pedantry exhibited by Eugenia's tutor, Dr Orkborne.

If the author of *Camilla* was learned in Latin, as we can surmise from the above satire on women's education, the author cannot have been Fanny Burney, who had no education in Latin. If the author was Eliza, we have here ironic comments on the importance of Latin to a woman's education, which were likely to have been written by somebody with a good education in Latin herself. Since we have previously indicated that, if Eliza was the author of *Fanny Burney's* works, she must have also been the author of *Jane Austen's* works, then logically this passage from *Camilla* also shows that *Jane Austen's* works were written by an author learned in Latin. Logically, if the author of *Jane Austen's* works was learned in Latin she would no doubt have been well acquainted with the works of Tacitus, which is confirmed by the above mentioned references to Tacitus's works in *Northanger Abbey*. From this we can conclude that the similarities in the style of Tacitus and *Jane Austen* are due to the influence of Tacitus **as he was read in the original Latin** and indicate Tacitus as a main stylistic influence on *Jane Austen*. Tacitus can only be deeply understood and appreciated in the original language, since

Latin (as a language with cases and without definite or indefinite articles) has a concision which English cannot match but only imitate.

To disprove, therefore, the authorship of Jane Austen, theoretically and logically it is only necessary to prove that Fanny Burney did not know Latin. It is unnecessary to prove that Jane Austen knew no Latin. I have seen no book about Fanny Burney which asserts she was learned in Latin. Fanny Burney, writing about herself in the third person in her *Memoirs of Doctor Burney* admitted that she had had no formal education whatsoever. She wrote: "Frances was the only one of Mr Burney's family who never was placed in any seminary, and never was put under any governess or instructor whatsoever." It is highly unlikely that she would have been able to teach herself Latin. Indeed, Kate Chisholm, in her biography of Fanny Burney, confidently asserts that Fanny Burney knew neither Greek nor Latin. She mentions that Dr Samuel Johnson offered to give her lessons in Greek and Latin, but Fanny Burney's father refused her permission to take up this offer. If what Kate Chisholm asserts is true, and Fanny Burney knew neither Latin nor Greek, logically the authorship of both Fanny Burney and Jane Austen is disproved.

We know that one of the Latin texts taught by Jane Austen's father was Virgil's *Aeneid*. This may have been where Eliza got the title name for *Fanny Burney's Camilla*, named after Virgil's woman warrior who fought against Aeneas. Another Latin author I suggest that Eliza had studied with George Austen is Horace, and I have already quoted from a letter from Eliza's husband, Henry, dated 5th June 1802 to Warren Hastings, in which Henry Austen's father, George, recommended to him a translation of Horace by Hastings. If George Austen also instructed Eliza in Latin, it is likely she would also have translated with him the works of Horace. I will put forward later on my evidence that Eliza was also the author of some of the works which are now attributed to *Elizabeth Hamilton*. In the preface to *Elizabeth Hamilton*'s *Memoirs of Modern Philosophers* of 1800, the author quotes Horace in the original Latin *"Ridiculum acri Fortius et melius magnas plerumque secat res"* and in the translation by Francis: "Ridicule shall frequently prevail, And cut the knot, when graver reasons fail". We can be fairly certain that the author of this book knows Latin as she also quotes from Horace's *Ars Poetica* at the beginning of Volume 1, Chapter VII, *"Spectatum admissi risum teneatis"*, without translating this into English.

In *Elizabeth Hamilton's Translations of the Letters of a Hindoo Rajah* of 1796 there is further support for the author *Elizabeth Hamilton* being able to read Latin and Greek (we know that Elizabeth Hamilton herself had not learnt these languages). In her Preliminary Dissertation to the book, the author confirms that she had learnt Latin and Greek as a child when she compares herself to those "who have not had the advantages of an early classical education":

"The many elegant translations from the different Oriental languages with which the world has been favoured within these last few years, have not failed to attract merited attention; and the curiosity awakened by these productions, concerning the people with whom they originated, has been gratified by the labours of men, who have enjoyed the first rank in literary fame.

Still, however, the writers in every branch of Oriental literature, have to contend with disadvantages, too numerous and too powerful to be easily overcome. The names of the Heroes of Greece and Rome, are rendered familiar at a period of life, when the mind receives every impression with facility, and tenaciously retains the impressions it receives. With the name of every Hero, the idea of his character is associated, and the whole becomes afterward so connected in the mind, with the blissful period of life at which it was first received, that the recollected scenes of juvenile felicity may frequently, even in the most accomplished minds, be found to give a zest to the charms of the ancient authors. To those, who have not had the advantages of an early classical education, the same objections which render the translations from the Oriental writers tiresome, and uninteresting, will operate with equal force on the most beautiful passages of Homer, or Virgil, and the names of Glaucus and Sarpedon, of Anchises and Eneas, be found as hard to remember, and as difficult to pronounce, as those of Krishna and Arjoun."

She is saying that it will be difficult for her readers to understand the characters and stories of the Indian writers if they have just read them in translation. She is saying that a person who had not learnt Latin or Greek as a child would face the same problems with Greek or Latin literature in translation. She contrasts this person with herself, who learned Latin and Greek at a young age. It was widely believed at the time that languages could only be easily learned at a very young age. Sir Hugh Tyrold, in *Fanny Burney's Camilla* is unable to learn Latin as an adult, mainly from his lack of intelligence, but also because he has taken it up too late. Mr Hancock wrote of Eliza's education on 17th January 1770 (when Eliza was eight years old) that he was in agreement with Warren Hastings that it should on no account be interrupted. He wrote: "It is very certain that neither Languages nor Exercises can be attained to any Degree of Perfection but in the earlier Years of Life".

Since writing the above, I was very pleased to find a published article which, in my opinion, although perhaps not the author's, gives complete support to the views I have expressed. This is an article entitled "Jane Austen: Closet Classicist" by Mary DeForest, who has a doctorate in Classics and teaches Latin at the University of Colorado at Denver (published in *Persuasions: The Jane Austen Journal* vol. 22, 2000). She discusses whether the author *Jane Austen* knew Latin or Greek, and her conclusion is that she almost certainly did. She remarks of Jane Austen's father, George, in relation to his teaching the classics "Would he not have taught a gifted child what he taught the sons of other people?" She mentions characters with classical names in *Jane Austen's* Juvenilia, such as Daphne and Corydon in a short play called *The Mystery*, and Damon and Corydon in another.

In *Jane Austen's The History of England* "The Author" writes about Lady Jane Grey, who was unsuccessfully put onto the English throne by the Protestants in 1553 for nine days after the death of Edward VI and before the accession of Mary Tudor. The passage is a direct satire on Oliver Goldsmith's description of Lady Jane Grey being visited by her tutor, Roger Ascham, in his *History of England*, where the tutor finds her reading Greek while the others are out hunting:

> "Lady Jane Grey... was... famous for reading Greek while other people were hunting...Whether she really understood that language or whether such a Study proceeded only from an excess of vanity for which I beleive she was always rather remarkable, is uncertain. Whatever might be the cause, she preserved the same appearance of knowledge, & contempt of what was generally esteemed pleasure, during the whole of her Life, for she declared herself displeased with being appointed Queen, and while conducting to the Scaffold, she wrote a Sentence in Latin & another in Greek on seeing the dead Body of her Husband accidentally passing that way".

In respect of her classical learning, Mary DeForest writes that "Lady Jane Grey may well be a humorous portrait of Austen herself." Ms DeForest cites other examples of the author's knowledge of Latin and Greek, but the most interesting part of her article is where she quotes the same words as myself from *Jane Austen's Northanger Abbey*, as spoken by Elinor Tilney:

> "If a speech be well drawn up, I read it with pleasure, by whomsoever it may be made – and probably with much

greater, if the production of Mr. Hume or Mr. Robertson, than if the genuine words of Caractacus, Agricola, or Alexander *[sic]* the Great".

Ms DeForest remarks that "The speeches of Agricola and Caractacus are not to be found in the histories of England by David Hume or William Robertson, as Elinor implies, but in the works of the Roman historian Tacitus (Agricola; Annals 12.37). With the exquisite manners of an Austen heroine, Elinor does not spring upon her new friend the name of a Roman historian… Instead, she substitutes the names of familiar British historians, without actually attributing the speeches to them". For the author *Jane Austen* to display her knowledge of Latin and Greek directly, would be for her to go against the literary ideals of the eighteenth century. These ideals are expressed as the "artless elegance and ease" for which the poet Lady Sophia Burrell praised Eliza. Ms DeForest agrees with this, saying that "although Austen only rarely alluded to classical literature, her sparing usage is artistry, not ignorance."

Ms DeForest also believes that the author of *Northanger Abbey* had read Tacitus in its original Latin, since she writes "The intellectual Elinor Tilney of Northanger Abbey could stand for the author herself, revealing a classical education without displaying one… Once we imagine Elinor reading Tacitus, however, it is an easy step to imagine her reading him in Latin".

What Ms DeForest writes in her article completely overturns the traditional case for Jane Austen being the author. The case made by biographers of Jane Austen for her authorship has usually been that she had only two years' basic primary education, but that she was able to learn the rest of her knowledge by reading from the extensive library of books belonging to her father (the famous "five hundred books") and by listening to the intelligent conversation of her better educated father and brothers. Deirdre Le Faye believes Jane Austen to have had just a smattering of Latin, solely from snippets overheard from her father's pupils whilst they were being taught the language. Mary DeForest's revelation that the author had been given a systematic and lengthy classical education from an early age and over several years completely explodes this theory. I have outlined previously that it is highly unlikely Jane Austen ever learnt Latin or Greek and why it was highly likely that Eliza did, since George Austen would not have been in a financial position to instruct his own daughter, whereas the education of Eliza would have been paid for by her mother from Eliza's trust fund.

Apart from Tacitus and other classical authors, the main influences on the works of *Jane Austen* and *Fanny Burney* appear to be French rather than English authors. In French literature, the influence of Voltaire on *Jane Austen* is very apparent, especially his dry and ironic sense of humour. It is likely, for instance, that the name and character of Mr Gardiner in *Pride and Prejudice*, the sensible and prosperous London merchant, makes reference to the conclusion in Voltaire's *Candide* that the best philosophy of life is "*Il faut cultiver son jardin*" (one should cultivate one's own garden).

If we are to look at which French authors had the most influence on the writings of *Fanny Burney* and *Jane Austen*, our main source of evidence is the Preface to *Fanny Burney's Evelina*, where the author specifically mentions two French authors. These are Jean-Jacques Rousseau (1712-78) whose works included *La Nouvelle Héloise, ou Julie* of 1761 and *Émile, ou De l'éducation* of 1762; and Pierre Marivaux, author of the novels *La Vie de Marianne* and *Le Paysan parvenu* (1735-36). When considering the strong influence of these authors on the novels of *Jane Austen* and *Fanny Burney*, we should bear in mind the observation of Jane Austen's nephew James Edward Austen-Leigh, that Eliza was "highly accomplished, after the French rather than the English mode".

There is little reason to believe that Jane Austen herself was fluent in French, since biographers have tended to attribute any knowledge she had of the language to tuition from Eliza. Jane Austen, unlike Eliza, had no French companion to teach her the language. Jane Austen never visited France (indeed she never left

England), while Eliza lived in France for several years before and after her first marriage. Another reason to doubt that Jane Austen knew very much French is that the French books bought for her by Eliza, such as Arnaud Berquin's *L'Ami des Enfans*, were of a very simple nature, intended for the instruction of children. Anna Lefroy was the daughter of James Edward Austen-Leigh, the son of Jane Austen's brother, James. She wrote in a letter of 16th April 1869 of Jane Austen and her sister Cassandra's knowledge of French that "I think it probable that they had very valuable assistance from their cousin, Uncle Henry's first wife [i.e. Eliza] , who was an extremely accomplished woman, not only for that day, but for any day". On the grounds of her lack of knowledge of French alone it would be unlikely, therefore, that Jane Austen was the author of the novels now bearing her name.

At the time of the writing of *Evelina* in 1778 we know that Eliza was completely fluent in French. She had learnt French from a French speaking companion provided to her. In one of his letters to his wife, Mr Hancock wrote to Eliza's mother on 26th August 1774 "Undoubtedly your Method of teaching Betsy French by giving Her a French Companion is the Shortest".

At this time, however, Fanny Burney herself was not fluent in French. Unlike her two sisters, she was not sent to France to be educated, as her father did not believe she was intelligent enough to benefit from this. In addition, we know that when she met her French husband later in life they were not able to communicate fluently in French with each other at first. Therefore, at the time of the writing of *Evelina*, Fanny Burney, unlike Eliza, would not have been able to read the works of Pierre Marivaux or Jean-Jacques Rousseau in their original language. Because of the influence of the novels of both of these French writers, as outlined in the Preface to *Evelina*, on *Fanny Burney*, it would appear that the author is likely to have read them in the original French, as only Eliza could have done.

At the time of the publication of the novels of *Fanny Burney*, Eliza was an ardent Francophile, as she had greatly enjoyed her visit to the French court of pre-revolutionary France and her involvement in Paris society in the early 1780s, as we know from her letters, and she had even married a Frenchman. The contrasting ambiguity shown by *Jane Austen* towards France and the French, however, can be easily explained by the execution of Eliza's husband in 1794 by guillotine and the other injustices she suffered from the French Revolution, in particular the confiscation of her husband's estate, perhaps a more severe blow to Eliza than the loss of the Comte himself. The Revolutionary France of *Jane Austen's* time was like a different country compared to the France of *Fanny Burney's* time, which was still the France of Louis XVI and the dying days of the *ancien régime*.

Of course, it is extremely odd how, according to most biographers, Eliza could have passed on so much knowledge of French literature to Jane Austen but have had no interest whatsoever in writing herself, so that not a single poem or any piece of writing by her survives, other than letters.

In English literature, the influences mentioned by the author in the Preface to *Evelina* are Samuel Johnson (1707-84), author of *Rasselas*; Henry Fielding (1707-54), most famous as the author of *Tom Jones*; Tobias Smollett (1721-71), author of *Roderick Random* and *Peregrine Pickle*; and finally Samuel Richardson (1689-1761), whose most famous novel was *Pamela*. It has been generally noted, however, that the novel with the greatest influence on both *Fanny Burney* and *Jane Austen's* works was Samuel Richardson's novel *Sir Charles Grandison* of 1753-54 and many articles and books have been written outlining the important connections between *Sir Charles Grandison* and the novels of *Jane Austen*.

One final interesting area I have not explored but which deserves more study would be whether Eliza was fluent in German and how much the novels of *Jane Austen* and *Fanny Burney* were influenced by German authors, and whether in the original German or in translation.

7.

Why Was the Author of "Fanny Burney" the Same as the Author of "Jane Austen"?

As steals the morn upon the night,
And melts the shades away:
So Truth does Fancy's charm dissolve,
And rising Reason puts to flight
The fumes that did the mind involve,
Restoring intellectual day.

(Handel: *L'Allegro, il Penseroso ed il Moderato*)

Fanny Burney's Evelina, her first novel, which appeared in 1778 in the same year as Eliza's seventeenth birthday, has been described with much truth by one well read literary critic as *"Jane Austen* lite". Many critics agree on the importance of *Fanny Burney's* influence on *Jane Austen*. Could this be because *Fanny Burney* was the pen name of Eliza before she used the name *Jane Austen*?

At first sight this might seem far-fetched. However, there are so many avenues which support this thesis that logically I believe it cannot be untrue. One of the many convincing arguments in this respect comes from the dedication of *Fanny Burney's Evelina*, as mentioned, the first of *Fanny Burney's* novels. None of the authors I have read have been able to explain this dedication satisfactorily. To other biographers, it is something of a loose end which has been discreetly swept under the carpet. However, I believe I have the solution below. Just as a serial killer is most likely to give himself away in his first murder, before he becomes more careful, so the author here gives us one of the largest clues to her identity in the preface to her first work. The dedication to *Evelina* reads as follows (with my own highlighting):

To _____ _____

Oh author of my being!–far more dear
   To me than light, than nourishment, or rest,
Hygieia's blessings, Rapture's burning tear,
   Or the life blood that mantles in my breast!

If in my heart the love of Virtue glows,
   'T was planted there by an unerring rule;
From thy example the pure flame arose,
   Thy life, my precept–thy good works, my school.

Could my weak pow'rs thy num'rous virtues trace,
   By filial love each fear should be repress'd;
The blush of Incapacity I'd chace,
   And stand, recorder of thy worth, confess'd:

Bu**t** s**in**ce my ni**gg**ard **s**tars **t**h**a**t gift refu**se**,
   Conc**ea**lment **is** th**e** only boon I cl**ai**m;
Obscure be still the unsuccessful Muse,
   Who cannot raise, but would not sink, thy fame.

Oh! of my life at once the source and joy!
   If e'er thy eyes these feeble lines survey,
Let not their folly their intent destroy;
   Accept the tribute–but forget the lay.

Conventional critics have portrayed this poem as a dedication by

Fanny Burney to Dr Charles Burney, her father, which of course they must do to uphold the authorship of Fanny Burney. However, they do not take into account that the novel was published anonymously and that the dedicatee, like the author, was unnamed. There are several reasons why I believe that this dedication is not to Fanny Burney's musician father, Dr Charles Burney, but rather to Warren Hastings, who, as we have seen, was almost certainly the biological father of Eliza. Its tone is very much in tune with Eliza's feelings towards her father, whom she idolised but naturally felt herself distant from.

Firstly, there is the general tone of the poem. The praise of the father is so overwhelming that it does not accord easily with praise for a parent who is ever present, who the author has lived with cheek by jowl, taken for granted, argued with, been annoyed and upset by. Fanny Burney lived with her father in London at this time and acted as his secretary. Warren Hastings, on the other hand, at this time was Governor General of India and living in Calcutta. There is something distant (both geographically and emotionally) and unobtainable about the father figure in this poem. The father figure is idealised.

The poem mainly deals with the father in the sense of him being the author of the author. His creation of the author is like that of the author of the book. It is only his "authorship" that is stressed, i.e. his biological creation of the author, not his physical presence as a father. Love of virtue is described as being "planted" like a seed. He is described as the "source" of the author's life. Nowhere in this poem is real fatherhood, the physical closeness of father and daughter, celebrated. Indeed, the word "father" is not mentioned in the poem at all, but instead "author of my being". It is likely that Eliza is here making the distinction between the man who was her "father", Tysoe Saul Hancock, and her biological father, the "author of my being", who was Warren Hastings. There is a distance between the father and the daughter in the poem, so that instead of speaking of the father's warmth, affection, kisses, embrace etc., the author of the poem only speaks of "rule", "example", "precept" and "school". The father is here represented as a distant teacher, or more clearly, a role model. Eliza is referring to Hastings both as the overseer of her education and as the example who she follows.

Instead of being praised for his affection and loving kisses, the father is lauded for his "unerring rule", "good works", "num'rous virtues", "worth" and "fame". He is described more as a public figure than as a close family member. In addition, he is described as a public figure whose fame cannot be raised, i.e. somebody who is at the very pinnacle of public life. The writer of the poem says she "cannot raise… thy fame". This would perfectly describe Warren Hastings who, as Governor General of India at this time, was one of the most important, wealthy and powerful Englishmen of his time. Even with the love of a daughter, it would be difficult for Fanny Burney to represent Dr Charles Burney in this light, a man of little wealth and consequence and who, in spite of all his abilities, was even considered a mediocrity in musical circles. In the light of the strict class distinctions of the time, it would have been laughable to describe a jobbing musician and teacher of keyboard instruments as somebody whose fame in the world could not be higher. To emphasise the "low fame" of Dr Burney, we also have the evidence of Mrs Hester Thrale, the literary hostess and famous friend of Dr Samuel Johnson, who was also a friend of Charles Burney (Burney was the music tutor to her famous daughter, Queeney). In spite of her friendship for Burney, Mrs Thrale nevertheless wrote that "The Burneys are I believe a very low Race of Mortals." In her poem to Dr Charles Burney she also emphasised his low social position when she described him thus [my highlighting]:

> "His Character form'd free, confiding, & kind
> Grown cautious by Habit, **by Station confin'd**"

By contrast, the line in the dedicatory poem to *Evelina* is cleverly phrased so that when the writer says that she "would not sink thy fame", she is also referring simultaneously to the other meaning of "fame" as reputation, i.e. that she does not wish to lower Warren Hastings' reputation by revealing herself to be his illegitimate daughter. Thus, the writer is saying that the dedicatee has such a high position in public life that it cannot be enhanced whatever the quality of the novel ("cannot raise... thy fame"). There is a subtle and clever contrast in the poem between "cannot raise" and "would not sink". The word "cannot" means she is not capable of raising his position in public life. But the words "would not sink" in this context imply "does not desire to (but could if she wanted to)". The author is saying that she could reveal her identity but does not wish to do so, for fear of damaging the reputation of the dedicatee. This could only apply to Warren Hastings. There could be no damage to the reputation of Charles Burney by Fanny Burney revealing herself to be the author, as, firstly there was no shame in his having a legitimate daughter and, more importantly, the reputation of a mere music tutor could only be enhanced by having a daughter who was a renowned author.

Far from being distant from her father, Fanny Burney lived in the same small house in London and acted as her father's secretary. The "distance" between father and daughter in the poem has been explained away by biographers of Fanny Burney rather unconvincingly by declaring that it is an emotional distance, because the relationship between the two was difficult and distant. However, this cannot be correct as it is patently contradicted by the words of the poem which are completely flattering towards the father and show only admiration for the father and no emotional distance whatsoever in this sense.

Above all, the poem reads more as a plea for acknowledgment by the father, rather than a dedication to a well loved family member. Warren Hastings had always refused to recognise Eliza as his daughter. Indeed, 1778 was a time of crisis for Eliza's relations with Hastings, as on 8th August 1777 he had married Anna Maria Chapuset (his "Marian") in Calcutta, which must have made it likely that Hastings would sever for ever any relations with Eliza's mother, and therefore with Eliza herself. Eliza's mother, Philadelphia, wrote to Hastings on 3rd March 1780, requesting his help to sort out her late husband's financial affairs and asking him "not to refuse me this request the last perhaps I shall ever make you."

The author of *Evelina* is not even sure that the father will read the book ("If e'er thy eyes these feeble lines survey"), suggesting he may live a long distance away and is in some way not in communication with his daughter. At the time of publication of *Evelina* in 1778 Hastings was still in Calcutta in India, as Governor General of India, and he was not to return to England until seven years later, in 1785.

But all this would be much less significant were it not for the plot of the novel *Evelina*, which bears striking similarities to the life of Eliza (it is a truism that first novels are autobiographical).

Evelina is the tale of an heiress like Eliza, of exactly the same age (seventeen) as Eliza was in the year the book was published, whose father refuses to acknowledge her publicly as his daughter, as Hastings always refused to recognise Eliza. Indeed, even on Eliza's death, when her husband visited him a few months later in August 1813, Jane Austen wrote in one letter that Hastings did not show any interest to him about her death. Jane Austen herself, normally a sympathetic letter writer, was shocked by this and wrote that "Mr. Hastings never <u>hinted</u> at Eliza in the smallest degree."

The heroine of the novel, Evelina, is forced to bear the surname of "Anville" because her father, Sir John Belmont, will not recognise her as his daughter. Thus, in the book it is Evelina Anville, and in real life Eliza Hancock, who may not bear their respective true names of Evelina Belmont and Eliza Hastings. Eliza was never to use the surname of Hastings, as she married a few years later. However, she was to name her son "Hastings" as if to make up for the lack of her true surname. The choice of the name "Belmont" as Evelina's true surname may refer obliquely to Hastings, since it is a conjunction of Hastings' two main residences in India. These were

The Belvedere in Alipur, Calcutta and The Mount in Madras. The character of Sir John Belmont in this book, Evelina's father, who is an Englishman living in Paris, is also reminiscent of the real life Sir John Lambert. He lived in Paris where he was also known as "*le Chevalier Lambert*". He was the friend and main business contact of Eliza's mother in Paris at this time, and it was he who probably helped her to arrange Eliza's marriage. We have records of money being sent through him to Eliza's mother and, in her letter of 27th June 1780 to Philadelphia Walter, Eliza gives her postal address in Paris as "*au soin du Chevalier Lambert*" (care of Le Chevalier Lambert).

The novel *Evelina* can thus be read on one level as a fantasy or wish fulfilment for Eliza for acknowledgment by her father, since Sir John Belmont in the book finally recognises his daughter at the end of the novel and it emerges that his refusal to recognise her previously as his daughter was merely due to a misunderstanding. By contrast with all of the above, the plot of *Evelina* bears no relation whatsoever to the life of Fanny Burney.

For those of a cryptic frame of mind, I have indicated in highlights how the letters in the first line of the fourth stanza consecutively spell "hastings" (when one starts from the sixth word, "that", and then, at the end of the line, reverts to the beginning of the line). The letters in the next line consecutively spell "elise" or "elisa", the French versions of Eliza's name. This is especially significant in view of the line "Concealment is the only boon I claim". At first sight this line seems conventional, i.e. it describes that the author is forced to conceal her identity. However, when we look at this line closely, we can see that it describes concealment not as a duty, as we would expect, but as a boon, i.e. a benefit. How can concealment be a benefit? Only if the concealment is in some sense not a concealment but rather a revelation, i.e. the name of the father is literally hidden in the poem, in the preceding line.

I also highlight in the poem how the initials of Warren Hastings have been deliberately hidden in the poem as a clue to readers in the future, not only at the beginning but also at the end. The first letters of the alternate lines of the first two stanzas form an obvious acrostic, reading downwards and spelling out "OHIF". In addition, the first two stanzas begin with "Oh" and "If" respectively. The same "Oh!" and "If" is spelt out at the beginning of the first two lines of the last stanza. This has obviously been done deliberately by the poet, as the chance of it occurring randomly is minuscule. As the poem is addressed to the father of the author, we would expect any message hidden by Eliza to be along the lines of "Warren Hastings made me". This is exactly what "OHIF" stands for in Latin: "*Ouarren Hastings ipse fecit*" which literally means "Warren Hastings himself made me". Latin has no letter "W" and this therefore cannot be used; it has been substituted by an "O" which is the first letter of the French spelling of the name, "Ouarren". The name is originally French.

This is confirmed by the German knowledge website "*wissen.de*" belonging to Wissen Media Verlag, which has a definition of the Latin "*ipse fecit*" as follows:

[lateinisch, "er hat (es) selbst gemacht"]
Abkürzung, i.f. , Vermerk des Künstlers neben der Signatur auf eigenständig hergestellten Kunstwerken.

This can be translated as:

[Latin, he made (it) himself]
Abbreviation i.f. , Artist's mark next to artist's signature on works of art he has produced himself.

Thus the initials OHIF on a painting or other work of art at the time would indicate "OH made me". The work of art in this case is Eliza herself, the author of whom, indicated by the initials OH, is Warren Hastings.

This poem in the introduction to *Evelina* may seem unimportant in the investigation of the authorship of *Fanny Burney* and irrelevant to the authorship of *Jane Austen*, but it goes to the very heart of the matter. It is the loose end which completely undermines those who support Fanny Burney's and Jane Austen's authorship. It cannot be stressed too strongly how important this poem is to the investigation of the authorship of *Jane Austen*. Anyone who defends the authorship of Jane Austen must be sure that this poem describes Dr Charles Burney, which seems most unlikely, given my above arguments. This is because, once they admit this poem (and therefore *Evelina* and other works of *Fanny Burney*) were written by Eliza de Feuillide, they must assert that Eliza gave up writing at the same time as Jane Austen began to become an author, which is highly improbable.

8

Other Similarities in Fanny Burney's Works to the Life of Eliza

Cecilia, Fanny Burney's second novel, published in 1782, like her first, *Evelina*, has certain elements in the plot which are similar to events in the life of Eliza. The heroine, Cecilia, like Eliza, is an heiress who inherits £10,000. She is aged twenty-one, the same age as Eliza in the year of publication of the book, and it was believed at the time that the anonymous author was the same age as the heroine. Like Eliza, Cecilia has guardians who are in charge of her trust fund. The name "Cecilia", the patron saint of music, was surely chosen to reflect Eliza's keen love of music.

There are also a number of plays attributed to Fanny Burney but never performed in her lifetime. One of them, staged at the Hen and Chicken pub theatre in Bedminster, Bristol by the Show of Strength Theatre Company in 1993 to great acclaim, is called *A Busy Day*. The plot of this play describes a young heiress called Eliza, known affectionately to her mother and father as Betsy, who returns from Calcutta in India where her guardian lived, who made her his heir. There is little resemblance here to Fanny Burney's life.

I have myself been fortunate enough to see the performance of another of *Fanny Burney's* plays, *The Woman Hater*, written around 1800 and staged for the first time at the Orange Tree Theatre in Richmond upon Thames, in a superb production by Sam Walters. This comedy is about a young woman who is not recognised as his daughter by her father, who has made his fortune in the West Indies.

Knowing how this play also was likely to be based on Eliza's life, I guessed that in the original version of the play the father was from the East Indies (as India was then known). Upon checking this in the introduction to my edition of the play, I found this to be the case. Another element of the plot is a suspected shipboard romance en route to the Indies. This is reminiscent of the real shipboard romance of Warren Hastings en route from England to India with his future second wife, Marian, then the wife of Count Imhoff.

Apart from *The Witlings*, written shortly after *Evelina* (*Evelina* was published in 1778) the only well written plays of *Fanny Burney* were the three plays written during and shortly after 1799 (*Love and Fashion*, *A Busy Day* and *The Woman Hater*), none of which were, however, performed in Fanny Burney's lifetime. These plays were written at a time when Fanny Burney was living at Camilla Cottage in West Humble, the closest village to Dorking in Surrey. Fanny Burney records in her diary how at least one of the plays, *Love and Fashion*, was sent in 1799 from this house to Thomas Harris, manager of Covent Garden Theatre in London, with a view for it to be performed there shortly, although it never was. It is extraordinary to note that during this period from 1799, Eliza was living at Dorking, less than a mile and a half from Fanny Burney. This was the only time during her life that Eliza lived in Dorking. It is likely that Fanny Burney was acting as Eliza's secretary and copyist at this time in the writing of the plays. In her letter from Dorking dated 29th October 1799 to her cousin Philadelphia, Eliza writes mysteriously of being a recluse and shunning all society, and preferring to remain at home with her books for six months. Curiously, she also refers to her home in Dorking as her "hermitage", the same term Fanny Burney uses in reference to her own home not far away, Camilla Cottage, at the time of writing of these plays. It cannot be coincidence that all of these plays now attributed to Fanny Burney were written at a time when she was in such close proximity to Eliza.

9.

Similarities in the Works of Fanny Burney and Jane Austen

We know from the novels of *Jane Austen* that the author was a huge admirer of the works of *Fanny Burney*, and especially of *Fanny Burney's* third novel, *Camilla*, published in 1796.

In *Jane Austen's Northanger Abbey* the author refers to *Fanny Burney's* novels directly more than in any of her other works, perhaps because *Northanger Abbey* was written at a time nearer to *Fanny Burney's* works than any of the other *Jane Austen* novels (*Fanny Burney's* third novel, *Camilla* was published in 1796 and *Northanger Abbey* is believed to have been written between 1798 and 1799). The most famous reference to *Fanny Burney's* novels is the following passage in *Jane Austen's Northanger Abbey*:

> "'And what are you reading, Miss _____?'
> 'Oh! It is only a novel!' replies the young lady; while she lays down her book with affected indifference, or momentary shame. – 'It is only Cecilia, or Camilla, or Belinda;' or, in short, only some work in which the greatest powers of the mind are displayed, in which the most thorough knowledge of human nature, the happiest delineation of its varieties, the liveliest effusions of wit and humour are conveyed to the world in the best-chosen language.'"

This paragraph of *Jane Austen's* brings to mind the Preface to *Fanny Burney's* first novel, *Evelina*, expressing very similar sentiments:

"In the republic of letters, there is no member of such inferior rank, or who is so much disdained by his brethren of the quill, as the humble Novelist: nor is his fate less hard in the world at large, since, among the whole class of writers, perhaps not one can be named of which the votaries are more numerous but less respectable."

Also, in *Jane Austen's Northanger Abbey*, the boorish and ignorant John Thorpe talks about *Fanny Burney's* novel *Camilla*, showing that he has only read the beginning of it:

"'I was thinking of that other stupid book, written by that woman they make such a fuss about, she who married the French emigrant.'

'I suppose you mean Camilla?'

'Yes, that's the book; such unnatural stuff! – An old man playing at see-saw, I took up the first volume once, and looked it over, but I soon found it would not do; indeed I guessed what sort of stuff it must be before I saw it: as soon as I heard she had married an emigrant, I was sure I should never be able to get through it.'

'I have never read it.'

'You had no loss I assure you; it is the horridest nonsense you can imagine; there is nothing in the world in it but an old man's playing at see-saw and learning Latin; upon my soul there is not.'"

It has been written that this is the only time in her fiction that *Jane Austen* refers to a living contemporary in an identifiable way but without naming them. However, how "identifiable" is the author of *Camilla* as described by John Thorpe? His description of the author as being someone who married "an emigrant" seems to be deliberately ambiguous, as "an emigrant" could apply as equally to Eliza's first husband, the Comte de Feuillide, as to

Fanny Burney's husband, Monsieur d'Arblay.

Camilla is also referred to in *Jane Austen's* final, unfinished masterpiece, *Sanditon*, when the heroine, Charlotte Heywood, visits the subscription library in Sanditon. In *Fanny Burney's* novel, Camilla mistakenly buys some jewellery in the library, without realising how expensive it is, and this leads her into trouble. In *Sanditon* the author refers to *Camilla* as follows:

"The library, of course, afforded every thing; all the useless things in the world that could not be done without, and among so many pretty temptations, and with so much good will for Mr. Parker to encourage expenditure, Charlotte began to feel that she must check herself – or rather she reflected that at two and twenty there could be no excuse for her doing otherwise – and that it would not do for her to be spending all her money the very first evening. She took up a book; it happened to be a volume of *Camilla*. She had not Camilla's youth, and no intention of having her distress, – so, she turned from the drawers of rings and brooches repressed farther solicitation and paid for what she bought."

Therefore, given *Jane Austen's* obvious regard for the novels of *Fanny Burney*, it is a huge puzzle why Jane Austen never met Fanny Burney. Jane Austen would have been living very close to Fanny Burney when she visited Eliza in the West End of London. Jane Austen also on occasions visited her relatives, the Reverend and Mrs Cooke, in Great Bookham in Surrey at the same time as Fanny Burney, a friend of the Cookes, was living only a few miles from Great Bookham, in West Humble. In any event, Jane Austen and Fanny Burney never lived a great distance apart and would have been able to call on each other whenever they wished to. If they did not meet each other, as seems to be the case, it could only have been because they deliberately chose to avoid each other. The only plausible explanation for this can be that Jane Austen and Fanny Burney were both merely secretaries to Eliza.

Anyone who studies the novels of *Jane Austen* and *Fanny Burney* may find countless resemblances between the novels of the two authors. There are many resemblances in names employed by each. Each, for example, uses a lot of surnames which belong to aristocratic families. There are also specific correspondences. In *Fanny Burney's Cecilia*, Miss Bennet is the humble companion of Lady Margaret Monckton and in *Jane Austen's Pride and Prejudice* the heroine is Eliza Bennet. Lady Honoria Pemberton is a character in *Cecilia* and it has been proposed by Stephen Derry that her surname suggested the name of Pemberley, the estate belonging to Mr Darcy in *Pride and Prejudice*. Derry supports this theory in his article *The Two Georgianas: The Duchess of Devonshire and Jane Austen's Miss Darcy*. He cites Georgiana, Duchess of Devonshire, wife of the owner of Chatsworth, as the inspiration for the name of Georgiana for Mr Darcy's sister. This Georgiana has, of course, recently become more famous as the subject of a biography by Amanda Foreman which has been adapted into the successful film *The Duchess* starring Keira Knightley. Stephen Derry says of the Duchess of Devonshire:

"The Duchess herself wrote a novel, *The Sylph* (1779), in which the name "Pemberton" occurs. Fanny Burney may have borrowed this name, as it is also found in her novel Cecilia (1782), which was a major source for the plot of *Pride and Prejudice* – both are studies in snobbery – and which provided it with its title; Jane Austen's "Pemberley" may therefore represent a double allusion, to both *Cecilia* and *The Sylph*. It would be appropriate if Miss Darcy's home ultimately owed its name to her namesake's imagination. (Jane Austen may have conflated "Pemberton" with "Beverley," the surname of the heroine of Cecilia, to make "Pemberley".)"

Since *Pride and Prejudice* was published thirty years after *Cecilia*, it is not surprising to see that the author Eliza, while retaining a similar tone, has a far greater technical ability in her writing. The former book shows a far more accomplished weaving of plot, theme, characters and style, which can be readily accounted for by the author being thirty years older. However, the above mentioned similarities in the two books make it astonishing that Jane Austen and Fanny Burney never met.

As well as the heroines, there are other women in the novels of both authors that resemble Eliza in character. We have mentioned the similarity in ages of the heroines of *Evelina* and *Cecilia* to Eliza when she wrote the novels. *Fanny Burney's Camilla*, however, was published in 1796 when Eliza was thirty-four, and its alternative title *A Picture of Youth* perhaps reflects an older woman looking back at her own youth. There is one character in *Camilla*, however, who reminds us of Eliza, and that is Mrs Arlbery, Camilla's friend who, although older, still has the power to attract younger men with her wit and charm, as Eliza was able to attract her husband Henry Austen, ten years her junior.

It seems that Eliza was also not unwilling to satirise herself in her novels. In her letters she often criticises herself, describing her flirting, her selfishness, her slowness to respond to letters, and her unwillingness to let her husband control her. This has been misrepresented by some authors as being evidence that Eliza was a shallow and vain woman. However, the fact she is able to criticise herself, on the contrary, shows her self-awareness and her good nature in being aware of her own weaknesses. Critics have correctly seen a portrayal of Eliza as Mary Crawford in *Mansfield Park* who, like Eliza, used the context of amateur dramatics to flirt with her fellow actor. But what condemns the character of Mary Crawford is that the unprincipled remarks that Eliza makes jokingly in her letters are echoed seriously by Mary Crawford. For instance, when Mary Crawford says "Selfishness must always be forgiven you know, because there is no hope of a cure" this reminds us of Eliza when she wrote in one letter "I always find that the most effectual mode of getting rid of temptation is to give way to it". Eliza paints an even more unflattering portrait of herself in one of her short works as the scheming Lady Susan.

Eliza was also willing to make fun of her friends in her novels, for instance her widowed friend Lady Sophia Burrell married Revd William Clay, a Church of England priest, on 23rd May 1797. The widow who tries to trap Sir Walter Elliot in *Persuasion* is a Mrs Penelope Clay (the name Penelope being a classical allusion to the Penelope of Homer's *Odyssey*). Eliza gave the unprincipled and rakish Henry Crawford in *Mansfield Park* the first name of her husband, and her husband is also alluded to in the name of Mr Wickham, the villain in *Pride and Prejudice* since her husband, like Wickham, was an officer in the local militia and also, as a former pupil of Winchester College, the famous public school, was a Wykhamist (pupils of this school are referred to in this way to commemorate the founder of Winchester College, William of Wykeham, Bishop of Winchester and Chancellor to Richard II).

When reading the novels of *Jane Austen* and *Fanny Burney*, one frequently comes across ideas and expressions resembling those of the other author, which are too numerous and too close to be coincidental. If Jane Austen had written the novels bearing her name, we are left once again with the huge puzzle of why she never contacted Fanny Burney. However, the connection between the two authors makes perfect sense if we look at the novels of *Jane Austen* as Eliza's adaptation of her earlier *Fanny Burney* novels, written fifteen to thirty years later. They demonstrate the greater accomplishment of Eliza as a writer in her later years. This also explains the perfection of *Jane Austen's* novels, the result of the author perfecting her craft over a period of thirty years.

10.

The Age of the Author of Fanny Burney's "Evelina"

One very striking fact is that the first two novels of *Fanny Burney*, *Evelina* and *Cecilia*, although published anonymously, were widely believed at the time to have been written by an author the same age as their respective protagonists. Indeed, even Anna Letitia Barbauld, in *The British Novelists*, published much later in 1810, stated that "Miss Burney composed her *Evelina* when she was in the early bloom of youth, about seventeen."

Also, John Wilson Croker, in his review of *The Wanderer* in 1814, wrote, "Her Evelina, published at the age of seventeen, was a most extraordinary instance of early talent." The author of *Evelina* also stresses her youth in the introduction to this novel when she writes to the critics "Remember, Gentlemen, you were all young writers once". Whilst Eliza was seventeen in 1778, the year *Evelina* was published, Fanny Burney herself was twenty-five, an age not considered particularly youthful in those days, particularly for a woman. Indeed, twenty-five was an age, according to *Jane Austen*, when "the early bloom of youth" had already passed. In *Pride and Prejudice Jane Austen* refers to the age of her friend Charlotte Lucas, twenty-seven, as being an age when a woman was no longer considered young. Marianne Dashwood in *Sense and Sensibility* declares "A woman of seven and twenty… can never hope to feel or inspire affection again". In his letter of 19th April 1772 Tysoe Hancock had written to Eliza's mother about Warren Hastings' new love, his "Marian", that "She is about twenty six Years old has a good person & *has been* very Pretty" [my italics].

131

The French writer, Pierre Choderlos de Laclos, author of *Les Liaisons Dangereuses*, in his review of *Fanny Burney's Cecilia*, also mentions the gossip at the time which identified the author, and especially her age, with the main character.

In fact, the ages of Evelina, seventeen, and Cecilia, twenty-one, correspond exactly to the ages of Eliza in the year of publication of both books. *Evelina* was published in 1778 when Eliza became seventeen years old and *Cecilia* was published in 1782 when Eliza became twenty-one. This confusion in the minds of the readership was so strong that it later led John Wilson Croker to accuse Fanny Burney of deliberately misleading the public about her age, and he even went so far as to apply for Fanny Burney's birth certificate from the vicar of St Margaret's, King's Lynn in Norfolk. That the belief persisted in the author of *Evelina* being seventeen years old is confirmed by Thomas Babington Macaulay writing in 1842:

> "The book had been admired while it was ascribed to men of letters long conversant with the world, and accustomed to composition. But when it was known that a reserved, silent young woman had produced the best work of fiction that had appeared since the death of Smollett, the acclamations were redoubled. What she had done was, indeed, extraordinary. But, as usual, various reports improved the story till it became miraculous. "Evelina", it was said, was the work of a girl of seventeen. Incredible as this tale was, it continued to be repeated down to our own time."

What is even more curious is that the author of *Evelina* was even believed to have been under twenty years of age in 1779, the year after *Evelina* was written. *The Gentleman's Magazine*, Volume 3, 1835, in its review of *Memoirs of the Life and Correspondence of Mrs Hannah More* by William Roberts includes the following passage:

> "We had expected, we hardly knew why, to have found not

a little concerning Miss Burney in this book, as well as those whose characters are of such interest in her Memoirs – but her name is almost a blank, though it appears that Hannah More was well acquainted with her. In 1779, she says, 'I was asked yesterday to meet Dr. Burney and Evelina at Mrs. Reynolds's, but was engaged at home. This Evelina is an extraordinary girl. She is not more than twenty, of a very retired disposition; and how she picked up her knowledge of nature and low life, her Brangtons, and her St. Giles's gentry, is astonishing !"

The idea of the author being seventeen was not at all "miraculous". The style of the author is not very different from the style of Eliza in her letter which she wrote from Paris aged eighteen, an extract from which I have quoted earlier.

After the publication of *Cecilia* in 1782 there is a gap in the novel writing of *Fanny Burney* which corresponds with Eliza's removal to France, her marriage to her French husband and her stay in France until her return to England in 1786. Between 1786 and 1796, Eliza was a frequent visitor to Jane Austen's home at Steventon in Hampshire and it was during this period that *Jane Austen's* short pieces, the so-called "Juvenilia" were written, while no further novels of *Fanny Burney* appeared. *Fanny Burney's* next novel, *Camilla*, was not published until 1796, soon after the last of *Jane Austen's* Juvenilia, long after Eliza's return from France and two years after the death of Eliza's husband at the guillotine in 1794. No further *Fanny Burney* novels were published during all the forty-four years after 1796 until Fanny Burney's death in 1840 (except the totally unsuccessful and truly dreadful *The Wanderer* in 1814, the year after Eliza's death (which I will discuss later)). At about the same time as the last successful novel of *Fanny Burney*, *Camilla*, was published (1796), the first full novels then began to be written which are now attributed to Jane Austen. These were the preliminary drafts to *Sense and Sensibility* (then called *Elinor and Marianne*), begun in 1795, and to *Pride and Prejudice* (then called *First Impressions*), begun in 1796.

It was only upon Eliza's return from France in 1786 and her stay with Jane Austen at Jane's parents' home at the Steventon Rectory in Hampshire in the late 1780s and early 1790s that *Jane Austen* suddenly produced some extremely mature works of literature to be read among her family group. No satisfactory explanation has ever been given for this spontaneous outpouring of literary ability by a poorly educated girl of thirteen years of age. Indeed, the date of the first writings of *Jane Austen* (1788) corresponds exactly with the arrival of Eliza to stay at Jane Austen's home at Steventon. From the surviving letters of Eliza, including one written by her from Steventon on 26th October 1792 to Phylly Walter, we know that she was probably staying at Steventon during the second half of 1792 and at least the first half of 1793. Once again, it is very strange that, in this letter, the literary Eliza makes no mention of Jane Austen being a gifted writer, although Eliza's stay was supposed to have been during the time when many of the best examples of *Jane Austen's* Juvenilia were written.

11.

Real Life Sources for Jane Austen's "Mansfield Park"

It is a truth generally acknowledged by the biographers of *Jane Austen* whose biographies I have read, that there is a real connection between the life of Jane Austen and the events of *Jane Austen's* novel *Mansfield Park*, published in 1814. Biographers of Jane Austen readily acknowledge that the character of Mary Crawford in *Mansfield Park* is to some extent a portrait of Eliza de Feuillide, who took the lead role in the amateur theatricals at the Austens' house in Steventon during the Christmas season of 1787-1788 and conducted a flirtation with two of Jane Austen's brothers, James and Henry, during the course of the acting.

However, the plot of *Mansfield Park* is also strikingly similar to the life of Fanny Burney. I discovered this independently for myself but later found it confirmed in the excellent biography of Fanny Burney by Claire Harman, which I quote from in detail later on. For many years I had been struck by the similarity between the names of Fanny Price and Fanny Burney. Reading about the life of Fanny Burney, there is also a striking resemblance in their characters. Fanny Burney described herself thus in *Memoirs of Doctor Burney*:

"in company, or before strangers, [Fanny] was silent, backward, timid, even to sheepishness: and, from her shyness, had such profound gravity and composure of features, that those of my friends who came often into my house, and entered into the different humours of the children, never called Fanny by any other name, from the time she had reached her eleventh year, than the The Old Lady."

Her sister Susan said that her characteristics were "sense, sensibility and bashfulness, and even a degree of prudery" and that "her diffidence gives her a bashfulness before company with whom she is not intimate, which is a disadvantage to her".

Similar amateur theatricals to those in *Mansfield Park* were also held in which Fanny Burney took part in her youth, and Fanny Burney had a similar shyness to Fanny Price, and needed to be persuaded to act in them. Also, Fanny Burney's family situation was very similar to that of Fanny Price. Like Fanny Price, who was treated like an inferior sister to her two cousins, Fanny Burney lived with two stepsisters who were perhaps treated more favourably than her, as Fanny was the daughter of Charles Burney's first wife and had very bad relations with her stepmother, Mrs Elizabeth Allen. One of her stepsisters, Maria Allen, was, like Maria Bertram in *Mansfield Park,* a keen amateur actress and of a strong and independent mind. Maria Allen took the main role in amateur theatricals at Dr Burney's home and at Chesington Hall in Surrey, the home of Samuel Crisp, a friend of the Burneys and an amateur playwright, just as Eliza was to do much later in the Austen household. In addition, in real life, Maria Allen eloped with a Mr Martin Rishton (sometimes spelled Rushton) while in *Mansfield Park* Maria Bertram elopes with Henry Crawford, and it is a Mr Rushworth who is Maria's jilted husband. The elopement of Maria Allen also led to her, like Maria Bertram, being abandoned, although she and Mr Rishton later married in 1772. The marriage, however, was to prove very unhappy for Maria Allen.

The name "Rushworth" in *Mansfield Park* seems to have been adapted by the author from the name of "Rushton" to emphasise the uselessness of Mr Rushworth, i.e. that he was not a rush's worth.

Curiously, the layout of the theatre in Mansfield Park also

resembles that of the Burneys at Barbourne Lodge, near Worcester, where Fanny Burney records herself acting with her cousins. Claire Harman in her biography of Fanny Burney talks of "the strange similarity of Fanny Price's experience in the famous 'Lovers Vows' episode in *Mansfield Park* with the account in Burney's early diary of her own terrifying amateur debut in *The Way to Keep Him* in Worcester back in the 1770s."

It is unlikely that such similarities could have been merely coincidental. Therefore, we must assume that the writer of *Mansfield Park* knew Fanny Burney well. It would have been totally impossible for Jane Austen to have known Fanny Burney at the time of the amateur dramatics at Barbourne Lodge in the 1770s, as Jane Austen was only born in 1775. She could not have incorporated these experiences into *Mansfield Park* and therefore cannot be the author of this novel. However, although younger than Fanny Burney, Eliza, born in 1761, would have been old enough to know about or witness such events and later incorporate them into the plot of *Mansfield Park*, interspersed with her own later experiences of amateur theatricals in the Austen household. Perhaps Eliza even took part in amateur theatricals with Fanny Burney. We know from a letter of 7th November 1772 from Mr Hancock to Eliza, that she had been acting in a play, with some success.

Another direct connection between Eliza and *Jane Austen's Mansfield Park* is the letters which Eliza wrote to her cousin, Philadelphia Walter, in which she tried to persuade her to act in the Austen family amateur theatricals at Jane Austen's home at Steventon. On 23rd November 1787 she wrote to her:

"I will only allow myself to take notice of the strong reluctance You express to what You call <u>appearing in Publick</u>. I assure You our performance is to be by no means a publick one, since only a select party of Friends will be present, and as to your very great apprehensions of not succeeding, You may be well convinced they are totally groundless. I think a consciousness of the many advantages which distinguish You might assure You of this, & besides if You do justice to my Friendship You cannot suppose I would press You to do any thing in which You could possibly appear either in an improper or a disadvantageous Light."

The arguments she uses are strikingly similar to those used in *Mansfield Park* to try to persuade Fanny Price to act in the theatricals. In the end Philadelphia Walter did not consent to come to Steventon to act for reasons of morality, either her own or her mother's. The resemblance between her situation and that of Fanny Price is striking. It is important to note that this source for *Mansfield Park* would have been unknown to Jane Austen. Since these letters between Eliza and Philadelphia Walter were confidential, and Eliza was generally regarded by her family as a woman of integrity and discretion, their contents would never have been made known to Jane Austen, who could not therefore have used them in *Mansfield Park*. Only if Eliza herself had been the author of *Mansfield Park* could such source material have been used.

12.

Modern Critical Reaction to the Works of Fanny Burney

At present the critical view of *Fanny Burney* stands lower than the critical view of the works of *Jane Austen*. How can this possibly be, how can the works of the same author at different times of her life be rated so differently? There may be several answers to this, some of them not particularly worthy.

1. The Length of the Novels of *Fanny Burney*

It is notable that the novel of *Fanny Burney's* which is the most well known and read today is the shortest, *Evelina* (being only about 300 pages long compared to the other two, which are nearly 1,000 pages each), although most impartial critics would have to agree with the author *Jane Austen* that *Camilla* is the one of the highest literary merit. This perhaps reflects the shorter attention span of modern readers, who are mostly working people with all the modern distractions of life. At the time the books were written, most readers would have been from the leisured class and especially women of this class, who had much more time to read and would have appreciated a longer work of fiction.

2. Modern Critical Reaction to *Fanny Burney's Camilla*

In my opinion it would not be an unrealistic claim to rank *Camilla*, published in 1796, as the greatest English novel of the eighteenth century. Its greatest weakness is its plot, which places rather artificial difficulties in the way of the marriage of Camilla, in order to prolong the book by several hundred pages, and the unduly prudish character of its hero, Edgar Mandlebert. However, if these aspects of the book are ignored and one examines the style of the book, the quality of the writing puts it far above any other English work of fiction of the eighteenth century. The style of writing is very comparable with the style of the novels of *Jane Austen*. In addition, we know that *Camilla* was greatly appreciated by contemporary readers, as the income that Fanny Burney obtained from it was huge for the time; it earned her £1,000 from the subscribers to the book and a further £1,000 for the sale of the copyright to the publisher.

Those critics of *Jane Austen* who do not agree with me in my opinion of *Camilla* unfortunately find themselves in direct opposition to the author *Jane Austen* herself, who obviously had an extremely high opinion of the work. The author referred to this book in her novels more than any other, and in terms of very high praise. From my point of view, I consider *Fanny Burney's Camilla* to be a much greater work of fiction than *Jane Austen's Persuasion*, for instance, but because it lacks the *Jane Austen* brand name it is treated by critics as a lesser work.

3. The "Branding" of Literary Works

As advertisers would say, *Jane Austen* has become a highly prestigious brand. Any works bearing her name are therefore automatically accorded higher status than those of *Fanny Burney*, just as a Volkswagen was at one time was regarded as being of a higher status than a Skoda, although at that time the two cars were made by the same manufacturer and were essentially the same. Surprisingly, literary critics apply similar criteria to novels as to motor cars, so that an inferior work of *Jane Austen*, such as *Persuasion*, is automatically regarded by them as being of higher merit than any work of *Fanny Burney*, even her most accomplished, *Camilla*.

13.

Was Fanny Burney Known to Eliza?

This question is one for which it has been hard to find concrete evidence. As we have seen above, we have evidence from *Jane Austen's Mansfield Park* that the author *Jane Austen* was intimately acquainted with many of the personal circumstances of Fanny Burney's life. However, there are other indications that it would have been very unusual if the two had not been acquainted. Eliza was keenly interested in music as a child and we know from the letters of her parents that she was learning the harpsichord. At this time she lived only yards from Fanny Burney among the limited number of families living in the fashionable part of the West End of London in the 1770s and 1780s, when *Fanny Burney's* first two books, *Evelina* and *Cecilia*, appeared in print. When studying London society in this period, it is remarkable how "confined and unvarying" it was and how intimately connected were most of the families in London society.

Eliza was a great lover of music and we know from Jane Austen that in her later years Eliza held a musical party at her house in London, at which leading professional performers of the day performed. This is described in Jane Austen's letter of 25th April 1811 to her sister, Cassandra. We also know that Eliza was a regular visitor to the opera. Eliza's cousin, Philadelphia Walter, describes a visit to the opera with Eliza in April 1788, where they sat in the private box belonging to Warren Hastings' wife, Marian. Eliza herself was an accomplished player of the harpsichord, pianoforte and harp, as we know from her letters and from the letters of Jane Austen. In a letter from France to her cousin Philadephia Walter of 27th June 1780, Eliza wrote, "I amuse myself with walking, reading, music, work &cc I have here both an harpsichord and harp." In a letter of 7th January 1791 to her she writes "I contrive by reading, Music Drawing and different kinds of study to fill up the twenty four Hours so as not to find them tedious". In a later letter to her of 29th October 1799 from Dorking she also wrote "I have not found it possible to persevere in my plan of shunning all society, to which I must honestly confess that I prefer my Books, my Harp & my Pianoforte". There is also evidence in her early letters that she may have learnt the guitar as a child. Mr Hancock wrote from India to her mother in London on 23rd September 1772:

"I am glad to hear that Betsy has a good Ear to Musick; if she attempts the Guitar at all I beg she may have the best Masters, otherwise she will get a Wrong method of Fingering which can never after be rectified."

Dr Charles Burney, Fanny's father, was the leading keyboard instrument teacher of his day in London, having invented a new way of fingering. His daughter Esther, known as Hetty, Fanny's sister, had been taught by him and was a child prodigy on the harpsichord. During the period of Eliza's literary and musical education in London she lived very close to the Burneys, who lived in Poland Street in Soho. Dr Burney must at least have been well known to the musical Eliza.

We know from the surviving letters of Tysoe Saul Hancock and Warren Hastings, in which they discuss their great project of education for Eliza, that they considered it imperative to employ only the best tutors for Eliza in writing and music, as well as all other subjects. In one of Mr Hancock's letters on 22nd June 1773 he mentions that Eliza's music tutor is a Mr Berg, but that they no longer wish to use his services because of his unkind manner. Mr

Hancock advised them to find another music tutor for Eliza. The obvious candidate to replace him would have been Charles Burney who, as well as being the best keyboard teacher of his day and in close proximity, because of his uncertain income and large family, was always willing to take on new pupils. In addition, he was well known, at least in his younger days, for his kindly disposition and easy manners (it may be that Charles Burney in this respect was a model for Charles Bingley in *Jane Austen's Pride and Prejudice*. Apart from the resemblance in names, both shared a similar obliging character).

Dr Burney was well known for his large number of young female pupils from polite society and, in a reference to this, in a painting by James Barry, 'The Thames, or the Triumph of Navigation', he was represented surrounded by young women as nereids. In some ways it would have been surprising if Eliza had not been one of these pupils. Indeed, I consider it is likely that Eliza first became acquainted with the Burney family through being a keyboard pupil of Charles Burney as a child, although I have no evidence of this. We know, however, that Eliza was being instructed in music as a child and Mr Hancock had insisted that the best harpsichord of the time, a Kirkman, be bought for her. Since Fanny Burney acted as a secretary for her father when he published his own works, she would have been a logical and natural choice for Eliza if she was looking for a secretary to help her with her first novel. This would be even more likely because of Fanny's interest in literature herself (which I discuss later).

Another, much later, connection between Eliza and Fanny Burney was that both were frequently present during the impeachment trial of Warren Hastings in Parliament and were amongst the most avid supporters of Warren Hastings. They must have encountered each other during the trial in Parliament. À propos of this, some writers have remarked upon the tremendous memory of Fanny Burney as evidenced by her accurate recall of the speech of Warren Hastings in this trial. A recent radio programme I have heard about parliament has however disabused me of this tale. It was apparently common practice at the time for the speeches to be taken down in one of the evolving forms of shorthand at the time, and therefore anyone who wanted a copy of any speech would only need to pay one of these shorthand writers for a transcript. In this case Fanny Burney's claims of having an extraordinary memory seem to tally with the general unreliability of her memoirs and her tendency to deception and self-aggrandisement, which is recognised by her biographer, Claire Harman.

Jacqueline Banerjee in her extremely interesting book *Literary Surrey* gives two characters in the works of *Jane Austen* which she, like myself, identifies with Fanny Burney. She believes, as I do, that these characters could only have been created if the author *Jane Austen* had been personally acquainted with Fanny Burney. She writes that "It is all very speculative, but there are two characters in the younger novelist's work who might owe something to a first-hand encounter with Fanny Burney". This would be further evidence that Fanny Burney was personally known to Eliza. The first of these characters based on Fanny Burney is Fanny Price in *Mansfield Park*. I have described the many connections that exist between the life of Fanny Burney and *Jane Austen's* novel *Mansfield Park*. Pat Rogers in an article in the *Times Literary Supplement* of 23rd August 1996 also sees reflections of Fanny Burney in the character of Fanny Price.

The second character of *Jane Austen* who resembles Fanny Burney is Mrs Elton in *Emma*. Like Fanny Burney, Mrs Elton calls her husband her "*caro sposo*". Fanny Burney used Italian in this way with her friends, including the Reverend Cooke and his wife, who lived in Bookham in Surrey. We know that she did this from the dialogue she describes in her journal and letters. She also addressed her father as "*Padre*" and talked of her child as her "*bambino*". Another way in which Jacqueline Banerjee shows that Fanny Burney resembles Mrs Elton is in the way "she gushes about grand houses, music and the Surrey countryside". Mrs Elton is also a representation of Fanny Burney in that she aspires to be a lady of fashion but is always inadvertently betraying her low social origins. The name "Elton" is surely an ironic anagram of the term "le ton", a French term used at that time for the leaders of fashionable London society.

I have also made a very important discovery in Fanny Burney's journals of an incident in which I believe she refers to Eliza. It is from her diary entry of Tuesday 9th December 1783. It talks of a visit Fanny Burney made to a literary party of one of the most famous London literary hostesses of the time, Mrs Elizabeth Vesey. Here Fanny Burney meets the writer Richard Owen Cambridge, who talks about his clergyman son, George Owen Cambridge:

"TUESDAY, DEC. 9.—This evening I went to Mrs. Vesey's at last. I was obliged to go alone, as my father would not be earlier than nine o'clock ; an hour too fine-ladyish for me to choose visiting at. But as I cannot bear entering a room full of company sola, I went soon after seven.

I found, as I wished, no creature but Mrs. Vesey and Mrs. Hancock, who lives with her. I soon made my peace, for several delays and excuses I have sent her, as she is excessively good-natured, and then we had near an hour to ourselves. And then, the first person who came,— who do you think it was? — Mr. Cambridge, senr. I leave you to guess whether or not I felt glad; and I leave you, also, to share in my surprise upon finding he was uninvited and unexpected; for Mrs. Vesey looked at him with open surprise.

As soon as the salutations were over, Mrs. Vesey, with her usual odd simplicity, asked him what had put him upon calling ?

'The desire,' cried he, 'to see you. But what! are there only you three?—nothing but women ?'

145

'Some more are coming,' answered she, 'and some of your friends; so you are in luck.'

'Poor Mr. Cambridge,' cried I, 'what will become of him? I know not, indeed, if the three women now present overpower him.' 'They are men, I hope,' cried he, laughing; 'for I can't bear being with only women !'

'To be sure they do,' cried he, 'for I like nothing in the world but men! So if you have not some men coming, I declare off.'

Mrs. Vesey and Mrs. Hancock stared, and I laughed; but neither of us could discover what he was aiming at, though he continued this raillery some time, till he exclaimed,—

'Well, I am sure of one friend, however, to stick by me, for one has promised me to come.'

'And who is that?' said Mrs. Vesey, staring more.

'A Christian-maker!—who's that?' 'Why a Christian-maker!'

'Why one who is gone to-night to make two Christians, and when they are made, will come to see if he can make any more here.'

'Who is it?'

'My son.'

Mr. Cambridge then ran on with other such speeches ; but Mrs. Vesey sat gravely pondering, and then called out,— 'O !—well, I am always glad to see him.'

'Pray how did your son know I should be at home?'

She said no more, but I saw she looked extremely perplexed. 'Why he does not know it,' answered Mr. C.; 'but he intends coming to try.'

Mr. Cambridge, during the reception, came up to me, and whispered with a laugh,— Soon after Miss E entered.

She is a sort of yea and nay young gentlewoman, to me very wearisome. I laughed, too, but thanked him, and we were going on with our own chat when Mrs. Vesey, as if from a sudden thought, came up to us, and patting Mr. Cambridge on the arm, said,— 'I called upon your friend, Mrs. Ord, this morning, and she told me you would be here to-night.' 'I dare say you came to meet Miss Burney?'

'Me?—no,' cried he, 'I came to meet Miss E;' and, immediately quitting me, he went to talk with her. Soon after came Mrs. Walsingham, and insisted upon sitting next me, to whom she is most marvellous civil. This was rather a home stroke to be sure, yet I really believe accidental."

It is very unusual that the full name of "Miss E" is not given, as Fanny Burney normally gives the full names of people in her diaries. To me the the last paragaraph of the above passage can only have one meaning. The clear implication in the last paragraph is that Mr Richard Owen Cambridge had come to see the authoress *Miss Burney* (Miss E) and not Miss Burney herself. "Miss E" is Eliza Hancock. This is what Fanny Burney describes as a "home stroke" or what we would call a home truth. I can see no other explanation for this passage. I have mentioned earlier how it seems Eliza had returned to London from France somewhat secretively over the winter of 1783-4 and so she would have been in London at this time.

When I came upon the above passage in Fanny Burney's diary I had not heard about the close relationship of Fanny Burney at this time with George Owen Cambridge, the son of the above Richard Owen Cambridge, who is mentioned above as the "Christian-maker", as George Owen Cambridge was a clergyman. However, the above passage solves the mystery about which Paula L. Stepankowsky, President of The Burney Society, has been seeking an answer. She states as follows in an article in the *British Library Newspaper Library News* No. 28 of summer 2000:

"Scholars have long speculated on what may have caused a promising relationship between George Owen Cambridge, a young clergyman, and the novelist, diarist, and playwright, Fanny Burney, to cool sometime in the spring of 1783. A team of six Burney Society members from Britain and the United States spent a day at the British Library Newspaper Library in early March seeking answers to that question by consulting microfilm copies of rare London newspapers of the day, which first became part of the British Museum Library in 1818, having been originally collected by the Revd Dr Charles Burney, Fanny's own brother.

Fanny Burney's letters and journals record many happy evenings she and George Owen Cambridge spent in London drawing rooms up until March or April of 1783. But Fanny appears to have agonised over the relationship, wondering why he seemed so interested, yet did not declare himself. Then, without explanation, the relationship, one that perhaps could have led to marriage had circumstances been different, appears to have come to an abrupt end. Collected editions of Burney's letters and journals published so far do not contain letters that refer to the cause of the rift in the relationship."

Stepankowsky has also written in an article in the *British Library Newspaper Library News* No. 30 of summer 2001:

"In the early 1980s, as I read Austin Dobson's *The Diary and Letters of Madame d'Arblay* (1904), then the most complete compilation of Fanny Burney's letters from the years 1782-1783, I was struck by her description of George Owen Cambridge. Cambridge was a young clergyman who frequented the salons of the Blue Stocking Circle, which took up Burney in 1778 when her first novel, *Evelina*, became a bestseller. The two met in 1782, the year *Cecilia* was published, something that increased Fanny's celebrity, although not her fortune. She enjoyed his wit, his conversation, and his evident pleasure in her company.

As I read through passages from late 1782 and January of 1783, the young, unmarried clergyman figures more prominently in her accounts, culminating in this sentence written in a letter dated 4th January 1783: 'Who, indeed, of all my new acquaintances, has so well understood me?' But after a big build-up, and a short account of a brief conversation on 23rd February, George makes no appearances in March in the Dobson edition and relatively few, and abbreviated, appearances in April."

I would suggest the reason George Owen Cambridge "seemed so interested" in Fanny Burney was because he believed her to be the author of *Evelina* and *Cecilia*. He himself, though a clergyman by profession, was also a literary man. He wrote the biography of his father, Richard Owen Cambridge, who himself was an author whose most famous work was *The Scribleriad*. It seems from the extract of Fanny Burney's diary above that by December 1783 both he and his father had found out that Fanny Burney was not the author of *Evelina* and *Cecilia* and that the true authoress was the mysterious "Miss E" (Eliza) to whom they then transferred their attentions. This explains the abrupt and mysterious ending of the relationship in 1783 between Fanny Burney and George Owen Cambridge and may also explain why there would have been some hostility from this time between Fanny Burney and Eliza, and why Fanny Burney described Eliza in her diary above as "wearisome" and "a sort of yea and nay young gentlewoman". It may also explain the length of time between the publication of *Cecilia* in 1782 and the next publication of a *Fanny Burney* novel, *Camilla* in 1796. The marriage of Fanny Burney on 28th July 1793 to Monsieur d'Arblay could have effected a reconciliation between Fanny Burney and Eliza, so that Fanny Burney was to collaborate as secretary for Eliza for *Fanny Burney's* novel *Camilla* and for the three *Fanny Burney* plays written at Dorking from 1799. In 1802 Fanny Burney left England to live in France, but was unable to return due to the political situation, and only returned to England on 15th August 1812 at the time of Eliza's final illness, and so in 1802 their collaboration ended.

14

Did Jane Austen Know Fanny Burney?

The Burney family and the Austen family had mutual acquaintances in Great Bookham in Surrey: the Cookes. The Reverend Samuel Cooke was vicar of Great Bookham, while his wife, Cassandra, was a cousin of Jane Austen's mother. There is also a very close connection between Jane Austen and Fanny Burney through the Reverend Cooke, as Jane Austen was his goddaughter and the Reverend Cooke also baptised Alex, Fanny Burney's son, in 1795. In fact the Reverend Cooke and his wife, Cassandra, were very close friends of Fanny Burney. It is all the more strange, therefore, that the two purported authors, Fanny Burney and Jane Austen, never met.

After the great financial success of *Camilla* in 1796, Fanny Burney was to build a house from the proceeds of *Camilla*, which she named "Camilla Cottage". It was built in the small hamlet of West Humble near Dorking, on a lease of a plot of land granted to her by her friends, William and Frederica Lock, on their estate of Norbury Park near Great Bookham in Surrey. On the opposite side of the Mole Valley to Norbury Park Estate, and visible from the large mansion of Norbury Park, was Box Hill, on which the famous picnic takes place in *Emma*. It would have been impossible for the author of *Emma* to have such an intimate knowledge of the area around Box Hill without being acquainted with both the Lock family and with Fanny Burney. The beautiful eighteenth century house of Norbury Park still stands at the top of a hill looking towards Box Hill and still resembles the magnificent mansion of a rich *Jane Austen* character.

It may be that Jane Austen did not wish to meet Fanny Burney, as is suggested by Jacqueline Banerjee in her admirable book, *Literary Surrey*. This is a fascinating book, especially for someone like myself who has lived in Surrey for most of his life. When a visit to Bookham was planned by Jane Austen's mother in 1799, Jane Austen was not keen on the idea. Jacqueline Banerjee writes:

> "Although the plan to visit Bookham comes up in a letter of 11th June 1799, and nothing happened to prevent her going, no letters exist from the visit. This in itself is significant, for they were apparently destroyed by her sister, whose eagerness to protect her reputation resulted in a number of such "deletions"… Jane had not been looking forward to the visit."

We must remember that in 1799 none of the *Jane Austen* novels had yet been published. However, both Jane and Cassandra would have been aware that Eliza was the true author of the *Fanny Burney* novels and so they would have "dreaded" the possibility of Fanny Burney visiting the Cookes during their stay with them. Although Fanny Burney was then living in Camilla Cottage in West Humble, a few miles away, at this time Jacqueline Banerjee notes that she was still on "dropping-in terms" with the Cookes. There is an intriguing clue in a letter of Jane Austen's to her sister Cassandra of 2nd June 1799 that she was well aware of the true author of the *Fanny Burney* novels. She wrote:

> "We had a Miss North and a Mr. Gould of our party; the latter walked home with me after tea. He is a very young man, just entered Oxford, wears spectacles, and has heard that 'Evelina' was written by Dr. Johnson."

It seems obvious that in the above extract she was sharing an in-joke with Cassandra. Only with the knowledge that Eliza was the author of *Evelina*, can we see the real point of the joke in the last sentence. Incidentally, is it not very strange that, according to Nigel Nicholson in the *The World of Jane Austen*, "to the general public she [Jane Austen] was quite unknown, and never in all her life did she meet another writer". This is confirmed by Jane Austen's nephew, James Edward Austen-Leigh, in the first biography of Jane Austen, his *A Memoir of Jane Austen* of 1870, Chapter VII:

> "Jane Austen lived in entire seclusion from the literary world: neither by correspondence, nor by personal intercourse was she known to any contemporary authors. It is probable that she never was in company with any person whose talents or whose celebrity equalled her own; so that her powers never could have been sharpened by collision with superior intellects, nor her imagination aided by their casual suggestions. Whatever she produced was a genuine home-made article. Even during the last two or three years of her life, when her works were rising in the estimation of the public, they did not enlarge the circle of her acquaintance. Few of her readers knew even her name, and none knew more of her than her name. I doubt whether it would be possible to mention any other author of note, whose personal obscurity was so complete."

According to James Edward Austen-Leigh, therefore, Jane Austen never even troubled to meet Fanny Burney, supposedly the author she most admired and who influenced her more than any other. Jane Austen could not even take the trouble in 1799 to make the short journey of a few miles from Bookham to West Humble to meet Fanny Burney, and it seems that she even deliberately avoided meeting her. James Edward Austen-Leigh also wrote of Jane Austen:

"Of events her life was singularly barren: few changes and no great crisis ever broke the smooth current of its course. Even her fame may be said to have been posthumous: it did not attain to any vigorous life till she had ceased to exist. Her talents did not introduce her to the notice of other writers, or connect her with the literary world, or in any degree pierce through the obscurity of her domestic retirement. I have therefore scarcely any materials for a detailed life of my aunt... We did not think of her as being clever, still less as being famous; but we valued her as one always kind, sympathising, and amusing."

It is hard to think of any other famous writer with no literary acquaintance at all. One wonders if it is possible for a writer to function while having no literary acquaintance. In fact, in addition to avoiding Fanny Burney, Jane Austen herself did everything she could to avoid meeting any literary figures. For example, her brother Henry Austen wrote in his *Memoir of Miss Austen* prefacing the 1833 edition of *Sense and Sensibility*:

"When Miss Austen was on a visit to London soon after the publication of Mansfield Park, a nobleman, personally unknown to her, but who had good reason for considering her to be the authoress of that work, was desirous of her joining a literary circle at his home. He communicated his wish in the politest manner, through a mutual friend adding, what his Lordship thought would be an irresistible enducement, that the celebrated Madame de Stael would be of the party. Miss Austen immediately declined the invitation."

From the address of Eliza's letter dated 29th October 1799, we can see that, at the time of Jane Austen's visit to Bookham above, Eliza was staying from 1799 probably up to 1800 in Dorking in Surrey, less than two miles from Fanny Burney's home in West Humble, where Fanny Burney lived from 1793 to 1802. During this stay in Dorking, Eliza records in her letter to her cousin Philadelphia that she was visited by some of her neighbours, including the poet and playwright Lady Sophia Burrell, who lived at The Deepdene in Dorking, and another acquaintance, Lady Talbot of Mickleham. From Dorking it is less than two miles to Fanny Burney's house, yet Eliza's letter does not even mention her. Eliza also, at other periods of her life, visited Lady Sophia Burrell at her estate at The Deepdene, close to Dorking. Lady Sophia Burrell's father, Sir Charles Raymond, was a large ship owner for the East India Company and a friend of Warren Hastings through this East India Company connection. His daughter, Lady Sophia, had married Sir William Burrell, a civil servant and antiquary, who had been a contemporary of Warren Hastings at Westminster School in London; they had both started at the school in 1743. Lady Sophia Burrell had inherited a large fortune from her father and devoted her time mainly to literature.

Considering Eliza was an intimate friend of the poet and playwright, Lady Sophia Burrell, who lived not far from Fanny Burney, supposedly the most famous writer of the age, surely either of them would have made the two mile trip to see Fanny Burney at some stage? It cannot be said that the reason Eliza avoided Fanny Burney was that she did not wish to have any literary acquaintance, as she was quite happy to be visited by the poet and playwright Lady Sophia Burrell.

Lady Sophia Burrell's tragedy, *Maximian*, (her translation of a tragedy by the French author Pierre Corneille) was published in 1800 and was dedicated to William Lock who, with his wife Frederica, lived at Norbury Park near Great Bookham. I have mentioned above how Mr and Mrs Lock were such close friends of Fanny Burney that they had leased to her the plot of land on their estate, on which she and her husband built Camilla Cottage. When Lady Sophia Burrell visited Eliza in Dorking, as mentioned in the letter above, they must have discussed her neighbours, the Locks, and in turn they must have discussed Fanny Burney who was living in Camilla Cottage in West Humble at this time. Had Fanny Burney been a writer, it is inconceivable that they would not have paid a visit on her. It is astonishing in particular that the poet Lady Sophia Burrell lived for many years only two miles from Fanny Burney, supposedly the most famous novelist of the time, and yet she never once considered visiting her, and never wrote any poems to her, as she did to her other literary friends including Eliza, Warren Hastings and Lord Mansfield.

What is perhaps even more astonishing is what happened when Lady Sophia Burrell met Eliza in 1799, while Eliza was staying at Dorking. By 1799, according to the conventional view, Jane Austen had written her first literary works, the so-called "Juvenilia", at a time when Eliza was staying with her at Steventon. In addition, Jane Austen is supposed to have written the novel *Susan* (later renamed as *Northanger Abbey*) by this time as well. Had Jane Austen been the true author of these, Eliza would have mentioned this to Lady Sophia Burrell who, as an enthusiastic writer, would have attempted to meet Jane Austen and cultivate her acquaintance. However, Lady Sophia Burrell never attempted to contact Jane Austen or to read any of her works, and wrote no poems praising her as a writer, as she wrote poems praising Eliza as a novelist. Lady Sophia Burrell did not even attempt to meet Jane Austen in 1799, when she was staying only about four or five miles away.

I have mentioned above the connections between Fanny Burney, her husband General d'Arblay, her sister Susan Phillips, Jane Austen, Eliza, Lady Sophia Burrell, Lady Talbot, the Cooke family and Mr and Mrs Lock, and how they seemed to centre on the area around Leatherhead, Mickleham, West Humble and Dorking, which all belong to this area in the Mole Valley. I have included a map of this beautiful valley (drawn by my wife) through which runs the River Mole, which is famous in this area for disappearing underground at certain points, a fact remarked on by the poet Edmund Spenser in his long poem, *The Faerie Queene*. The area is a landscape created by rich landowners to their ideal of beauty, often described nowadays erroneously as natural and unspoilt. It was also an area where the playwright Richard Brinsley Sheridan had an estate at Polesden Lacey; the area was truly the "Beverly Hills" of eighteenth century London.

Peter Brandon, in his wonderful local history book *A History of Surrey* gives us some fascinating information about the Mole Valley at this time between Leatherhead and Dorking, which he calls "The Vale of Mickleham". It had first been opened up to Londoners by the London to Worthing turnpike road of 1755. Mr Brandon writes that "One of the earliest Surrey districts to be remade was the Vale of Mickleham, pierced by the river Mole in its passage through the North Downs. Its delightful wooded landscape blends so harmoniously with its contour, and so forgotten is the care lavished upon its making, that such scenery is often wrongly regarded as 'natural' to Surrey. This is the reverse of the truth." He attributes this in the main to Fanny Burney's friends, Mr and Mrs Lock, who bought the Norbury Park estate in 1774 and rebuilt the house shortly afterwards. William Lock included in the house a famous "landscape room" (which still exists) painted with landscapes to create the illusion that one is outside the room amongst the scenery, and Mr Brandon writes that "the windows on the south framed the picturesque scenery then being remade in the Vale of Mickleham." As a result of the Locks' landscaping of the Vale of Mickleham Mr Brandon says "Soon after the building of Norbury the surrounding hills were crowded with decorative mansions overlooking parks, neat bow-fronted *cottage ornées* and thickly wooded clumps of yew and box."

To conclude, if we were to hypothesise that Eliza wrote the works of *Jane Austen* but not those of *Fanny Burney*, we would have to believe that Eliza stayed from 1799 to 1800 two miles from the author she most admired and was most influenced by, and never even considered visiting her. The only possible logical explanation for this highly unusual state of affairs is that Eliza wrote under both the above names. If Jane Austen had been the author of the works bearing her name, it would have been inconceivable also that she would not have been intimately acquainted with Fanny Burney, had she too been an author. *Fanny Burney* was the most celebrated author of her day and is acknowledged by most biographers of *Jane Austen* as the greatest literary "influence" on *Jane Austen*. It is therefore completely astonishing that we know of no correspondence between them and that there is no record of them ever meeting, when they moved in the same circles and were in such close geographical proximity, and when Jane Austen's cousin was staying less than two miles from Ms Burney.

This is even more extraordinary given the strength of the acknowledged "influence" on *Jane Austen* of the writings of *Fanny Burney*. For instance, the title and plot of *Pride and Prejudice* both come from *Fanny Burney's Cecilia* and there are many other examples, e.g the anti-heros in *Evelina* and *Sense and Sensibility* both share the name of Willoughby, and there is a Ms Bennet and a Mrs Hill in *Cecilia* and *Pride and Prejudice*. The name "Willoughby", incidentally, appears to have come from the Austen family connection to one Cassandra Willoughby, wife of the first Duke of Chandos. Further examples of this close connection between the works of *Fanny Burney* and *Jane Austen* are mentioned later in this book and especially in the quotation I will give from Claire Harman's excellent biography of Fanny Burney.

The similarity in style of the works of *Fanny Burney* and *Jane Austen*, bearing in mind the works of *Jane Austen* are written at a later date, is more than striking. The sense of humour of both authors is very similar, as is also their sense of decorum and style of writing. The authors both deal with similar plots (i.e. intelligent, lively, independent woman meets educated, gentlemanly man, there are misunderstandings until both are married.) However, it is not just in the similarity of style that the works of *Fanny Burney* and *Jane Austen* are similar. They both share the same philosophy of life and the same moral and religious code. They both believe that novels should reflect real life rather than being fantastic. *Fanny Burney* wrote in the Preface to *Evelina*:

> "To draw characters from nature, though not from life, and to mark the manners of the times, is the attempted plan of the following letters.... Let me, therefore, prepare for disappointment those who, in the perusal of these sheets, entertain the gentle expectation of being transported to the fantastic regions of Romance, where Fiction is coloured by all the gay tints of luxurious Imagination, where Reason is an outcast, and where the sublimity of the Marvellous, rejects all aid from sober Probability. The heroine of these memoirs, young, artless and inexperienced, is:
>
> "No faultless Monster that the world ne'er saw"
>
> but the offspring of Nature, and of Nature in her simplest attire".

Similarly, *Jane Austen* satirises the fantastic in contemporary literature in *Northanger Abbey*:

> "No one who had ever seen Catherine Morland in her infancy, would have supposed her born to be an heroine. Her situation in life, the character of her father and mother, her own person and disposition, were all equally against her. Her father was a clergyman, without being neglected, or poor, and a very respectable man, though his name was Richard – and he had never been handsome. He had a considerable independence, besides two good livings – and he was not in the least addicted to locking up his daughters. Her mother was a woman of useful plain sense, with a good temper, and, what is more remarkable, with a good constitution. She had three sons before Catherine was born; and instead of dying in bringing the latter into the

world, as any body might expect, she still lived on – lived to have six children more – to see them growing up around her, and to enjoy excellent health herself."

It is noticeable how the good characters in the works of both authors show a similar abhorrence of debt and a moral code that all debts should be paid as soon as possible. This was the view of Eliza herself. In a letter to her brother, James Walter, of 19th September 1787, Philadelphia Walter wrote of Eliza: "her principles are strictly just, making it a rule never to bespeak anything that she is not quite sure of being able to pay for directly, never contracting debts of any kind". Both authors dislike a show of religion and lean to the rather heretical view that Christianity is shown through good works and not faith. In this respect the philosophy of both authors has been linked to the views of the Swedish philosopher, Swedenborg.

Both authors are critical of insincerity but also critical of deliberate non-compliance with the normal manners of society. Both Mrs Arlbery in *Fanny Burney's Camilla* and Mr Darcy in *Jane Austen's Pride and Prejudice* put forward this view. Elinor in *Jane Austen's Sense and Sensibility* regrets her sister Marianne's unwillingness to conform to society's rules, although she does not believe one has to accept society's values. Above all, both authors approve thoughts over action in their heroes and heroines. A hero for *Fanny Burney* or *Jane Austen* is not a man of action, but a man of reflection. Both authors condemn the cult of "sensibility" in such characters as Mrs Berlinton in *Camilla* and Marianne in *Sense and Sensibility* and argue for moderation and the tempering of the feelings as the best method to cure affliction. Both condemn marriage which is carried out for ambition rather than love, for example the marriages of Mr Monckton to a rich elderly widow in *Cecilia* and the marriage of Willoughby in *Sense and Sensibility* to a Miss Grey with a fortune of fifty thousand pounds. Both contain heroes and heroines who are intellectually and morally superior to those that surround them. Both ridicule the proud and ambitious, while showing more compassion to other faults when they are accompanied by a kind heart. It cannot be said of either that they do not suffer fools, and we can compare the kind treatment given to the well-meaning but "mentally negligible" baronet Sir Hugh Tyrold in *Camilla* and the kind but meddlesome Mrs Jennings in *Sense and Sensibility*. In fact I have not come across a single instance in any of the novels of *Jane Austen* and *Fanny Burney* where their basic opinions and philosophy differ in any respect.

Fanny Burney and *Jane Austen* heroes are of a similar mould, being idealised and attractive for their intelligence and depth of character. They also tend to be of a somewhat feminine and intellectual cast, something which put them out of favour with Victorian audiences, who preferred a more muscular, manly hero. They often act as mentors to the younger heroines. Both authors tend to give their heroes surnames of Norman French origin (Ferrers, Darcy, Bertram in *Jane Austen*; Orville, Delville in *Fanny Burney*) whereas their villains have names of Anglo Saxon or Danish origin (Willoughby, Wickham, Crawford in *Jane Austen* and Willoughby and Monckton in *Fanny Burney*).

Camilla has been described as being the book of *Fanny Burney*'s closest in style to *Jane Austen* and I would concur with this. I believe this is because it is much closer in time of composition (1796) to *Jane Austen*'s works than *Evelina* (1778) or *Cecilia* (1782). *Camilla* is written in a fuller, more rounded and less sparing style and in my opinion the style of *Camilla* is in this respect far closer to the style of *Jane Austen* than it is to the style of *Evelina* or *Cecilia*.

One curious argument against Jane Austen's authorship that has been largely overlooked by biographers of Jane Austen concerns the fact that among the list of subscribers to *Fanny Burney's Camilla*, printed at the beginning of the first edition of 1796, is the name of a "Miss J. Austen" of Steventon in Hampshire. This is, interestingly, the only contemporary printed reference that exists to Jane Austen during her lifetime. Biographers to date have missed the relevance of Jane Austen's inclusion on this list. Without thinking, they have seen this unquestioningly as a confirmation that Jane Austen was a writer and that she was influenced by *Fanny Burney*.

However, if we examine the matter more closely, it seems to argue strongly to the contrary. We know that the subscribers each paid one guinea to subscribe to the new book, which was a large sum at the time and would have been beyond the means of Jane Austen herself, who would normally have been forced to borrow such books from a circulating library. Therefore, the subscription must have been taken out for her by a rich relation. The most likely person to have subscribed for her would have been Eliza, as her close friend and the wife of her favourite brother, Henry. The one guinea price would have been well within Eliza's purchasing power. The point that is very strange is that Eliza subscribed to one copy for her cousin, Jane Austen, but she is not on the list of subscribers herself. Since Eliza herself was an avid reader of English and French literature (we know from surviving letters I mention elsewhere that she visited the theatre often and her letters often refer to her preferring to stay at home with her books and study rather than to go out), the only logical explanation can be that Eliza was herself the author of the book and therefore had no need to subscribe to it. In addition, if Jane Austen was a subscriber to *Fanny Burney's Camilla*, why on earth did she make no attempt to contact or meet Fanny Burney herself?

Looking at the main novels of *Fanny Burney* and *Jane Austen* as a whole, I believe it is possible to see a progression in the style of the novels. *Evelina* and *Cecilia* are early works, then there are the middle period works, *Camilla*, *Northanger Abbey* and *Persuasion*, the "classic period" of *Sense and Sensibility*, *Pride and Prejudice* and *Mansfield Park* and the final mature works, *Emma* and the unfinished novel *Sanditon*. If one was to compare *Jane Austen* novels to Mozart operas, *Pride and Prejudice* and *Mansfield Park* correspond to *The Marriage of Figaro* and *Cosi fan Tutte*, while *Emma* corresponds to *The Magic Flute* and *Sanditon* to Mozart's last opera, *La Clemenza di Tito*.

There is one novel of *Jane Austen's* in my scheme above which does not fit into the traditional dating of the novels by Jane's sister, Cassandra. By examining its style, I personally estimated *Persuasion* at 1803/4. I later found out that Eliza visited Lyme Regis, where the novel is set, in 1804. *Persuasion* was first advertised in *The Courier* for sale in 1817, shortly after Jane Austen's death, in the same advert as *Northanger Abbey*, and both were published together. Both novels are set in Bath where Eliza met up with Jane Austen prior to visiting Lyme Regis. Since *Northanger Abbey* was first advertised for publication in 1803 under the name of *Susan* but never published at the time, it would appear that the publication of these two books together at the end of December 1817 was a "clearing up" process for publishing the remaining unpublished novels of *Jane Austen*. The main indications we have that *Persuasion* was written at a later date than 1804, other than the revision of its timescale prior to publishing, is the chronology of Jane Austen's sister, Cassandra, and final versions of the novel written at this time. Since Cassandra was responsible for burning and censoring most of Jane Austen's correspondence, no doubt to prevent knowledge of Eliza's authorship, it is likely that she would also have constructed a chronology showing erroneously that some novels were written after Eliza's death. I have already quoted from a letter of Jane Austen's dated 29th January 1813 in which Jane Austen confirms that all of *Jane Austen's* novels had already been written by this date. In addition, some critics believe that *Persuasion* when published was in an unfinished state. This would explain why, although written earlier, it was not published until after all the properly finished novels had been published.

The next reason to suppose that Eliza was the author of *Jane Austen's* works is the obvious one that *Jane Austen* only became a writer when Eliza appeared at Steventon in Hampshire, Jane's home, from 1786 onwards. Eliza's husband, the Comte de Feuillide, having been executed by guillotine in Paris in 1794 and Eliza's mother having died in 1792, Eliza often spent the summers, and sometimes the whole year, with her cousins at Steventon Rectory in Hampshire. If Jane Austen had been the author of the works written at this time, surely the literary Eliza would have made some contribution to them as well, or mentioned Jane as a writer in her letters?

At the same time, after the appearance of *Camilla* in 1796, *Fanny Burney* ceased to write any more novels, apart from the appearance in print of *The Wanderer* in 1814, a year after Eliza's death, which had a disastrous reception. *The Wanderer* will be discussed later. After 1814, Fanny Burney went on to live for twenty-six more years until her death in 1840 without publishing any further novels.

If we admit that Eliza was the author of *Fanny Burney's* novels, it would have been very strange for her to cease writing in the 1790s and for her cousin, Jane, to have started at the same time. Similarly, if we concede that Eliza was the author of *Jane Austen's* works, it would have been highly unusual for her to have not started writing until such an advanced age (Eliza was thirty-five when the first major novels we now know as those of *Jane Austen* were composed). Indeed, the first of the *Jane Austen* novels was not published until 1811, when Eliza was forty-nine years old. However, well before this time, as I will show later, Eliza had been acknowledged in writing as a novelist by her friend, the poet and playwright, Lady Sophia Burrell. The evidence points to *Fanny Burney* ceasing to "write" novels for a time once Eliza arrived at Jane Austen's home at Steventon in the late 1780s, and *Jane Austen* beginning to "write" at exactly the same time.

Another reason for the transference of the name of the author may have been that Fanny Burney married on 28th July 1793. She married an exile from France, General Alexandre-Jean-Baptiste d'Arblay, who she met when visiting her sister, Susan Phillips, in Mickleham in Surrey. M. d'Arblay had been living with other French exiles at Juniper Hall in Mickleham. As I have mentioned previously, after 1796 Fanny Burney was also no longer in need of financial assistance from Eliza, as that year she had received £1,000 in total from the subscribers to *Camilla* and £1,000 for the sale of its copyright to the publishers, Payne, Cadell & Davies. With this sum of money she was able to build herself and her husband a cottage on a lease of land on the estate of her friends, William and Frederica Lock, near Dorking in Surrey, which they aptly named "Camilla Cottage".

We know from *Jane Austen's* novels that Eliza had considerable sympathy for the plight of unmarried women. *Jane Austen* shows her sympathy for unmarried women especially in *Emma*. Mr Knightley tells Emma that any ridicule of Miss Bates cannot be tolerated because, as a single unmarried woman, she is poor and likely to sink into even more poverty:

> "were she prosperous, I could allow much for the occasional prevelance of the ridiculous over the good. Were she a woman of fortune, I would leave every harmless absurdity to take its chance, I would not quarrel with you for any liberties of manner. Were she your equal in situation – but, Emma, consider how far this is from being the case. She is poor; she has sunk from the comforts she was born to; and, if she live to old age, must probably sink more. Her situation should secure your compassion. It was badly done, indeed! – You, whom she had known from an infant, whom she had seen grow up from a period when her notice was an honour, to have you now, in thoughtless spirits, and the pride of the moment, laugh at her, humble her – and before her niece, too – and before others, many of whom (certainly *some*,) would be entirely guided by your treatment of her. – This is not pleasant to you, Emma – and it is very far from pleasant to me; but I must, I will, – I will tell you truths while I can, satisfied with proving myself your friend by very faithful counsel, and trusting that you will some time or other do me greater justice than you can do now."

In *Emma*, *Jane Austen* also expresses the contrast in the position of the poor Jane Fairfax, forced to be a governess, and Frank Churchill's rich aunt, saying that in the eyes of the world one was nothing and the other everything. This shows her compassion for the fate of women of the time, who had few ways of earning a living other than becoming a governess in another family's house. This sympathy is a reflection of Eliza's compassion for the unmarried Fanny Burney and Jane Austen. The proceeds of the *Jane Austen* books went to Jane Austen since, unlike her sister Cassandra, who had inherited £1,000 upon the death of her fiancé, Tom Fowle, Jane had no substantial means of support.

With Eliza, "sympathy" or, as it was then known, "sensibility", was not enough. She took practical steps to help unmarried women by engaging them as her secretaries and proofreaders, and rewarding them with the credit and financial profits of her books. She was well aware that it would be impossible for her ever to be known as the author of her books, because of her relationship with Warren Hastings, who was still living, which would no doubt be brought out into the light if she became famous. This would bring terrible shame not just on Warren Hastings, but on the whole Austen family.

Claire Harman, in her excellent biography of Fanny Burney, outlines many connections between *Fanny Burney* and *Jane Austen*, which even reveal knowledge by the author *Jane Austen* of Fanny Burney's private life. Claire Harman outlines the many and various connections between *Jane Austen* and *Fanny Burney* thus:

"Among the list of subscribers were Fanny Burney's fellow-novelists Ann Radcliffe and Maria Edgeworth and a 'Miss J. Austen' of Steventon in Hampshire. Austen was only twenty when *Camilla* was published, and four months later she began writing her own first adult work, a novel called 'First Impressions' (later *Pride and Prejudice*), the manuscript of which was circulating among the Austen family by August 1797. In her famous defence of the novel in *Northanger Abbey* (which, as we shall see later, was almost certainly addressed specifically to Madame d'Arblay), Austen singled out *Camilla*, along with *Cecilia* and Maria Edgeworth's *Belinda*, as examples of works in which 'the most thorough knowledge of human nature, the happiest delineation of its varieties, the liveliest effusions of wit and humour are conveyed to the world in the best chosen language'. Austen was a devoted fan of Burney, and seems to have particularly admired *Camilla* (along with *Sir Charles Grandison*, it is the novel most frequently mentioned in her letters), reusing several situations and jokes from it in her own much more famous work. Any close reader of *Camilla* who is familiar with *Pride and Prejudice* will get a feeling of *déjà lu* from the similarity of Sir Sedley Clarendel's haughty behaviour at the provincial ball to that of Darcy at Meryton; Camilla's detention at Mrs Arlbery's house because of the rain to that of Elizabeth Bennet and her sister at Netherfield; and the musical ineptitude of Indiana, who 'with the utmost difficulty, played some very easy lessons' on the piano-forte, to that of Mary Bennet, who so famously 'delighted us long enough'. The fate of Mr Bennet is foreshadowed in Mrs Arlbery's warning to Macdersey that the man who chooses a pretty, silly wife to gratify his own sense of superiority will end up 'looking like a fool himself, when youth and beauty take flight, and when his ugly old wife exposes her ignorance or folly at every word'. Even the famous first sentence of Austen's book finds an echo in Burney's '[It is] received wisdom among match-makers, that a young lady without fortune has a less and less chance of getting off upon every public appearance', and the main narrative of both books – couple get engaged but then break off and struggle back together – is of course identical.

There are connections from *Camilla* to other Austen novels too: to *Emma*, which like *Camilla* features a charming, imperfect heroine and a disapproving monitor/lover, and to

Persuasion, in which the famous Lyme Cobb accident recalls Indiana Lynmere coquettishly insisting on jumping into the yacht without assistance. The very title of *Pride and Prejudice* is thought to derive from Burney's repeated use of the phrase in the closing pages of *Cecilia*. These evidences of influence are easily traced through Austen's reading but there are other, more enigmatic echoes in Austen of Burney which are more difficult to account for, notably the strange similarity of Fanny Price's experience in the famous 'Lovers Vows' episode in *Mansfield Park* with the account in Burney's early diary of her own terrifying amateur debut in *The Way to Keep Him* in Worcester back in the 1770s. There is, more particularly, what looks like a pastiche of Madame d'Arblay's frequent use of the terms 'caro sposo' and 'cara sposa' in Mrs Elton's affected talk in *Emma*. In a fascinating article tracing the 'in-group language' common to the Burney and Austen families, 'Sposi in Surrey', the critic Pat Rogers elucidates the connection between the two writers through the d'Arblays' friends and neighbours at Bookham, the Reverend and Mrs Samuel Cooke. Mrs Cooke was a first cousin of Mrs Austen, Jane's mother, and the reverend gentleman was Jane's godfather. Jane Austen knew Bookham and its environs well (*Emma* is set in this part of Surrey), and kept in touch with the Cookes all her life."

15.

The "Juvenilia"

The first works attributed by conventional biographers to Jane Austen appeared in the late 1780s and first half of the 1790s in the form of short stories and parodies written privately at Steventon Rectory, the house of Jane Austen's father, George Austen, where Eliza was a frequent guest at this time. Such biographers omit to mention the fact that these works were not written under Jane Austen's name, but were merely inscribed by "The Author". To fit them into the timetable of Jane Austen's life (Jane Austen was born in 1775), critics have labelled these works as her "Juvenilia". There is no evidence from the texts of them, however, to support the label of these works as "Juvenilia" (the works of a young author) other than the age of Jane Austen at this period. As clever parodies of authors of the time (including the English playwright and "historian" Oliver Goldsmith) they are more in the style of a mature author. They appear to have been written for the amusement of the whole Austen family, with Jane Austen acting as a secretary and copyist for Eliza in preparation for her similar duties in the future for Eliza's complete novels.

Indeed, the time when these Juvenilia were written coincides exactly with the period from 1788 to 1796 when Eliza was a frequent visitor to Jane Austen's home in Steventon. A few of these short pieces are dated as follows:

Love and Freindship is dated Sunday June 13th 1790. Deirdre Le Faye in *Jane Austen's Outlandish Cousin* suggests that Eliza visited Steventon at this time.

Catharine, or the Bower is dated August 1792. We can be fairly sure that Eliza was at Steventon at this time, for in her letter of 16th July 1792 to her cousin Phylly Walter she writes "You may direct to me as usual for this whole month, for my letters will be carefully forwarded to me & when once August is begun direct to me at Steventon for I hope to be there by that time".

The Three Sisters is dated 2nd June 1793. There are no records of Eliza's movements for eighteen months after her letter from Steventon of 16th July 1792, as Deirdre Le Faye records, but in March 1793 Phylly Walter wrote to her brother James that she thought Eliza was still at Steventon. It is likely therefore that Eliza was still there in June 1793.

It is highly suspicious that no letters of Jane Austen remain from this period; presumably they were all destroyed by her sister Cassandra as they referred to the true circumstances behind the composition of these so-called "Juvenilia". In addition, Claire Tomalin notes that Eliza appears so little in the Steventon Austens' records of the time as to suggest a deliberate exclusion by them.

The Juvenilia are often prefaced with a joky dedication but they are not stated to be by "Jane Austen" or even by "J.A." but by "The Author".

One of these pieces, *Lesley Castle*, is dedicated as follows:

"To Henry Thomas Austen Esqre.
　Sir
　I AM now availing myself of the Liberty you have frequently honoured me with of dedicating one of my Novels to you. That it is unfinished, I greive; yet fear that from me, it will always remain so; that as far as it is carried, it should be so trifling and so unworthy of you, is another concern to your obliged humble
　Servant
　The Author

170

Messrs Demand and Co. – please to pay Jane Austen
Spinster the sum of one hundred guineas on account of
your Humble Servant.
H. T. Austen
£105. 0. 0"

This is a curious dedication. When the author writes "That it is
unfinished, I greive; yet fear that from me, it will always remain so",
it seems to me that Eliza is sending Henry Austen a coded message
that she will never consent to be his wife. Otherwise, what is the
meaning of the words "from me"? Then there is the curious cheque
for one hundred guineas made payable to "Jane Austen Spinster".
There is no indication here that "The Author" is the same person
as "Jane Austen Spinster". The jokiness of the cheque seems to
indicate that, although "Jane Austen Spinster" is not the author, she
is to be the financial beneficiary of the work. Like Fanny Burney,
Jane Austen is to receive the financial benefit of Eliza's writing in
return for helping her as a secretary, copyist and proofreader.

The very fact that these works are parodies would indicate that
they are much more likely to be the work of a mature writer than to
be juvenilia, since to write an effective parody one needs to be a
mature writer who is a master of the style they are parodying. What
annoys me more than the inaccuracy of the description of these
pieces as "Juvenilia" is the complete misrepresentation such a
description provides of how an artist develops. That educated critics
can be under the impression that a creative artist starts off writing
parodies before later creating serious works shows either a complete
ignorance of the creative process or a lack of professional ability on
their part. According to these critics, Jane Austen is the only example
ever known of such literary development *à l'envers*.

For instance, Mozart's *Ein Musikalischer Spaß* (A Musical Joke),
K.522 (Divertimento for two horns and strings) is understood by
many to be a masterful musical parody on bad composers of the era.
To suggest it was part of Mozart's juvenilia, written while Mozart

was still learning to write music correctly, would be ridiculous, since only a master of music could produce such a parody. In fact it was written by Mozart on 14th June 1787, when he was aged thirty-one, in the later years of his short life. I would take issue with the claim that *Jane Austen's* so-called "Juvenilia" were early works. These works, although short, are of a satirical nature and thus clearly the production of a mature writer. We only need to look at *Fanny Burney's Evelina*, written when Eliza was seventeen, to see that a young writer aspires to maturity of style, not to immaturity. Immaturity in writing is the affectation of later years.

Two of the main works in the Juvenilia are *Henry and Eliza* and the *The History of England*. *Henry and Eliza*, humbly dedicated to Miss Cooper by "The Author", is a very short satire of a few pages erroneously described by the author as "A Novel". This satire refers to Eliza in a number of ways. Firstly, the title is generally accepted by most biographers to refer to Eliza and Henry Austen. The character of Eliza in the story is, like Eliza herself, an illegitimate child looking for her real father. There is one paragraph which shows that Eliza is the author of *Henry and Eliza*, where the author mocks the youthful pomposity of her dedication to *Fanny Burney's Evelina* in 1778. In the dedication to *Evelina* she wrote to her father, Warren Hastings:

> "If in my heart the love of Virtue glows,
>   'T was planted there by an unerring rule;
> From thy example the pure flame arose,
>   Thy life, my precept,–thy good works, my school."

In *Henry and Eliza* the author says of Sir George and Lady Harcourt, who find Eliza as a three month old baby in a Haycock:

> "Being good People themselves, their first & principal care was to incite in her a Love of Virtue & a Hatred of Vice, in which they so well succeeded (Eliza having a natural turn

that way herself) that when she grew up, she was the delight of all who knew her."

Eliza here alludes to her "natural turn" to a "Love of Virtue", mocking the youthful pomposity of her own dedication to *Evelina* where she refers to the "Love of Virtue" glowing in her heart. In the story the baby Eliza is an illegitimate child found in a Haycock. This is a far from subtle pun on the illegitimate Eliza's surname at birth, Hancock. The author in *Henry and Eliza* also twice makes a joke similar to that made by Eliza in her letter to her cousin Phylly, dated 16th February 1798, where she wrote:

> "however I do believe that they [the French] will make an attempt on this Country, and Government appears to be convinced of it, for we have received orders to add one hundred & fifty Men to our Regiment, and hold ourselves in readiness to march at the shortest notice, so that I am going to be drilled and to bespeak my Regimentals without further delay".

In *Henry and Eliza* the author writes "Eliza, being perfectly conscious of the derangement in their affairs, immediately on her Husband's death set sail for England, in a man of War of 55 Guns, which they had built in their more prosperous Days" and "No sooner was she reinstated in her accustomed power at Harcourt Hall, than she raised an Army, with which she entirely demolished the Dutchess's Newgate, snug as it was, and by that act, gained the Blessings of thousands, & the Applause of her own Heart."

Another of the Juvenilia, *The History of England*, is a sophisticated parody of a history textbook written by Eliza. As a satire, it clearly shows the deep knowledge of English history required on the part of the author in order for her to make such clever jokes about the reign of each monarch she reviews. It is also generally agreed to be a parody of the informal historical style of the popular historian of the time, Oliver Goldsmith. Its humour is similar to that of Sellar and Yeatman's parody of schoolboy history *1066 and all That* in that it can only be appreciated fully by someone who has a very good education in English history. Nobody would seriously suggest that Sellar and Yeatman wrote their book whilst still schoolchildren, prior to writing proper history books when they grew up. In *The History of England*, the author shows a hatred of Queen Elizabeth and sympathy towards Mary Queen of Scots. This may be because of Eliza's Roman Catholic leanings. In her entry for James the 1st, the author of *The History of England* states that "As I am myself partial to the roman catholic religion, it is with infinite regret that I am obliged to blame the Behaviour of any Member of it." It is not likely that Jane Austen would have shared Eliza's Roman Catholic views, as she was the daughter of a protestant Church of England clergyman. On the other hand, given Eliza's connections with France and her Catholic friends in Paris, this is much more likely to be a view expressed by her.

The tone of *Jane Austen's* Juvenilia is very similar to the tone of Eliza's letters of the time, and many of the jokes made are also similar. Just as she wrote her letters for the amusement of her cousin Philadelphia, the Juvenilia were short pieces copied down by Jane Austen which Eliza wrote for the amusement of the Austen family when staying at their home in Steventon in Hampshire. The lively Eliza would have found such writing an amusing way to spend her otherwise empty time in a quiet rural backwater. Used to the fast pace of London, she would have had to find such employment to occupy herself.

There is, moreover, one extraordinary coincidence, only explicable if we accept Eliza was the author of both the works of *Jane Austen* and those of *Fanny Burney*. Many of the names that are used by *Jane Austen* in her Juvenilia are the same as names used by *Fanny Burney* in her plays written shortly afterwards. As the Juvenilia were not seen outside the Austen household, and the plays of *Fanny Burney* were never performed, this cannot be explained, unless we acknowledge that Eliza was the true author of both. For instance, *Jane Austen's Edgar & Emma* features a Mr and Mrs Willmot, while in *Fanny Burney's The Woman Hater* two of the principal characters are Wilmot and Miss Wilmot. *Jane Austen's Sir William Mountague* features a Lady Percival and her *Catharine, or the Bower* includes a Mrs Percival, while Miss Percival is a character in *Fanny Burney's A Busy Day*. *Jane Austen's The Three Sisters* includes a Mr Watts, while in *A Busy Day* there is a Mr and Mrs Watts and their daughter, the heroine Eliza (this is the Eliza who in the play was called Betsy by her parents and was the heiress of her guardian who lived in Calcutta in India). *Jane Austen's Lesley Castle* includes a Mr Cleveland, while Cleveland is the hero of *Fanny Burney's A Busy Day* (Cleveland Row was also the London street in which Eliza's husband had his office at this time). Wilhelminus is a character in a short scrap by *Jane Austen* called *A Tale* while there is a character called Lady Wilhelmina in *A Busy Day*.

In *Jane Austen's Frederic & Elfrida* one of Mrs Fitzroy's daughters lengthens her name to the ridiculous "Jezelinda" and in *Jane Austen's Love and Freindship* the daughter of the Macdonalds calls herself "Janetta" instead of Jane. In a similar way Miss Watts in *Fanny Burney's A Busy Day* wants to be called "Margarella" instead of Margaret, and she calls her sister "Eliziana".

In addition, Henry Tilney is the hero of *Jane Austen's Northanger Abbey*, begun in 1798 under the name of *Susan*, and one of the characters in *Fanny Burney's* play *A Busy Day* of 1799 is Sir Marmaduke Tylney. *Northanger Abbey* was not published until 1817 and *A Busy Day* was never performed until the twentieth century.

None of the above surnames are particularly common. Dr Roland Ennos, Reader in the Faculty of Life Sciences at Manchester University, and author of *Statistical and Data Handling Skills in Biology* has carried out a statistical review of this coincidence of names. His conclusion is that such a coincidence of names is very unlikely to appear by chance alone, and therefore it is very likely that the two authors either knew each other or were the same. Since we know that Jane Austen never met Fanny Burney, we must conclude that the pieces are statistically very likely to have been written by the same author.

Indeed, there is one telling piece of evidence I have come across which seems to prove without doubt that the so-called "Juvenilia" were not written by Jane Austen at all. This is the short story which is called *Catharine, or the Bower*. This, it is generally agreed by biographers of *Jane Austen*, is the most accomplished literary work among the Juvenilia and it is clearly the work of a very accomplished writer. George Holbert Tucker in his book *Jane Austen the Woman* is able to date this work from its reference to "Regency bonnets" to the narrow field of 1788-9. In *Jane Austen the Woman* he writes:

"More important, as far as Jane Austen was concerned, the prince's visits to Kempshott coincided with the first regency crisis of 1788-89, brought on by the insanity of George III. Although *Catharine, or the Bower,* her first attempt at serious fiction, was dedicated in its unfinished state in 1792 to her sister, Cassandra, it contains evidence that portions of it date from a slightly earlier period. The original manuscript of the unfinished novel in Jane's notebook *Volume the Third* contains numerous emendations that are not included in the standard published version of *Catharine*. For example, two mentions of a "Regency Bonnet" are made but were later erased by Jane, who substituted the names of other articles of clothing in their places. The original entries are still decipherable, however, and suggest that Jane was aware of the role her rakish neighbor, the Prince of Wales, was then playing in national politics.

To elucidate: At the time of George III's attack of mental illness in 1788-89, party feeling between the Whigs and the Tories mounted to fever pitch when it appeared that the Prince of Wales, who was supported by the Whigs, would become regent in the event that his father did not recover. 'The Opposition,' wrote one loyalist in castigating the Whigs, 'have been taking inconceivable pains to spread the idea that the disorder is incurable'. Still another Tory declared: 'The acrimony is beyond anything that you can conceive. The ladies are, as usual, at the head of all animosity, and are distinguished by caps, ribbands and other emblems of party.' At that time, Regency caps and bonnets, such as those mentioned by Jane Austen in *Catharine*, sold briskly from seven guineas up and were described by one fashion writer as 'a mountain of tumbled gauze, with three large feathers in front, tied together with a knot of ribbons on which was printed in gold letters *Honi soit qui mal y pense de la Regence*'... Jane's mention of "Regency bonnets" in *Catharine* (bearing the dedication date of 1792) therefore indicates that her novel was actually begun around the time of or shortly before the regency crisis of 1788-89. Otherwise, she would hardly have mentioned that particular type of millinery in the original draft of *Catharine*, only to erase the reference later as the passing of the regency crisis had rendered that style of female adornment unfashionable."

This would mean that Jane Austen would have had to have written *Catharine, or the Bower* at the age of thirteen to fourteen. *Catharine, or the Bower* is a thoroughly mature work which could not possibly have been written by a girl of thirteen to fourteen with only two years' primary school education. It is for this reason that the book is traditionally but wrongly dated, e.g. by Claire Tomalin and by Jon Spence, at the date of its dedication in 1792 when Jane Austen was sixteen years old, in order to make Jane Austen's authorship just squeeze into the bounds of possibility. The book discusses London society at a time when Jane Austen knew nothing of London society. At the age of thirteen or fourteen, living in the countryside, how could she possibly have known about it? In addition, the work specifically discusses the fate of women who are obliged, as was Eliza's mother, to travel to Bengal to find a husband, and laments their fate, in details only those acquainted at first hand with such matters would be likely to relate. In the story Miss Wynne is in a very similar position to that in which Eliza's mother found herself when young:

"It was now two years since the death of Mr Wynne, and the consequent dispersion of his Family who had been left by it in great distress. They had been reduced to a state of absolute dependence on some relations, who though very opulent and very nearly connected with them, had with difficulty been prevailed on to contribute anything towards their Support. Mrs Wynne was fortunately spared the knowledge & participation of their distress, by her release from a painful illness a few months before the death of her husband. – The eldest daughter has been obliged to accept the offer of one of her cousins to equip her for the East Indies, and tho' infinitely against her inclinations had been necessitated to embrace the only possibility that was offered to her, of a Maintenance; Yet it was one, so opposite to all her ideas of Propriety, so contrary to her Wishes, so repugnant to her feelings, that she would almost have preferred Servitude to it, had Choice been allowed her–. Her personal Attractions had gained her a husband as soon as she had arrived in Bengal, and she had now been married nearly a twelvemonth. Splendidly, yet unhappily married. United to a Man of double her own age, whose disposition was not amiable, and whose Manners were unpleasing, though his Character was respectable. Kitty had heard twice from her freind since her marriage, but her Letters were always unsatisfactory, and though she did not openly avow her feelings, yet every line proved her to be Unhappy."

The heroine, Catharine, states "But do you call it lucky, for a Girl of Genius & Feeling to be sent in quest of a husband to Bengal, to be married there to a Man of whose Disposition she has no opportunity of judging till her Judgement is of no use to her, who may be a Tyrant or a Fool or both for what she knows to the Contrary? Do you call *that* fortunate?"

The author of *Catharine* also discusses female education. She describes how a woman ought to be educated, contrasting the education given to Eliza in real life to that given to Camilla Stanley in the novel. This was a subject about which the poorly educated Jane Austen knew nothing:

> "they were therefore most agreably necessitated to reside half the Year in Town; where Miss Stanley had been attended by the most capital Masters from the time of her being six years old to the last Spring, which comprehending a period of twelve Years had been dedicated to the acquirement of Accomplishments which were now to be displayed and in a few Years entirely neglected. She was not inelegant in her appearance, rather handsome, and naturally not deficient in Abilities; but those Years which ought to have been spent in the attainment of useful knowledge and Mental Improvement, had been all bestowed in learning Drawing, Italian and Music, more especially the latter, and she now united to these Accomplishments, an Understanding unimproved by reading and a Mind totally devoid either of Taste or Judgement."

It is easy to imagine how Eliza wrote these lines. She is contrasting her own academic education under her Masters in London, organised by her highly intellectual father, Warren Hastings, with the inferior education received by most fashionable young women at the time. It is impossible that Jane Austen wrote these lines. When these lines were written, she had only received a primary education for two years at a basic provincial school, and was therefore in no position to criticise even an inferior form of London education, which would still have been vastly superior to the paltry one she had received. The author of *Catharine, or the Bower* also shows an easy familiarity with the style of Tacitus in describing Camilla Stanley thus: "She professed a love of Books without Reading, was Lively without Wit, and generally good humoured without Merit".

F B Pinion in his book *A Jane Austen Companion* expresses astonishment that Jane Austen wrote *Love and Freindship* at the age of fourteen and *Catharine* at the age of sixteen. He would be even more astonished to learn Jane Austen had written *Catharine* at the age of thirteen. Indeed, in style, *Catharine, or the Bower* fits in with what we would expect of *Fanny Burney's* style during the period between the publication of *Cecilia* in 1782 and *Camilla* in 1796. Moreover, two of the characters in *Catharine, or the Bower* are named Cecilia and Camilla. Another interesting coincidence is that Camilla Stanley in *Catharine, or the Bower* shares her surname with Cecilia Stanley, the heroine of *Fanny Burney's The Witlings*, an early play of hers that was never performed and was suppressed by Fanny Burney's father, and so could not have been seen by Jane Austen.

Eliza's Northern Journey

To Washington, Co Durham
(E de F only)

Chapel en
le Frith

Castleton

Tideswell

Buxton

Baslow

Old
Brampton
(Lambton)

Chesterfield

Bake-
well

Chatsworth
('Pemberley')

to London
(EB only)

Dove Dale

Matlock

Ashbourne

from London, Birmingham

The Vale of Mickleham

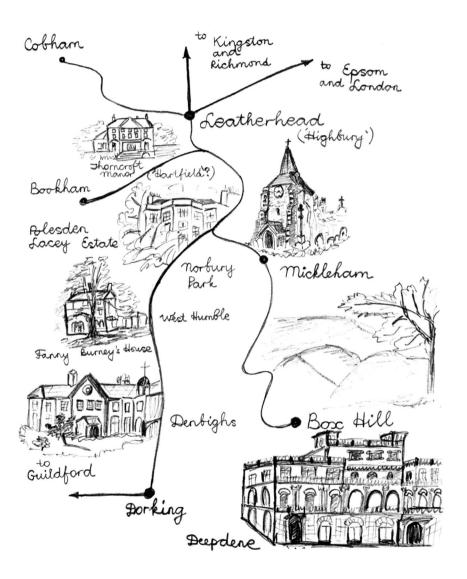

Cobham

to Kingston and Richmond

to Epsom and London

Leatherhead ('Highbury')

Thorncroft Manor ('Hartfield'?)

Bookham

Polesden Lacey Estate

Norbury Park

Mickleham

West Humble

Fanny Burney's House

Denbighs

Box Hill

to Guildford

Dorking

Deepdene

Stoneleigh Abbey ("Northanger Abbey")

High Tor, Matlock, Derbyshire

Anna Maria Appolonia Hastings when Mrs Imhoff by William
Dickinson; after Robert Edge Pine
© National Portrait Gallery, London

Lady Sophia Burrell (1750-1802). Poet, dramatist and friend of
Eliza. In her poems she praised Eliza as a great novelist.

Warren Hastings (1732-1818) by Sir Joshua Reynolds, painted
1767-68
© National Portrait Gallery, London

Portrait of Warren Hastings Anonymous, © Ashmolean Museum, University of Oxford. Believed by the author to be by Christoph Carl Adam von Imhoff

Portrait of Sir William Murray, 1st Earl of Mansfield William Russell Birch, © Ashmolean Museum, University of Oxford

Chipperfield Manor ("Netherfield Park")

Langley House (now called Breakspear Place) ("Longbourn")

Chatsworth ("Pemberley")

The Church of St Peter and St Paul, Old Brampton ("Lambton")

Thorncroft Manor ("Hartfield")

The Grave of Eliza Austen (the flat slab in the foreground) in the corner of the churchyard of St John-at-Hampstead, London

Frances d'Arblay ("Fanny Burney") (1752-1840) by Edward
Francisco Burney, painted 1784-85
© National Portrait Gallery, London

16.

Authorship of Jane Austen Denied by her Brother and Nephew

Readers of biographies of Jane Austen will have been convinced that her family was certain of her authorship. However, this was definitely not the case. I mentioned in my introduction the fact that the very idea that Jane Austen was an author was considered laughable by her brother and nephew and other close relations. This may come as a great surprise to most readers. I have never seen this admitted in any book but I present the following evidence to support this.

Jane Austen's brother James was a highly accomplished poet. He has been associated by many biographers with the character of Edmund Bertram in *Jane Austen's Mansfield Park*, since he was a clergyman and, as well as his brother Henry, was known to have flirted with Eliza during the amateur theatricals performed at Steventon over the Christmas of 1787-88. Upon the death of his first wife, Anne Matthew, in May 1795, it seems that he, like his brother Henry, may have courted Eliza and wished to marry her. No doubt in addition to her physical charms, he admired her literary ability. Just as Edmund was rejected by Mary Crawford because he was a clergyman, this seems to have been an objection for Eliza to marry James and she was later, of course, to marry his brother Henry, but only after Henry gave up his own plans to become a clergyman.

It seems that Eliza's objection would have been, in part, her irreverent outlook on life, which would not sit easy with the wife of a clergyman, but a much stronger impediment was her wish to live in London, where she indeed lived after marriage with Henry Austen, in the fashionable West End. Eliza loved to attend balls, the theatre and the opera. She would not have been happy living in the countryside as the wife of a country parson. We see in the works of *Jane Austen* that the narrowness of the life of a country parson is often satirised in such characters as Mr Collins in *Pride and Prejudice* and Dr Grant in *Mansfield Park*. This would have been a very unlikely view coming from Jane Austen; her beloved father was a country clergyman, and she enjoyed living in the small village of Steventon in Hampshire, becoming very upset when the family moved to Bath in 1801 on her father's retirement aged seventy. Also, at this time in the eighteenth century, it would have been normal for the daughter of a clergyman to look for a husband among the clergy.

In contrast to Henry Austen, we have no record of James Austen ever claiming that Jane Austen was the writer of the books which bear her name. Indeed, he impliedly denies it. James Austen was a poet of some talent himself, and it seems that one of the reasons he wished to marry Eliza was because of their shared interest in literature and his admiration for her in this regard. James Austen wrote a poem *Venta! within they sacred fane* upon the death of Jane Austen, which included the following lines:

"Ne'er did this venerable Fane
More beauty, sense & worth contain
Than when upon a Sister's bier
Her Brothers dropt the bitter tear.

In her (rare union) were combined
A fair form & a fairer mind;
Hers, Fancy quick and clear good sense
And wit that never gave offense;
A heart as warm as ever beat,
A Temper, even, calm, & sweet

...

Yet not a word she ever penn'd
Which hurt the feelings of a friend,
And not one line she ever wrote
Which dying she would wish to blot;
But to her family alone
Her real, genuine worth was known.
Yes, they whose lot it was to prove
Her Sisterly, her filial love,
They saw her ready still to share
The labours of domestic care,
...

To have thee with us it was given,
A special behest of heaven
...

When by the Body unconfined
All Sense, Intelligence & Mind
By Seraphs borne through realms of light
(While Angels gladden at the sight)
The Aetherial Spirit wings its way
To regions of Eternal day."

Rev. James Austen, (1817)

There is deep irony in the lines "not a word she ever penned", "But to her family alone her real genuine worth was known", and "not one line she ever wrote". We must remember that this must be deliberate, as James was a poet skilled in the craft of poetry. The only tasks he mentions that Jane **did** carry out are "The labours of domestic care". He is saying indirectly that Jane Austen was not a writer.

Thus, although James, as an accomplished poet himself, would have above all appreciated *Jane Austen* as the finest novelist of her time, there is no mention in the above poem of Jane Austen even being a writer. Perhaps it was because James was a clergyman that he found it impossible to tell a lie about his sister. In spite of James Austen being an enthusiastic and gifted poet, we have no record of him ever discussing literature with his sister Jane at any time. As far as we know, he never visited Jane Austen in order to talk to her about any literary matters whatsoever. Had Jane Austen been a writer, he would have spent much more time with her. However, we know that he did collaborate in a literary way with Eliza, in that he wrote the prologues for some of the plays which he performed with her at Steventon. Any contact he had with Eliza was broken, however, after his second marriage to Jane Austen's friend, Mary Lloyd, in 1797. Perhaps jealous of her husband's previous admiration for Eliza, Mary Lloyd always refused to meet her.

Jane Austen's nephew and James Austen's son, James Edward Austen (known to the family as "Edward") was a much less accomplished poet (more McGonagall than Milton) but he was more direct in denying Jane Austen's authorship and asserting that of Eliza (presumably he had this knowledge through his father). He wrote a poem to Miss J Austen when he was fifteen which included the following lines: [with my highlighting]:

No words can express, my dear Aunt, my surprise
Or make you conceive how I opened my eyes,
Like a pig Butcher **Pile has** just struck with his knife,
When I heard for the very first time in my life
That I had the honor to have a relation
Whose works were dispersed
Through the whole of the nation.
…

Now if you will take your poor nephew's advice
Your works to Sir William pray send in a trice,
If he'll undertake to some grandees to show it,
By whose means at last the Prince Regent might know it,
For I am sure if he did, in reward for your tale,

He'd make you a countess at least, without fail,
And Indeed, if the Princess should lose her dear life
You might have a good chance of becoming his wife."

The poem starts out by saying he is astonished to find his aunt (Jane Austen) is an author. Next, a crude anagram appears in the line "Like a pig Butcher **Pile has** just struck with his knife." It will be obvious to the least accomplished crossword solver that the letters in "Pile has" need to be re-arranged ("struck with his knife") to find the solution of this riddle, which is, of course "Elisa Ph". The Austen family were very fond of riddles and there are examples of charades and riddles in *Jane Austen's Emma*. The only conceivable reason for the Butcher's surname to be "Pile" in this poem is for this anagram to work. Later in the poem, the poet says that his aunt Jane Austen should be made a countess, at least, without fail. This refers to the fact that Eliza was by marriage a French Countess (Comtesse), while the word "fail" refers to the French word for failure, "*faillite*", which is the closest French word to her title as a countess, which was "*Feuillide*". There is no conceivable reason why the poet should otherwise mention a countess, or indeed failing, in the poem, unless to point to the authorship of Eliza. Indeed, the line in the poem makes no sense otherwise, since it was impossible for a woman to be made a countess. In England a woman could only acquire this title by marrying an earl. Because of the young age of James Edward Austen, it is notable how obvious the clues to Eliza's authorship are in this poem, compared to the more subtle clues left in his father's preceding poem.

Thus, while all the biographies of Jane Austen published since her death imply that her authorship was well known to her family, these poems show that in fact her close family did not believe in her authorship at all, and knew Eliza to be the true author.

The only close relative of Jane Austen who attributed the novels to her was Eliza's husband, Henry. After their publication he talked of the authorship of Jane Austen to various acquaintances and after

Jane Austen's death on 18th July 1817 he included a biographical notice of "the author" at the beginning of *Northanger Abbey* when it was published late in the same year. We should bear in mind that Henry was the person from whose house in London the novels had been published and, as the closest person to Eliza, had presumably been asked by her to conceal her identity as author. The main reason for this concealment was without doubt because Warren Hastings was still alive (he died on 22nd August 1818), and Eliza, as a loving daughter, wished to protect his reputation and spare him any embarrassment. This is the same reason outlined in the poem in the dedication to *Fanny Burney's Evelina*. A secondary reason was no doubt to spare the embarrassment of the Austen family.

Henry Austen himself had no wish to reveal Eliza as the author and cause embarrassment to Hastings or his wife and stepchildren. This is why he gradually spread the rumour of his sister, Jane Austen's, authorship. Henry had previously requested the help of Warren Hastings to set up his bank, and he wished to remain in favour with Hastings, perhaps in hope of some reward or recommendation in return for his discretion. We know that he visited Warren Hastings at his estate at Daylesford shortly after Eliza's death, perhaps to request some particular favour from him.

The first official mention of Jane Austen as the author of the works now attributed to her only appears in the obituary columns of the *Hampshire Chronicle and Courier* of 22nd July 1817:

"On the 18th inst. , at Winchester, Miss Jane Austen, youngest daughter of the late George Austen, Rector of Steventon, in Hampshire, and the authoress of Emma, Mansfield Park, Pride and Prejudice and Sense and Sensibility. Her manners were most gentle; her affections ardent; her candor was not to be surpassed; and she lived and died as became a humble Christian."

No doubt this notice was inserted by her brother Henry.

Strangely, for such a distinguished author, nothing further was published about the life of Jane Austen for another fifty years after her death, when her above-mentioned nephew, James Edward, by now styling himself James Edward Austen-Leigh, published the first biography of her, *A Memoir of Jane Austen*, in 1870. As mentioned, James Edward was the author of the above poem hinting that Eliza, and not Jane Austen, was the true author. Not surprisingly, therefore, he had undertaken the task of writing the life of Jane Austen most reluctantly. The topic of her life was not a subject that held much fascination for him and he saw the writing of her biography as a burdensome duty which had fallen on him but which he owed to the rest of the Austen family. In his biography he states blandly of Jane Austen: "Of events her life was singularly barren: few changes and no great crisis ever broke the smooth current of its course." A strange epitaph to a woman whose novels describe life in all its fullness.

17.

The Reaction of Other People to Jane Austen's Authorship

Contemporary descriptions of the character of Jane Austen are hard to find but when we do find them they are less than flattering. This has been a matter of embarrassment for biographers of Jane Austen, who have tended to play down these descriptions. Philadelphia Walter, Eliza's cousin, admired Jane's sister Cassandra but described Jane in a letter to her brother James of 23rd July 1788 as "whimsical and affected" and "not at all pretty & very prim, unlike a girl of twelve". That she had some justification in holding this opinion and was not motivated by malice is shown by the marked contrast of the very high opinion she gives of Eliza and her mother. Of them Philadelphia Walter wrote to her brother James on 19th September 1787:

> "[Eliza] has many amiable qualities, such as the highest duty, love and respect for her mother; for whom there is not any sacrifice she would not make, and certainly contributes entirely to her happiness;… her principles are strictly just, making it a rule never to bespeak anything that she is not quite sure of being able to pay for directly, never contracting debts of any kind."

She also described Eliza's mother as "so strictly just and honourable in all her dealings, so kind and obliging to all her friends and acquaintance, so religious in all her actions, in short I do not know a person that has more the appearance of perfection".

Philadelphia Walter was also generous in her praise of Warren Hastings' wife, Marian, after she met her in London. In a letter to her brother James Walter of 21st April 1788 she wrote of her, "Mrs. Hastings I admire exceedingly, very affable, lively and pleasing."

Therefore we can be reasonably sure that Philadelphia Walter was a fair judge of people and was giving an accurate portrait of Jane Austen. However, some Jane Austen biographers have never been able to accept Philadelphia Walter's comments on Jane Austen as being justified. Philadelphia's opinion of Jane Austen is, however, confirmed by Mary Russell Mitford, whose mother had lived in Steventon when the Austens were residing there. In a letter to Sir William Elford in December 1814, she says her mother described Jane Austen as "the prettiest, silliest, most affected husband-hunting butterfly she ever remembers".

Miss Mitford also said the following about Jane Austen in her later years:

"A friend of mine who visits her now, says that she has stiffened into the most perpendicular, precise, taciturn piece of 'single blessedness' that ever existed, and that, till Pride and Prejudice showed what a precious gem was hidden in that unbending case, she was no more regarded in society than a poker or a firescreen, or any other thin, upright piece of wood or iron that fills the corner in peace and quietness. The case is very different now: she is still a poker – but a poker of whom everyone is afraid."

Jane Austen's niece, Lady Fanny Knatchbull, writing in 1869, also recalled her as "not so *refined* as she ought to have been from her *talent*". She also said of Jane Austen and her sister:

"Both the Aunts (Cassandra & Jane) were brought up in the most complete ignorance of the World & its ways (I mean as to fashion &c) & if it had not been for Papa's marriage which brought them into Kent, & the kindness of Mrs. Knight, who used often to have one or other of the sisters staying with her, they would have been, tho' not less clever & agreeable in themselves, very much below par as to good Society & its ways".

Jane Austen's nephew, James Edward Austen-Leigh, also emphasised Jane Austen's ignorance of the fashionable world:

"I believe that she and her sister were generally thought to have taken to the garb of middle age earlier than their years or their looks required; and that, though remarkably neat in their dress as in all their ways, they were scarcely sufficiently regardful of the fashionable, or the becoming."

These are the most reliable first-hand descriptions we have of Jane Austen herself, and they could not contrast more strongly with the author *Jane Austen*, whose books demonstrate an intimate knowledge of the manners and fashions of prosperous gentry and of London society and the fashionable world. In her opinion of *Mansfield Park*, collected by Jane Austen at the time of its publication with the opinions of others, a Mrs Pole wrote:

"There is a particular satisfaction in reading all Miss A-s works – they are so evidently written by a Gentlewoman – most Novellists fail & betray themselves in attempting to describe familiar scenes in high Life , some little vulgarism escapes & shews that they are not experimentally acquainted with what they describe, but here it is quite different. Everything is natural, & the situations & incidents are told in a manner which clearly evinces the Writer to belong to the Society whose Manners she so ably delineates."

Mrs Pole is saying that the author must have been someone in high society herself or she could not have portrayed high society in her books so accurately. As we have seen from the first-hand testimony we have of Jane Austen above, she was in no way a woman of fashion and she had little experience of "high Life". Therefore she could not have written the novel without making mistakes in her description of London high life. This was in marked contrast to Eliza, who moved in the highest circles of London society, visiting such fashionable London destinations as Almacks Rooms and the Court of St James'. She also mixed with people of very high social standing such as Warren Hastings and Lady Sophia Burrell. Interestingly, in the same opinion of *Mansfield Park*, Mrs Pole also talks of speculation as to the true author at the time of the appearance of the novels:

"Mrs Pole also said that no Books had ever occasioned so much canvassing & doubt, & that everybody was desirous to attribute them to some of their own freinds, or to some person of whom they thought highly."

How on earth could the author of *Jane Austen's* novels be ignorant of fashion? Jane Austen was not, like Eliza, a rich woman (a "lady of fashion"). In the other sense of the word "fashion", nothing could be of more importance in these books than the (often rather vapid) discussion of the latest fashions of the day between the various women characters, as where Mrs Gardiner tells the Bennets about the latest fashion for long sleeves in London in *Pride and Prejudice*. Indeed, the especial interest shown in fashion in the works of *Jane Austen* and *Fanny Burney* can perhaps be traced to Eliza's mother having worked as a milliner before her marriage. Certainly Eliza in one of her letters describes the fashions at the court of Marie Antoinette in great detail. Because of Eliza's wealth she was often more fashionably dressed than those around her, and her cousin Philadelphia Walter wrote of Eliza's dress being greatly admired during their time together in Tunbridge Wells.

Another niece, Caroline Austen, wrote of Jane Austen:

"She was fond of work – and she was a great adept at overcast and satin stitch" and "she generally sat in the drawing room till luncheon: when visitors were there, chiefly at work [i.e. sewing and embroidery]…"

It is extraordinary that an author of the quality of *Jane Austen* should spend her whole mornings sewing. This is in stark contrast to the occupations Eliza mentions in her letters, i.e. her books, her study, her pianoforte and her harp.

Jon Spence in *Becoming Jane Austen* makes the following statement:

"Eliza's love of pugs [pug dogs] was unforgettably given to Lady Bertram in Mansfield Park; perhaps the older Eliza of whom we hear so little also spent her time nicely dressed sitting on a sofa doing some long piece of needlework of little use and no beauty. The picture has a certain ring of truth. Austen perceived in Eliza that the fate of a Mary Crawford – or of an Eliza de Feuillide – might be nothing so dramatic as a descent into a 'vortex of Dissipation' but a gradual decline into vacuous dullness."

Jon Spence imagines that, because Eliza liked pug dogs and Lady Bertram liked pug dogs and liked to do needlework, therefore Eliza liked to do needlework. However, there is no evidence or logical reason to reach this conclusion. We know from her letter of 29th October 1799, when Eliza was thirty-seven, that Eliza wrote from Dorking in Surrey that she spent her time there with "my Books, my Harp & my Pianoforte". The only person who we have direct evidence spent most of her time in needlework was Jane Austen herself, as described by her niece, Caroline Austen, above.

Caroline's brother, James Edward, also expressed astonishment that Jane Austen could have produced the novels attributed to her:

"How she was able to effect all this is surprising, for she had no separate study to retire to, and most of the work must have been done in the general sitting-room, subject to all kinds of casual interruptions".

The information at Jane Austen's house in Chawton in Hampshire would have us believe that Jane Austen wrote in the sitting room downstairs, but that the door to the sitting room was creaky and whenever she heard someone coming she hid her writing away. This supplies a romantic but less than convincing explanation as to why no one ever saw her writing any novels.

To conclude, it would seem that the idea of Jane Austen as a literary genius was one people who knew her found very difficult to believe.

18.

The Burning of Jane Austen's Correspondence

The most suspicious circumstance surrounding the authorship of *Jane Austen* is that, some time after Jane Austen's death in 1817, the larger part of her letters were burnt by her sister, Cassandra.

Jane Austen's niece, Caroline Austen, wrote of the letters: "My Aunt [Cassandra] looked them over and burnt the greater part, (as she told me), 2 or 3 years before her own death – She left, or gave some as legacies to the Nieces – but of those I have seen, several had portions cut out." This is confirmed by Jane Austen's nephew, James Edward Austen-Leigh, who wrote in his *A Memoir of Jane Austen* of 1870:

> "The grave closed over my aunt fifty-two years ago; and during that long period no idea of writing her life had been entertained by any of her family. Her nearest relatives, far from making provision for such a purpose, had actually destroyed many of the letters and papers by which it might have been facilitated."

It is highly probable that Eliza wrote many letters to her cousin Jane Austen, as what we know of Eliza's life comes chiefly from several of her letters to another cousin, Philadelphia Walter, which still survive. Eliza was on much closer terms with her first cousin, Jane Austen, than with her more distantly related step-cousin, Philadelphia Walter, and Eliza and Jane Austen often visited each other's houses, so they must have written to each other frequently. Indeed, Henry was the favourite brother of Jane Austen and of course it would have been impossible for Jane to see him without seeing Eliza.

We know that there must have been a frequent correspondence between Jane Austen and Henry and Eliza. This is confirmed by a letter of 8th April 1805 from Jane Austen to her sister, Cassandra, in which she describes a letter she received from Henry and Eliza after sending them the gift of a screen and a brooch. In other letters of Jane Austen that survive, she refers on several occasions to writing to Henry or Eliza. In turn, Eliza mentions in one of her letters to Phylly Walter that she has received a letter from Jane Austen. Of all the letters written between Henry and Eliza and Jane Austen, however, none survive. Therefore it seems that Cassandra burned all of the letters Jane received from Eliza or Henry in order to prevent Eliza from becoming known as the author. Any letters Eliza received from Jane Austen would have been kept by Eliza's husband, Henry, but there is no trace of them, so it is presumed that they must have been destroyed by Henry. It is only by pure accident that the letters from Eliza to her cousin Philadelpia Walter survive, because the Walters were from a distant branch of the family and so it was out of the power of Cassandra or the immediate Austen family in the nineteenth century to destroy them, and these letters did not re-surface to biographers until long after Jane Austen's death. All the letters from Philadelphia Walter to Eliza, on the other hand, would have been the property of Henry Austen who no doubt destroyed them. In any event, none of them exist any longer. We are left with a completely one-sided correspondence from Eliza to Philadelphia Walter.

The correspondence between Jane Austen and Henry and Eliza must have been extensive, judging by the many times they stayed together in London or Steventon, especially when Jane Austen was staying at their house in London from 1811 to correct the proofs of the novels. They also travelled around together, for instance Henry and Eliza travelled from Bath to Lyme Regis with Jane Austen and her sister Cassandra in 1804. That no correspondence survives cannot be an accident. The systematic destruction of Jane Austen's letters by the Austen family in the nineteenth century can only have been for one purpose; to conceal that she was not the author.

There is a parallel here to Fanny Burney, who also destroyed quantities of her own papers during the last decade of her life, and burnt her diary and correspondence from the period leading up to the publication of *Fanny Burney's* first novel, *Evelina,* in 1778.

19.

Is There Any Evidence that Eliza was an Author?

There is no direct evidence that Eliza was an author of any poem or story at all. However, perversely, this total lack of documentation is strong evidence that her authorship has been concealed. We have examples of short literary pieces by most of the rest of the Austen family, which have been published by David Selwyn in *The Poetry of Jane Austen and the Austen family*. In addition to poems by James, Jane Austen's brother, and his son James Edward, there are poems by Jane Austen's mother, Jane's sister Cassandra, three of her other brothers, and Fanny and Anna, her nieces. And yet the most well-educated, cultivated and artistic person in the whole family has left nothing.

Many of the surviving letters of Eliza refer to her spending much of her time in reading, books and study. If her authorship had not been concealed, we could expect to find at least a poem or two from her pen, especially considering her fine education, her strong interest in literature, reading, acting and the theatre, and the beauty of the prose in her letters. As I will explain, Eliza's friend, Lady Sophia Burrell, stated in writing that Eliza was a novelist. We also know from Eliza's letters that she was a keen and frequent visitor to the theatre in London and she even commissioned plays to be put on at the spa town of Tunbridge Wells in Kent. She was also a keen amateur actress and played roles in her childhood and later as an adult in France and in the amateur theatricals the Austens put on at their home in Steventon. She was the natural daughter of Warren Hastings, who as a schoolboy had been the first king's scholar of his year in 1747 at the famous Westminster School in London. Hastings, as well as being a fine scholar in Greek and Latin, had taught himself to translate Persian and had learnt other languages used in India, in which he conversed with the native princes. Hastings also wrote poetry in English that was praised by Eliza's friend, the poet Lady Sophia Burrell. The love of literature and language literally ran in Eliza's blood. Why, then, is there no surviving poem or prose writing by Eliza, unless all such writing has been either destroyed or hidden under another name? Indeed, this poses another fundamental question: if Eliza was not a writer, what did she do all her life and, if she lived a life of idleness, why was she so admired by others, including her husband Henry, his brother James, Jane Austen, and the poet Lady Sophia Burrell?

We know from Eliza's letters and her enthusiasm for both visiting the theatre and acting in amateur theatricals that she had very strong literary interests. Unlike Jane Austen, she also had literary friends, like Lady Sophia Burrell, who was herself an accomplished writer and a published playwright, poet and novelist, and of course Warren Hastings himself. Lady Sophia Burrell was a close friend of both Eliza and Warren Hastings and indeed, in her collection of poems published in 1793, her poem to Warren Hastings stands next to one to Eliza, hinting perhaps at their blood relationship. Eliza wrote movingly to Hastings about Lady Sophia Burrell's final illness in a letter probably dated 6th March 1802:

"My dear Sir,
    Lady Burrell has a house in Chesterfield Street, but in consequence of Sr. Lucas Pepys directions has been for many months past at Richmond – I grieve to say that her health is in a deplorable state, and that the nature of her complaint which appears to be a confirmed decline, leaves but little hope of her restoration to the many friends who love and esteem her."

Lady Sophia Burrell's father, Sir Charles Raymond, had been the owner of a large number of ships which traded for the East India Company and was in consequence extremely rich, and Lady Sophia Burrell inherited from him part of his fortune of at least £100,000. Sir Charles Raymond was also, through his connection with the East India Company, a friend of Warren Hastings.

Lady Sophia Burrell referred to Eliza in one of the poems she dedicated to her as being "dear to the muse". I can find no other explanation for using this term than that Eliza was a writer, and an accomplished one at that. The poem is as follows [my highlighting]:

"And will Eliza then return?
Shall I once more behold her here,
And from her eyes, delighted learn
Her generous heart is still sincere?

Shall we retrace those happy days
When first we knew each other's mind,
When first I spake Eliza's praise
When first I found her good, and kind?

Ah! friend, so lov'd – so long deplor'd,
Welcome again to Britain's shore!
May health, may peace, their sweets afford;
May ev'ry blessing crowd thy door.

And when thy many friends have shar'd
The language of thy tuneful tongue,
Let a few hours to me be spar'd,
At distance from the busy throng.

If you can love our beechen trees,
Sequester'd cells, romantic views,

I court you to such scenes as these,
Dear to your friend, and to the muse.

While the gay birds their carols sing,
and to the sun their plumes display ,
We will enjoy the sweets of spring
As grateful, and as blest as they."

We can in fact be completely certain that Lady Sophia Burrell was here referring to Eliza as an accomplished writer. This is because she refers to the Lord Chief Justice, the Earl of Mansfield, in the same terms in her poem to him "On the Anniversary of the Earl of Mansfield's Birthday" in which she wrote [my highlighting]:

"Him virtue tutor'd, genius fir'd,
His words by Hermes were inspired,
His works the Muses loved;
Learning unfolded all her stores
Fancy illumin'd his leisure hours,
And POPE his thoughts approved."

In Lady Sophia Burrell's own notes to this poem, published in her edition of 1793, she writes that the line "His works the Muses loved" alludes to Lord Mansfield "having been a very elegant Poet in the juvenile part of his life" and that "Mr [Alexander] Pope was a friend of Lord Mansfield, and a particular admirer of his talents". Therefore when she describes Eliza as "dear to the muse" we can be certain she is saying that she is a writer.

Lady Sophia Burrell also notes that the poet Pope had praised Lord Mansfield (who was then just plain Mr Murray) in his *Essay on Satire*, Vol III. Page 19 as follows:

"With joy she sees the stream of Roman art [poetry]
From Murray's tongue flow purer to the heart"

Lord Mansfield's ability as a poet is confirmed not only by the poet Pope, but also by another famous poet, William Cowper, who was, according to Henry Austen in his *Biographical Notice of the Author, Jane Austen's* favourite poet. In one of his poems, Cowper laments the destruction of Lord Mansfield's library in the Gordon Riots of 1780. A Protestant mob had attacked Lord Mansfield's house in Bloomsbury in London because of Lord Mansfield's support for Catholic emancipation. In the poem Cowper shows his great admiration of Lord Mansfield's poetry as he lamented the loss of Lord Mansfield's own poems in the fire. The poem is as follows:

"On the burning of Lord Mansfield's library together with his manuscripts by the mob, in the month of June, 1780.

So then-the Vandals of our isle,
Sworn foes to sense and law,
Have burnt to dust a nobler pile
Than ever Roman saw!

And Murray sighs o'er Pope and Swift,
And many a treasure more,
The well judged purchase, and the gift
That graced his letter'd store.

Their pages mangled, burnt, and torn,
The loss was his alone;
But ages yet to come shall mourn
The burning of his own."

Cowper also wrote the following poem, *Lord Mansfield's Library*, on the same subject:

"O'er Murray's loss the Muses wept,
They felt the rude alarm,

201

Yet bless'd the guardian care that kept
His sacred head from harm.

There Memory, like the bee that's fed
From Flora's balmy store,
The quintessence of all he read
Had treasured up before.

The lawless herd, with fury blind,
Have done him cruel wrong;
The flowers are gone – but still we find
The honey on his tongue."

William Cowper was also a near contemporary of Warren Hastings
at Westminster School and addressed one poem to Hastings. In it
Cowper defended Hastings against his accusers in his trial in
Parliament, and remembered his schoolday admiration for Hastings:

"Hastings! I knew thee young, and of a mind,
While young, humane, conversable, and kind,
Nor can I well believe thee, gentle then,
Now grown a villain, and the worst of men.
But rather some suspect, who have oppress'd
And worried thee, as not themselves the best."

In describing Eliza as being "dear to the muse", we can be certain
that Lady Sophia Burrell was saying that Eliza, like Lord Mansfield,
was an accomplished writer. We also know that Lady Sophia Burrell
was praising Eliza not as a poet, however, but as a novelist. This is
made explicit in another poem of Lady Sophia's which I have already
quoted but will quote again [my highlighting]:

"To Eliza –
When you no more have power to please

By artless elegance and ease;
When that dear guileless heart shall grow
Cold as the Pyrenean snow;
Light and inconstant as the wind,
Artful, capricious, and unkind,
Devoid of honour, virtue, sense,
And ev'ry claim to excellence,
Then will Eliza cease to be
Thus tenderly esteem'd by me;
(Whose friendship ev'rything defies,
But cold neglect – and mean disguise.)"

The first two lines quote from the poet William Mason's *Epistle to Sir Joshua Reynolds* of 10th October 1782. William Mason, little known now, was considered an important poet at this time and the quotation from Mason's poem would have been recognised by most educated people. An *Essay on Epic Poetry* was addressed to Mason by the poet William Hayley, who later became a friend of William Cowper. Mason himself was the close friend and biographer of the poet Thomas Gray, now most famous for his *Elegy Written in a Country Churchyard* of 1751. William Mason wrote in his *Epistle to Sir Joshua Reynolds* [my highlighting]:

"Yet still he pleas'd; for *Dryden* still must please,
Whether with artless elegance and ease
He glides in prose, or from its tinkling chime,
By varied pauses, purifies his rhyme,
And mounts on Maro's plumes, and soars his heights
    sublime."

John Dryden (1631–1700) was a famous poet and playwright but above all influential in creating the English prose style that was to be the most copied during the eighteenth century. William Mason contrasts Dryden's prose style of "artless elegance and ease" with the "tinkling chime" of his poetic style and compares his poetic style, but not his prose style, to that of Maro (Publius Virgilius Maro, the full name of the Roman poet Virgil). Lady Sophia Burrell, however, compares Eliza's writing only with the **prose** style of Dryden. From these poems of Lady Sophia Burrell's we can therefore understand she is saying that Eliza was not a poet, but a novelist of great accomplishment. The most notable and novel feature of the prose style of Dryden was its smoothness which enabled it to be read easily. William Mason describes this smoothness in the above poem with the word "glides". This is the same feature which most strikes the reader about the style of *Jane Austen* and *Fanny Burney*. Readers of their novels are often struck above all by how smooth and easy they are to read.

Mason's theme of "elegance and ease" is discussed by the author in *Jane Austen's Emma*. Emma gives her opinion of Mrs Elton as follows:

> "She did not really like her. She would not be in a hurry to find fault, but she suspected that there was no elegance;– ease, but not elegance. – She was almost sure that for a young woman, a stranger, a bride, there was too much ease Her person was rather good; her face not unpretty; but neither feature, nor air, nor voice, nor manner, were elegant."

In *Jane Austen's Sense and Sensibility* the author also talks of artlessness and elegance, saying of the Steele sisters:

> "The vulgar freedom and folly of the eldest left her no recommendation, and as Elinor was not blinded by the beauty, or the shrewd look of the youngest, to her want of real elegance and artlessness, she left the house without any wish of knowing them better."

When Lady Sophia Burrell describes Eliza as being "dear to the muse" she is here referring to Eliza specifically as a writer, since the muse of literature was the muse with which Lady Sophia chiefly concerned herself. Lady Sophia considered herself chiefly as a poet, and there are at least three full length portraits of her, which all portray her with a book of her own poems on her lap. As Lady Sophia was a published poet and playwright herself, and from her published works it appears she had some talent (she even has her own entry in the *Oxford Dictionary of National Biography*) she would have been speaking from the point of view of an author of literary merit herself, who admired Eliza's published works, it seems from her enthusiasm, well above her own. How could this be when there is no record of Eliza ever writing or publishing anything?

In the same poem above, Lady Sophia Burrell also refers to "the language of thy tuneful tongue". This was another phrase often used to describe the language of an accomplished poet or writer. For example, the poet William Cowper, in his poem quoted previously, *Lord Mansfield's Library,* described Lord Mansfield's literary ability as "The honey on his tongue".

Incidentally, the poems of Lady Sophia Burrell, published in 1793, were written a long time before any of the works we know as those of *Jane Austen* appeared in print. In any event Lady Sophia Burrell died in 1802, long before any of the works of *Jane Austen* were published. Since Lady Sophia Burrell praises Eliza as a published author of high quality novels, she could only be praising her as the author of the works of *Fanny Burney*, and not of the works of *Jane Austen*. This is another vital link between Eliza and Fanny Burney.

There is little other direct evidence that Eliza was an author, no doubt because of the comprehensive "weeding" of the archives by the Austen family in the nineteenth century, and especially their destruction and censorship of Eliza's and Jane Austen's letters. In fact only forty-six letters written by Eliza have survived; thirty-six of them are to her distant cousin, Philadelphia Walter, six of them to her trustee, Mr Woodman, and four to Warren Hastings. Tellingly, no letter of Eliza's to any member of the Austen family survives, suggesting that they were all deliberately destroyed after her death. Also, not a single letter received by Eliza from anyone else survives. However, there are indirect hints as to Eliza's authorship in some remaining letters. For instance, shortly after the publication of *Evelina* in 1778, Eliza's cousin, Philadelphia Walter, wrote to Eliza congratulating her on being *a phenomenon*. The letter from Phylly does not survive. However, in her letter of reply to Phylly from Paris of 16ᵗʰ May 1780 Eliza writes:

> "I know not my dear friend whom You can have seen that have given You such accounts of me, but of this You may be assured that You or Whoever else expects a <u>phenomenon</u> or anything very accomplished in me will be much disappointed when ever they see me, & indeed to have had so much said in my favor is enough to make me afraid of ever presenting myself, as I am sensible how very far The reality will fall short of people's expectations."

There is no explanation of what she was referring to, why so many people were saying so much in her favour. However, a logical explanation seems to be that she was called a phenomenon (in the sense of a prodigy) because she was known by her cousin to be the youthful author of *Evelina*. Suspiciously, we do not have the original letter from Phylly to Eliza, but only Eliza's reply.

In the letters of Jane Austen which survived the destruction of Jane Austen's sister, Cassandra, and the Austen family in the nineteenth century, one or two hints remain that Eliza was the true author of the *Jane Austen* novels, which Cassandra and the family seemed to have overlooked at this time in their efforts to expunge any evidence. One of these which is particularly convincing is a letter of Jane Austen of 1ˢᵗ October 1808 where Jane talks about a certain Colonel Powlett:

> "Colonel Powlett and his brother have taken Argyle's inner

house,… If the brother should luckily be a little sillier than the Colonel, what a treasure for Eliza!"

This can only suggest to me that Jane Austen means Colonel Powlett's brother would make an interesting character for one of Eliza's books. One is reminded of the scene in *Pride and Prejudice* where Mr Bennet has high hopes of finding Mr Collins not a sensible man.

Another hint from Jane Austen herself that she is not educated enough to be the true author is met with in her letter of 11th December 1815 to the Prince Regent's secretary, James Stanier Clarke, in their correspondence concerning the dedication of *Emma* to the Prince Regent:

"I am quite honoured by your thinking me capable of drawing such a clergyman as you gave the sketch of in your note of Nov. 16th. But I assure you I am not. The comic part of the character I might be equal to, but not the good, the enthusiastic, the literary. Such a man's conversation must at times be on subjects of science and philosophy, of which I know nothing; or at least be occasionally abundant in allusions and quotations which a woman who, like me, knows only her mother tongue, and has read very little in that, would be totally without the power of giving. A classical education, or at any rate a very extensive acquaintance with English literature, ancient and modern, appears to me quite indispensable for the person who would do justice to your clergyman; and I think I may boast myself to be, with all possible vanity, the most unlearned and ill-informed female who ever dared to be an authoress."

Here Jane Austen admits that she is not well educated and has not received a classical education, as has the author *Jane Austen*.

However, as this letter is in a much more educated style than her letters to her sister Cassandra, I believe it could well have been dictated to her by Henry Austen.

One strong indication that Eliza was the writer of *Jane Austen's* novels is that they were sent out to the world to be published from Eliza's home at 64 Sloane Street in the West End of London, and not from Jane Austen's house in Chawton, Hampshire, which is stated incorrectly on a plaque on the wall of the Chawton cottage. Jane Austen visited Eliza at her London house from 1811 onwards to correct the proofs of *Sense and Sensibility*, but it would seem that she was only engaged in proofreading the work and other secretarial duties. Indeed, it was normal practice at the time for the proofreader to be someone other than the author, as they would be much more likely than the author to pick up any mistakes. I believe the same holds true today. It is a rare author who relies on their own proofreading. The fact that Jane Austen was proofreading the book is evidence that she was not the author of it. One curious coincidence is that Fanny Burney mentions in her diaries a dialogue with King George III in which she also stated that she proofread her own books, which surprised the King who believed that authors nearly always employed someone else to carry out this service for them.

20.

A Comparison of the Letters of Eliza and Jane Austen

If one is to compare the quality of the letters of Jane Austen with those of Eliza, the comparison can only be vastly to the former's detriment. Many commentators have criticised the letters of Jane Austen as being unworthy of the writer. The collected letters of Jane Austen have been compiled by Deirdre Le Faye and there are a large number of them. Truth to tell, they are not very different in style from many other women's letters of the period that survive. They are comparable in style and substance with the surviving letters of other female members of the wider Austen family, and even show a less educated style than those of her mother and of her cousin, Philadelphia Walter. There is little in them to betray a literary genius. They tend to consist largely of the reporting of everyday events to her sister, Cassandra. Indeed, Caroline Austen, daughter of Jane's brother James, when writing to her brother James Edward Austen-Leigh (Jane Austen's nephew), wrote in 1867 of Jane Austen's letters in *My Aunt Jane Austen: A Memoir*:

"There is nothing in those letters which I have seen that would be acceptable to the public – They were very well expressed, and they must have been very interesting to those who received them – but they detailed chiefly home and family events: and she seldom committed herself even to an *opinion* – so that to strangers they could be no transcript of her mind – they would not feel that they knew her any the better for having read them".

Caroline Austen also wrote of Jane Austen's letters that "My Aunt [Cassandra] looked them over and burnt the greater part, (as she told me), 2 or 3 years before her own death – She left, or *gave* some as legacies to the Nieces – but of those that *I* have seen, several had portions cut out –"

If Jane Austen had been such a great writer, surely Cassandra would have realised the importance of preserving the letters for posterity. The fact that they were destroyed or had parts cut out suggests she knew that they were without worth, and she was covering something up, deleting any suggestions that Eliza was the true author.

Caroline Austen also wrote in a letter to her brother, James Edward Austen-Leigh:

> "I am sure you will do justice to what there is – but I feel that it must be a difficult task to dig up the materials, so carefully have they been buried out of our sight by the past generat[ion]…"

Caroline Austen thus in the above letter also confirms that the Austen family had carefully "buried out of our sight" in the nineteenth century certain materials about the authorship of Jane Austen.

The learned editor of the Dictionary of National Biography and father of Virginia Woolf, Leslie Stephen, considered the letters of Jane Austen, when published in Lord Brabourne's 1884 edition, as trivial. Authors of the twentieth century have also been less than impressed by them. Susan J Wolfson of Princeton University, in her article *Boxing Emma; or the Reader's Dilemma at the Box Hill Games* sums up excellently the reaction of educated readers to the appearance in print of the letters of Jane Austen, comparing them to the tedious ramblings of the impoverished spinster, Miss Bates, in *Jane Austen's Emma*:

> "The appearance in 1932 of a volume of her Batesy-letters

"profoundly disillusioned some of the more fastidious admirers of her novels," Robert Donovan reminds us; "Harold Nicolson and E. M. Forster professed themselves disenchanted with the triviality of the letters and the vulgarity of the mind which produced them" (109, referring to reviews in *New Statesman* and *TLS*). "Trivial and dull," Nicolson sighed; a "desert of family gossip." If Miss Bates is "a great talker upon trivial matters" (I.iii, 18), so seems Austen. Forster implied the link, and *Virginia Quarterly Review* was explicit: the letters "contain the raw materials" for Miss Bates. "Triviality, varied by touches of ill-breeding and sententiousness," it elaborated; "she has nothing in her mind except the wish to tell her sister everything; and so she flits from the cows to the currant bushes, from the currant bushes to Mrs. Hall of Sherborne, gives Mrs. Hall a tap, and flits back again" (362-63; cf. even Austen-Leigh's Memoir 207). A habitually dyspeptic H. W. Garrod was inspired to fresh bile: "a desert of trivialities punctuated by occasional oases of clever malice," he sneered, setting the lexicon; "wearying lengths in which one meets nothing but the most uninspired talk about petticoats and drawing-room curtains, colds, coquelicots and magnesia" (23); "feminine triviality interests her immensely and entertains her adequately" (26)."

Even the best of the modern biographers of Jane Austen, Claire Tomalin, agrees that the letters of Jane Austen are, in the main, disappointing. To explain this, she is only able to put forward the theory that the "interesting" letters were all destroyed by Jane's sister, Cassandra:

"Cassandra took particular care to destroy personal family material... Cassandra's culling, made for her own good reasons, leaves the impression that her sister was dedicated to trivia. The letters rattle on, sometimes almost like a comedian's patter. Not much feeling, warmth or sorrow has been allowed through. They never pause or meditate but hurry, as though she is moving her mind as fast as possible from one subject to the next. You have to keep reminding yourself how little they represent of her real life, how much they are an edited and contrived version."

Claire Tomalin does not attempt to explain why Jane Austen's sister decided to destroy all the interesting letters of Jane Austen and only keep the dull ones. She asks us just to accept that the decision to do this was made "for her own good reasons".

This obvious evidence that Jane Austen's letters were without interest has, however, become subject to the looking glass world of *Jane Austen* scholarship. *Jane Austen* scholars, in working backwards from the assumption that Jane Austen wrote the novels, paint themselves into this corner. Carol Houlihan Flynn exemplifies this looking glass world when she writes about Jane Austen's letters in *The Cambridge Companion to Jane Austen*:

> "Jo Modert suggests that the very banal domestic surface of the letters offers us a tool for understanding the foundations of Austen's creative production, while Deborah Kaplan and Susan Whealler read Austen's depictions of self-denial and housewifery as subtle productions emerging from a feminine culture which supports the self-expression of women who are conscious of dual allegiances to claims of social class and gender."

Because of the assumption that Jane Austen wrote the novels, Flynn stresses the importance to the writer *Jane Austen* of the purely domestic sphere (Jane Austen did not stir very much from home and was not well travelled or a member of fashionable London society like Eliza) when she writes "It is Austen's awareness of the

212

texture of domestic life that generates her densely realized novels". Flynn provides the following example in Jane Austen's letters as evidence of Jane Austen's genius, however:

> "I wonder whether the Ink bottle has been filled. Does Butcher's meat keep up at the same price? & is not Bread lower than 2/6 – Mary's blue gown! My Mother must be in agonies."

Flynn reads the simple shopping list above as "a stream of consciousness located somewhere between Sterne and Samuel Beckett." Flynn also criticises Caroline Austen for expecting from Jane Austen's letters "a proper 'transcript' of an elegant, composed mind" and states that Jane Austen's letters have "a jolting, frustrating style" (this is in contrast to the "elegance and ease" and beautiful writing style of Eliza's letters). She does not give any reason, however, why Jane Austen chose to write in a jolting, frustrating style when writing letters and then change to an elegant and stylish one in her novels. In fact, Flynn's theory that the author wrote in different styles in her letters and in her novels cannot be justified, as it is flatly contradicted by Henry Austen in his *Biographical Notice of the Author*. In it he writes of the "authoress":

> "The style of her familiar correspondence was in all respects the same as that of her novels. Every thing came finished from her pen; for on all subjects she had ideas as clear as expressions were well chosen. It is not hazarding too much to say that she never dispatched a note or letter unworthy of publication."

The above remarks by Henry Austen most definitely apply to the beautifully written and constructed letters of Eliza.

As mentioned in the above article by Ms Wolfson, when reading the letters of Jane Austen, unfortunately the character of *Jane Austen's* that springs to mind as their author would be Miss Bates, the talkative spinster in *Jane Austen's Emma* who at the party on Box Hill is memorably regrettably "limited as to number" in the number of dull things she is able to relate. A typical extract from a letter of Jane Austen, taken at random (from a letter of 20th June 1808) confirms this resemblance:

> "Mary thanks Anna for her letter, and wishes her to buy enough of her new coloured frock to make a shirt handkerchief. I am glad to hear of her Aunt Maitland's kind present. We want you to send us Anna's height, that we may know whether she is as tall as Fanny; and pray can you tell me of any little thing that would be probably acceptable to Mrs. F. A.? I wish to bring her something: has she a silver knife, or would you recommend a brooch? I shall not spend more than half a guinea about it. Our Tuesday's engagement went off very pleasantly; we called first on Mrs. Knight, and found her very well; and at dinner had only the Milles' of Nackington, in addition to Goodnestone and Godmersham, and Mrs. Moore. Lady Bridges looked very well, and would have been very agreeable, I am sure, had there been time enough for her to talk to me; but as it was, she could only be kind and amiable, give one good-humoured smiles, and make friendly inquiries. Her son Edward was also looking very well, and with manners as unaltered as hers. In the evening came Mr. Moore, Mr. Toke, Dr. and Mrs. Walsby, and others. One card-table was formed, the rest of us sat and talked, and at half after nine we came away."

This is just one paragraph from this long-winded and tedious letter. There are countless other letters of Jane Austen in a similar style. Jane Austen scholars, however, undeterred by the dullness of their heroine's letters, have nevertheless gamely trawled through them to try to find at least a spark of wit. They have come up with such witticisms as the following:

> "I bought some Japan Ink likewise, and next week shall begin my operations on my hat, on which you know my principal hopes of happiness depend."

and

> "You know how interesting the purchase of a sponge-cake is to me."

Other critics have conceded that the letters of Jane Austen are without any merit but they say that the reason for this is that they were family letters not written for publication. However, this argument cannot be sustained, since the surviving letters of Eliza to Philadelphia Walter were also written to a close relative and also not intended for publication. It also contradicts the evidence of Henry Austen quoted above, where he expressly states that even in intimate family letters ("familiar correspondence") the author wrote in the same beautiful writing style as in the novels (as Eliza did).

Compare the many surviving letters of Jane Austen with the few that remain written by Eliza. Eliza's letters are full of the wit and wisdom of *Jane Austen* and we can also see direct parallels between them and incidents in *Jane Austen's* novels. No less a personage than the former Chairman of the Jane Austen Society, Brian Southam, has written of Eliza's letters, in comparison to *Jane Austen's* short novel unpublished in her lifetime *Lady Susan*: "indeed, many passages might well be mistaken for Jane Austen's own work" (in *Jane Austen's Literary Manuscripts: a Study of the Novelist's Development*).

For instance, there is an interesting connection to *Jane Austen's Northanger Abbey* in one of the letters from Eliza to her cousin, Philadelphia Walter. There is a famous episode in *Northanger Abbey* parodying a scene in Ann Radcliffe's gothic novel *The Romance of the*

Forest where Monsieur La Motte opens an old wooden chest to reveal a skeleton. The heroine, Catherine Morland, suspects that the old wooden chest in her bedroom in Northanger Abbey contains something sinister, perhaps something, she thinks, like "Laurentina's skeleton" which in Ann Radcliffe's *The Mysteries of Udolpho* the heroine, Emily St. Aubert, suspects is hidden behind a black veil (there appears to be some confusion in Catherine's mind between the two novels). Eventually Catherine summons up the courage to open the old chest:

> "With this spirit she sprang forward, and her confidence did not deceive her. Her resolute effort threw back the lid, and gave to her astonished eyes the view of a white cotton counterpane, properly folded, reposing at one end of the chest in undisputed possession!"

We can compare this passage to an extract from Eliza's letter to her cousin Philadelphia Walter of 7th November 1796, never seen by Jane Austen, where Eliza is shown into her doctor's study:

> "[I] was accordingly shut into a Study where an empty grate announced the <u>cold reception</u> which I had to depend on. Here I waited nearly two Hours which gave me an opportunity of reading various physical Books filled with shocking cases, and also of inspecting two large presses (this part of the Story you must keep secret) where I expected to find Skeletons, but however met with nothing but crooked Scissors and other formidable Surgical Instruments, and a few <u>Embryos</u> in Spirits".

Jon Spence in *Becoming Jane Austen* writes that through the above letter of Eliza's "the famous episode of the mock-Gothic discovery of the laundry lists *[sic]* in the old chest can be directly connected to Eliza herself." He admits that "it is not likely that [Jane] Austen read this letter" but he then goes on to say that "the echo of it in *Northanger Abbey* is too strong to be coincidental". The obvious conclusion is that Eliza was the author of *Northanger Abbey*. However, Jon Spence decides instead, without any evidence, that Eliza told the story to Jane Austen, who then incorporated it into *Northanger Abbey*. One is faced throughout Jane Austen biographies with this strange paradox, why a woman of Eliza's education and literary interests would choose never to write; why she should pass on information of this sort to Jane Austen; why Eliza chose never to mention to her literary friends that her cousin Jane was a great writer, or to include Jane Austen in her literary circle. In fact the whole of the above letter of Eliza's is very representative of *Jane Austen's* humour. In the same letter Eliza also laughs at the pretensions of her doctor, who is a baronet:

"This Note I addressed to <u>Dr. Farquhar</u>, whereas it should have been to <u>Sr. Walter Farquhar Bart</u>."

It is noticeable in the works of both *Fanny Burney* and of *Jane Austen* how the author likes to laugh at baronets. As a well read historian, Eliza would have been aware of the absurdity of the title of baronet, which is a hereditary knighthood invented by James I of England in the early seventeenth century in order to be openly sold to raise money.

In *Persuasion* the author describes the baronet Sir Walter Elliott as "a man who, for his own amusement, never took up any book but the baronetage where he could read his own history with an interest that never failed." Sir William Lucas in *Pride and Prejudice* was not a baronet but one rank lower, a non-hereditary knight. The author, however, feels the same way about the awarding of knighthoods to those in trade such as Sir William Lucas, as she would to the awarding of a baronetage. She says of Sir William Lucas's award of his knighthood that perhaps it had been felt too keenly, and it leads Sir William Lucas to give up his business and talk of nothing but being presented at the Court of St James'. Similarly, in *Fanny Burney's Camilla*, the baronet Sir Hugh Tyrold is gently poked fun at for his limited intellect. We know that Eliza shared this amused view of the baronetage because in her letter of 7th November 1796 to Philadelphia Walter, as previously mentioned, she writes of her own doctor:

> "I thought myself materially worse, and accordingly dispatched a Note to Farquhar requesting him to appoint a time for seeing me – This Note I addressed to Dr. Farquhar, whereas it should have been to Sr. Walter Farquhar Bart., but this impropriety he forgave".

Indeed, it must have been a source of amusement for ladies of fashion such as Eliza that, at this time, it was not uncommon for their personal physicians to be made baronets. In this respect her friend Lady Sophia Burrell's doctor, Sir Lucas Pepys, may have been the model for Sir William Lucas in *Pride and Prejudice*. The name of Eliza's own physician, Sir Walter Farquhar, also has echoes of the pompous baronet in *Persuasion*, Sir Walter Elliot.

The above letter also creates humour out of Eliza's treatment with leeches by the good doctor:

> "The idea of these Leeches was very terrible to me, but I mustered up what courage I could, and the odious Beasts were stuck on – They obligingly staid with me above two Hours, and Sr. Walter who saw me again the next day was well satisfied with their effect, tho' I could not see any apparent difference in the Swelling – He desired me to continue my Medicines, and in the course of a few days the Leeches were again applied. They then favored me with their Company still longer than the first time..."

The letters of Eliza were a surprise to me. At first I thought they would be very literary but they are of an almost classical restraint, although one senses the passion underlying them. The letters are amusing, informative, playful with words and meanings, sometimes "superficial" but also deeply moving. These elegant letters reflect the world of the novels of *Jane Austen* far more than the mundane letters of Jane Austen. Apart from including many familiar phrases that occur in the novels, Eliza's letters display the same playful use of language, the same irony, and the same highly educated and balanced style of writing as the novels and, of course, the same humour. Perhaps if there is one word to describe the style of *Jane Austen* and *Fanny Burney*, also reflected in Eliza's letters, it is "balance". The destruction of Eliza's correspondence must represent the most serious act of literary vandalism that has ever been carried out. The letters of Eliza that remain are a treasure trove of the wit and wisdom of *Jane Austen*, and the destruction of the others has probably deprived us of a literary heritage almost equal to the novels themselves. Far from being congratulated for commemorating *Jane Austen*, the Austen family of the nineteenth century should be condemned by the literary world for this unprecedented act of destruction of world culture.

À propos of these letters, the full texts of all Eliza's surviving letters are included in Deirdre Le Faye's *Jane Austen's Outlandish Cousin: The Life and Letters of Eliza de Feuillide*, a marvellous book which I strongly recommend. I would recommend anyone interested in *Jane Austen* to read here the full texts of all of Eliza's wonderful letters. I include for your amusement and delight just a selection of quotations from the letters of Eliza, which are very much in the style of *Jane Austen* and illustrate Eliza's humour, indistinguishable from that of *Fanny Burney* and *Jane Austen*.

Paris 16th May 1780

> "There is perhaps no place in the world where dress is so well understood & carried to so great a perfection as in Paris & no wonder it should be so since people make it the chief

business & study of their Lives. Powder is universally worn, & in very large quantities, no one would dare to appear in public without it, The Heads in general look as if they had been dipped in a meal tub;"

Comblaville, [near Paris] 27th June 1780
"rouge is I acknowledge much worn here, but not so universally as you imagine, no single ladies ever make use of it, & were they to do it would be much disapproved of; When once married I own in general they make themselves ample amends for this denial;".

Paris, 7th May 1784
"It is still the fashion to translate or rather murder, Shakespear; Romeo & Juliet, Lear, Macbeth & Coriolanus have successively made their appearance on the French stage, in my opinion they make but an uncouth figure in their foreign attire".

Chateau de Jourdan, 17th January 1786
"This uncommon & striking Landscape [the Pyrenees] is added to & heightened, by literally chrystal streams such as I had till now imagined to exist no where but in a Poets Brain, Vines formed into festoons more regular & more beautiful than the Decorations of any Theatre ever exhibited, Villages dispersed here & there, & a thousand other objects still more picturesque, concur to finish the Picture & render the Environs of Bagnères really inchanting".

Paris, 11th February 1789
"I must therefore tell You that this said Son of mine is notwithstanding what I have already said most exceedingly good tempered and I do not think he will ever be either

Alderman or Lord Mayor as he has not the least of the greediness and Love of Dainties which children usually shew, and will absolutely offer his half muncht apples or cakes to the whole company altho' I have remonstrated on the impropriety of the proceeding."

Margate, 7th January 1791
[on her delay in replying to Philadelphia Walter's last letter]
"Alas My Dear Friend, for with both Sorrow and Shame do I speak it – it seems to be decreed that I should ever be faulty in regard to you – That Fate must have something to do with it I am the more convinced as my Heart bears testimony it has had no share in it nay that my inclination dictates very different proceedings, remember therefore the Lines of the Poet who affirms that 'If weak women go astray / Their stars are more in fault than they' and once more graciously extend your mercy and pardon to me. I will not tease You with a tedious and insipid detail of the many avocations by which I have been engrossed, the odious letters of business which have not suffered me to devote my pen to more agreeable correspondents &cc &cc it would be taking up your time in no very entertaining manner and therefore I think it better to plead guilty in every thing but what relates to my affection for You and throw myself entirely on your lenity for a remission of my transgression."

23rd June 1791
"He [Edward Austen] is now proposing to visit the Lakes, with Mr. & Mrs. K. and a large party as I understood, no less than twelve in number, but his beloved alas is not to bless him with her presence on this occasion. I asked him how he would be able to exist? which enquiry he answered with that calm smile of resignation which his Sex generally wear under circumstances of this nature."

7th November 1796

"I am so much of a prisoner, for I do not stir of an evening for fear of fresh cold, that I cannot tell how the world goes. I saw some of it however in the Park this Morning where the Princess of Wales & myself took an Airing – We were however so unsociable as to go in different Carriages".

30th December 1796

"She [Lady Frances B] certainly pays a great Compliment to the married state by wishing to engage in it a fourth time."

"I beg you will send Captn. Anderson to me with all speed for his £100,000 will suit me wonderfully well [it is] indeed very unfair in such a disinterested Being as yourself [to ma]ke such conquests, you ought to leave them to those females who like myself have a great relish for all the pretty things that are not to be had without plenty of Cash".

3rd May 1797

"Great Preparations are now making for the Nuptials of the above mentioned Royal Fair [the Princess Royal], whose Intended [the Prince of Württemberg] is said to be the greatest man in Europe – I am assured it is a fact that he cannot eat with any comfort if the Table has not been hollowed out in such a manner as to make room for what delicate Ladies would denominate his long Stomach."

Manchester Street, London 3rd July 1797

"I have a variety of rural Plans and cannot determine which to adopt. I believe however that I shall neither climb the Welsh Mountains, retire into the embowering shades of the Rectory, or quarter myself near a Camp, but rather hearken to the dashing Billows on the Sussex Coast. I certainly do feel a very strong Propensity towards revisiting that retired quiet Spot usually called Brighton and perhaps in this case as in many others the only effectual means of getting rid of the temptation, will be to give way to it".

Ipswich 16th February 1798
"Matrimony is generally accused of spoiling Correspondents, but I was so bad a one before I entered the holy state, that it could not well make me worse"

Steventon 26th October 1792
[on her first (arranged) marriage to the Comte de Feuillide]
"I never was but at one Wedding in my Life and that appeared a very stupid Business to me."

In a letter to Phylly Walter of 22nd August 1788, Eliza writes: "As to our Friends, those sweet creatures called Jack & Tom F– I know but little of them & I think I need not add that I care still less about the matter". This is reminiscent of the conversation in *Jane Austen's Mansfield Park* between Fanny Price and Mary Crawford:

'I know nothing of the Miss Owens,' said Fanny calmly.
'You know nothing and you care less, as people say.'

Another letter to Phylly Walter of 11th February 1789 also reminds one of Mary Crawford. Eliza wrote: "but to return that so important thing (I mean, important to myself) called Self." This reminds us of Mary Crawford who says in Mansfield Park:

"Selfishness must always be forgiven you know, because there is no hope of a cure."

Eliza had also written on 16th February 1798 of her marriage to her second husband, Henry:

"to say nothing of the pleasure of having my own way in every thing, for Henry well knows that I have not been much accustomed to controul and should probably behave rather awkwardly under it, and therefore like a wise Man he has no will but mine, which to be sure some people would call spoiling me, but [I] know it is the best way of managing me".

The letters of Eliza reflect the lively mind, wit and imagination of a literary genius. The letters of Jane Austen reveal nothing to those unaware of her purported authorship.

21.

The Epitaphs of Eliza and Jane Austen

"Who sayes that fictions onely and false hair
Become a verse? Is there in truth no beautie?
Is all good structure in a winding stair?
May no lines passe, except they do their dutie
Not to a true, but painted chair?
Is it no verse, except enchanted groves
And sudden arbours shadow course-spunne lines?
Must purling streams refresh a lovers loves?
Must all be vail'd, while he that reads, divines,
Catching the sense at two removes?"

(George Herbert, *Jordan* (1))

It has often been remarked on by biographers and readers of *Jane Austen* that the epitaph on the tomb of Jane Austen does not make any mention of her being a writer. Indeed, the fact that she was buried in Winchester Cathedral was not because she was a person of any importance, but merely because she had travelled to this town before her death, for medical reasons. Indeed, her death went completely unremarked in literary circles for a full five decades after her death. This was not surprising as we have no record that Jane Austen had any literary acquaintances whatsoever.

Her epitaph on a stone plaque on the floor of Winchester Cathedral in Hampshire reads as follows:

In memory of
JANE AUSTEN,
youngest daughter of the late
Revd. GEORGE AUSTEN,
formerly Rector of Steventon in this County.
She departed this Life on the 18th July 1817,
aged 41, after a long illness supported with
the patience and the hopes of a Christian.

The benevolence of her heart,
the sweetness of her temper, and
the extraordinary endowments of her mind
obtained the regard of all who knew her, and
the warmest love of her intimate connections.

Their grief is in proportion to their affection
they know their loss to be irreparable,
but in the deepest affliction they are consoled
by a firm though humble hope that her charity,
devotion, faith and purity have rendered
her soul acceptable in the sight of her
REDEEMER.

Indeed, if you visit Winchester Cathedral you will see on the wall above Jane Austen's memorial that it was found necessary to erect much later, in 1872, after the publication of her nephew James Edward Austen Leigh's biography *A Memoir of Jane Austen*, a brass plaque to rectify this omission and to explain who the lady was:

JANE AUSTEN
known to many by her
writings, endeared to
her family by the
varied charms of her

Character and ennobled
by Christian faith
and piety, was born
at Steventon in the
County of Hants Dec.
XVI MDCCLXXV, and buried
in this Cathedral
July XXIV MDCCCXVII.
"She opened her
mouth with wisdom
and in her tongue is
the law of kindness."
— Prov. XXXI v. XXVI.

Even this plaque is highly ambiguous, referring merely to Jane Austen as "known to many by her writings". Perhaps the author of the plaque feared the consequences of writing direct falsehoods in the house of God. The quotation from the Old Testament from the Book of Proverbs in its context referred to the qualities of a good wife.

The epitaph to Eliza is much less well known. She was buried alongside her mother in the churchyard of the Parish Church of St John-at-Hampstead in North London and her epitaph was written no doubt by her husband Henry, Jane's brother. Although Eliza's grave survives, her epitaph has long since been erased by time. However, fortunately it was recorded from her gravestone before it faded away. It read as follows:

"Also in memory of Elizabeth wife of H.T. Austen Esq. formerly widow of the Comt. Feuillide a woman of brilliant generous and cultivated mind just disinterested and charitable she died after long and severe suffering on the 25th April 1813 aged 50 much regretted by the wise and good and deeply lamented by the poor."

Without saying expressly that Eliza was a writer, the epitaph mentions that she was of "brilliant generous and cultivated mind" (a very unusual way at this time on a tombstone to describe a deceased wife; wives were normally praised for their loving devotion to their family, piety and charity, as was the case with Eliza's mother, as I mentioned earlier) and that her death will be regretted by "the wise" i.e. the intellectual world in general. By contrast, the epitaph of Jane Austen emphasises she will be missed only by her family and friends and those who knew her personally ("all who knew her, and... her intimate connections"). When her obituary refers to Eliza's death as being much regretted by "the wise" there is a clear implication that Eliza was a writer. In her opinion of *Mansfield Park* at the time of its first publication Lady Robert Kerr wrote that *Mansfield Park* was "Universally admired in Edinburgh, by all the *wise ones*" [her italics]. The clear implication is that the "wise ones" was a euphemism for the literary critics. Therefore, to describe Eliza's death as being much regretted by the wise has the clear implication that she was a famous author. Indeed, taken all in all, Eliza's obituary, unlike Jane's, is what we would expect of the obituary for a writer of genius. In any event, if Eliza was of brilliant, generous and cultivated mind, as her epitaph states, how is it that this mind bore no fruit?

Incidentally, her epitaph also refers to Eliza as being "charitable", which ties in with the tone of the books of *Fanny Burney* and *Jane Austen* whose heroines, such as Cecilia and Emma, often perform acts of charity to the poor. The reference to Eliza being "disinterested" as well as "charitable" could also refer to the fact that she allowed her work to be published under the names of poor women, who also benefited financially from the sale of the novels.

I have visited the grave of Eliza, hidden away obscurely in the bushes and trees of Hampstead churchyard. The London branch of The Jane Austen Society have re-engraved the names of Eliza, her mother and her son on the gravestone but, for reasons best known to them, have omitted to re-engrave this obituary which was so fitting for Eliza.

22.

The Life and Works of Fanny Burney

The life of Fanny Burney is much less well known to the general public than that of Jane Austen. The popularity of her novels waned after her death and has only begun to revive again in recent times.

Frances Burney (now more often referred to as "Fanny") was born in Kings Lynn in Norfolk on 13th June 1752, the second eldest daughter of Dr Charles Burney, a musician who is chiefly remembered now for his writings about the musicians of the time, especially Handel. After working as organist in Kings Lynn in Norfolk for a time, Dr Burney returned with his family to Poland Street in Soho in the West End of London, where Dr Burney earned his living principally as a music teacher teaching the harpsichord, mainly to the daughters of the rich. He was especially well known as a keyboard teacher to "young ladies of fashion" including, most famously, Queeney, the daughter of Dr Samuel Johnson's friend, Mrs Hester Thrale. In James Barry's painting of 1783 'The Thames, or the Triumph of Navigation', Charles Burney is depicted surrounded by such young pupils who are depicted as naked Nereids. Whilst Fanny Burney's older sister, Esther (known as "Hetty"), was a child prodigy on the harpsichord, Fanny Burney herself was described by her father as "wholly unnoticed in the nursery for any talents, or quickness of study". She was thought by her father to be backward and called "a little dunce" by a family friend. Fanny Burney's mother, Esther Burney, died on 29th September 1762 and Charles Burney was remarried on 2nd October

1767 to Elizabeth Allen, a rich widow who Fanny Burney disliked intensely.

Thomas Babington Macaulay wrote of Fanny Burney's childhood:

> "Nothing in her childhood indicated that she would, while still a young woman, have secured for herself an honourable and permanent place among English writers. She was shy and silent. Her brothers and sisters called her a dunce, and not altogether without some show of reason; for at eight years old she did not know her letters."

It is possible that Fanny Burney had what we would now call learning difficulties. Fanny and her younger sister, Susan, did not have a governess. Fanny's two sisters, Susan and Esther, were sent to France in 1764 to be educated by boarding with a Protestant woman in Paris. Fanny, although older than Susan, was not sent to be educated there but remained with her father because of her "backwardness" in her education. She acted as his housekeeper and secretary. Fanny Burney had no formal education whatsoever. Any education she gained was through reading. Kate Chisholm writes that from scraps and notebooks kept by her in her teenage years, it appears she was keen on female conduct books such as Fordyce's *Sermons to Young Women*, a book later satirised by *Jane Austen* in *Pride and Prejudice*. In this respect Fanny Burney resembled Mary Bennet in *Pride and Prejudice*. Fanny Burney wrote of herself in her later years in her memoirs of her father, in the third person and in her peculiar stilted style:

> "Frances was the only one of Mr Burney's family who never was placed in any seminary, and never was put under any governess or instructor whatsoever."

She also wrote that her father "had not, at the time, a moment to spare for giving her any personal lessons; or even for directing her pursuits".

Her father was later, not surprisingly, at a loss to explain how she was able to write. He wrote of his daughter "nor did any of the family ever know how the talent was acquired". Thus any education she might have obtained through reading was haphazard and unsupervised, totally different from the education of the author of *Fanny Burney's* works who, as we have seen, was fluent in French and had been instructed for several years in Latin and Greek. However, Fanny Burney herself had literary ambitions, although she lacked the education or talent to be a success in this field. The only works she published in her name after 1813, the year of Eliza's death, were the novel *The Wanderer* and her memoirs of her father, and both of these were extremely badly received by the critics. She also wrote some equally bad plays in her own name during her years at court, one of which was literally laughed off the stage of the London theatre.

In 1768 Fanny Burney began to write her journal or diary, for which she is now principally remembered. I believe she is remembered for this not from its literary merit, but from the cast of famous people she was acquainted with in London through her father, such as the author Samuel Johnson, his friend Mrs Hester Thrale and the artist Sir Joshua Reynolds, and from her life at the court of George III, especially during the period of the king's "madness" (an illness now thought to have been porphyria). In addition, her diary shows a little more literary talent than her other works published in her name after Eliza's death, perhaps because the style of the diary is more natural and she is not here trying to imitate the style of a great writer. These journals or diaries purport to be a relation of events at the time, but in fact they were re-ordered towards the end of Fanny Burney's life. Claire Harman describes Fanny Burney as a "creative autobiographer". She accuses her of making up "private correspondence" specially for publication. According to her, many of Fanny Burney's documents were altered or erased. Harman writes that "none of the best-known stories about her life bears close inspection; each is riddled with contradictory statements, inconsistencies, evidence of editing or elaboration." Because of the many fabrications in Fanny Burney's correspondence and journals, Claire Harman sees the large amount of documentation left by Fanny Burney as a burden, rather than a benefit to the biographer.

The musicians, writers, actors and singers that Fanny Burney became acquainted with while working for her father as his secretary do not figure as major characters in any of the *Fanny Burney* novels or plays prior to Eliza's death in 1813. These novels are peopled by the same class of leisured and wealthy people to which Eliza belonged. By contrast, the characters Fanny Burney knew are described in *The Wanderer*, the disastrously bad novel which appeared in 1814, written by Fanny Burney herself and published after Eliza's death.

In the autumn of 1760, Charles Burney returned from Kings Lynn to London and lived with his family in Poland Street in Soho. They later moved to Queen Square and in 1774 to St Martin's Street.

It is notable that Fanny Burney burned her diary and correspondence for part of the years 1776 and 1777, which would have been the years in which any communication with Eliza over the novel *Evelina* would have taken place. The only explanation given for this by her was that the documents were "upon Family matters or anecdotes". Much later in her life, in her unreliable *Memoirs of Doctor Burney* Fanny Burney also claimed to have destroyed an earlier manuscript version of the novel called *Caroline Evelyn* in 1766 or 1767. Had this been true, it would have been an extraordinary and irrational thing to do. I will explain later her real reason for inventing this story.

It was in 1777 that *Evelina; or, the History of a Young Lady's Entrance into the World* was taken up by the publisher Thomas Lowndes and on 29th January 1778 published by him, with the author remaining anonymous. In *Evelina* the author drew a tale from characters of fashionable London life, contrasting the polite characters of the West End of London, with whom the author identified, with the rather common characters, the Branghtons and the "genteel" Mr Smith, who inhabit the City of London, London's business centre. Fanny Burney and her father had themselves lived in the City of London before moving to the West End. In this and the other novels and plays of *Fanny Burney* it is notable how accurately the author captures the "cockney" speech of the "Cit" characters. To somebody who has lived near London for most of their lives like myself it is easy to see how much of this cockney speech is still unchanged. Even some London slang used in *Fanny Burney's* novels still persists, such as "rhino" for money. Only a true Londoner, as Eliza was, would be able to transcribe this speech so accurately.

Once *Evelina* was published in 1778 and became popular, there was immediate speculation as to who the author was. The title page did not even indicate if the author was a man or a woman. It was strange how such lengths were taken to publish *Evelina* anonymously and yet in the year of its publication, 1778, Fanny Burney became known as the author to her own father. This was in spite of the author writing to the publisher when submitting the novel "such is my situation in Life that I have objections unconquerable to being known in this transaction". The unconquerable objections to Eliza being known as the author were of course, Warren Hastings being her father, which was hinted at in the poem prefacing *Evelina*.

The authorship of Fanny Burney was further promulgated, in spite of the supposed anonymity she craved, through the relationship of Dr Charles Burney with Mr and Mrs Thrale. Mrs Hester Thrale, married to the rich brewer Henry Thrale in a loveless marriage, was famous for her literary circle in Streatham, south of London, and above all for her literary friendship with Dr Samuel Johnson. Charles Burney was engaged as music master to the Thrales' celebrated daughter, Queeney. Charles Burney's character is strongly reminiscent of that of Charles Bingley in *Pride and Prejudice*. His recollection of "the hops I had seen in my early youth, in a village, where those ballets were literally Country dances, not Contre-danse, as the French pretend" reminds one of Mr Bingley's enthusiasm for a country dance. Mrs Thrale wrote of Charles Burney that "Few People possess such Talents for general Conversation". Those who regarded him less kindly gave him the nickname of "The Hare with Many Friends" after the animal in a well known children's fable of the time by John Gay, whose many friends proved worthless when he was in trouble. Mrs Elton in *Jane Austen's Emma* quotes from this poem.

It seems, from the confused history that we have, that Mrs Thrale enjoyed *Evelina* and recommended it to Dr Johnson who also appreciated the book, especially the character of Mr Smith. The knowledge of how Fanny Burney became known to them as the author is somewhat mysterious. The social-climbing Dr Burney may have engineered the revelation himself, as being known as the father of the author was very valuable to him in his career and social life (this does not tally with the words of the dedicatory poem to *Evelina* that knowledge of the identity of the author would harm the reputation of her father). There is a mystery as to whether Dr Burney was aware of the true author or whether he was sincere in believing throughout his life that Fanny Burney was the true author of the books written under her name. I incline to the belief, from his attitude towards his daughter, that he was unaware of the true author.

Mrs Thrale, for all her qualities, was not a woman to judge people solely on their personal merits and as soon as Fanny Burney was known as the author of *Evelina* she took her under her wing as her protégée. It was a decision that Mrs Thrale was later to bitterly regret. However, even at this time, Mrs Thrale could not help noticing the discrepancy between Fanny Burney the woman and *Fanny Burney* the author. She wrote in 1779 that Fanny Burney was:

"A graceful looking Girl, but 'tis the Grace of an Actress not a Woman of Fashion – how should it? Her Conversation would be more pleasing if She thought less of herself; but her early Reputation embarrasses her Talk, & clouds her Mind with scruples about Elegancies which either come uncalled for or will not come at all: I love her more for her Father's sake than for her own".

She also wrote that "The Burneys are I believe a very low Race of Mortals" and that Fanny was "not a Woman of Fashion", an extraordinary description for the author of *Evelina* who describes with such accuracy the fashionable life of London high society.

It seems that later in life Mrs Thrale discovered somehow that Fanny Burney was not the true author as she was then to describe her as "*l'aimable traitresse*" (the amiable traitor). In addition, there exists the copy of *Evelina* that was presented to Mrs Thrale from Fanny Burney which she originally dedicated to Mrs Thrale "From the Scribler". Upon the book Mrs Thrale has written "N.B. *Scribler with one B*, Madame Dab". This was perhaps a reference to Mr Dabler, an untalented dilettante writer in *Fanny Burney's* early play *The Witlings*, a play which though not performed had been read by Mrs Thrale. By describing Fanny Burney as "Madame Dab" it seems that Mrs Thrale was accusing her of being an untalented dilettante herself and not the real author of the book.

The second production of *Fanny Burney* was not a novel but this play, *The Witlings*, which satirised two of the most famous literary hostesses of the time, known as Blue Stockings, Elizabeth Montagu and Mrs Thrale, who appear in the play disguised as Lady Smatter and Mrs Sapient. Mrs Montagu had disapproved of the novel *Evelina* and could not have been popular with its author, and this may have been the reason the play was written satirising her. Although the play was witty and well written, Charles Burney feared the opinion of these two women and, under his influence, the play was never performed. The play deals with an orphan heiress called Cecilia

Stanley and her lover, Beaufort. Mrs Montagu was a rich widow with an adopted son whose inheritance depended on him assuming her surname, just like Lady Smatter and Beaufort in the play, and so it would not have been difficult for her to see the parallel and to have taken offence.

The second novel of *Fanny Burney, Cecilia, or Memoirs of an Heiress*, derived some of its material from *The Witlings* (which also had a heroine named Cecilia). *Cecilia* appeared in June 1782 and sold out very quickly. It was published by T. Payne and Son, and T. Cadell. *Cecilia* is the story of an heiress initially of just £10,000, whose potential marriage to the hero, Mortimer Delville, is hampered by the fact that her new husband, under the terms of her inheritance from her uncle, the Dean, must take her surname. The novel is widely believed to be the model for *Jane Austen's Pride and Prejudice* and indeed one character, Dr Lyster, declares at the end of *Cecilia*: "The whole of this unfortunate business... has been the result of PRIDE and PREJUDICE".

The hero's family, the Delvilles, are of an old aristocratic lineage and the parents of the hero, Mortimer Delville, will thus not contemplate his marriage on the terms that they lose their family name. Several factors in *Cecilia* remind us of the life of Eliza, principally her being an heiress of £10,000, the differing views of her guardians towards the use of her inheritance, the question of the importance of her surname (to some extent the inheritance given to Eliza was morally dependent on her never using the surname of her father – a term she betrayed by naming her son Hastings). The novel also touches on the responsibility of an heiress to use some of her money for charitable works, which we know was an important concern for Eliza. *Cecilia* displayed Eliza's growing ability as a novelist and in the novel she created some of her most striking characters, including the scheming Mr Monckton and the loquacious Miss Larolles, a character well known to Jane Austen and mentioned in one of her letters.

Meanwhile, the life of Fanny Burney herself took an

unexpected turn when she was offered a place at court by Queen Charlotte at a salary of £200 a year as Second Keeper of the Robes. This unusual event seems to have been compensation to her father, Charles Burney, who had hoped unsuccessfully to secure the post of Master of the King's Band. As Fanny was now a thirty-four-year-old woman who was unlikely to marry, Charles Burney was no doubt glad that he would not have to provide for her further. Fanny Burney took up this position at Windsor in 1786 and was to remain in post until the summer of 1791. Her duties involving waiting on and dressing the queen were of a rather dull ceremonial nature. Her time here was unhappy, as she did not like working under Juliana Elizabeth Schwellenberg, the German companion who acted as the Queen's lady-in-waiting, whose imperiousness probably reminded her of her stepmother, Mrs Allen. This Ms Schwellenberg was the same lady who had been so helpful and kind to Count Imhoff and his wife Anna Maria (later Warren Hastings' second wife, Marian) before their journey to India, which I will discuss later.

During this time the trial of Warren Hastings for corruption and other misdeeds in his role as Governor General of India began on 13th February 1788 in Parliament at Westminster. Fanny Burney attended this in support of Warren Hastings and described some of the speeches in her diary.

On the literary front, Fanny Burney's time at court was significant for her own disastrous attempts at play writing. She wrote two historical plays, *Edwy and Elgiva*, and *The Siege of Pevensey*, and two Gothic romances, *Hubert de Vere* and *Elberta*. Even Claire Harman in her biography of Fanny Burney admits that these "court plays", "have little claim to literary or dramatic merit". This is an astounding admission, that the greatest novelist of her age was unable to produce a single play with any literary merit. In addition, this is in contrast to the skilful and witty dialogue produced earlier by the writer of *Fanny Burney's* play, *The Witlings*. The only reason for this can be that these court plays were written by Fanny Burney herself, and they are comparable in merit only to Fanny Burney's later literary works written after Eliza's death. *Fanny Burney's* fame as a novelist, however, led to the production of Fanny Burney's play *Edwy and Elgiva* at the Theatre Royal, Drury Lane on 21st March 1795, with disastrous consequences. Reviewers described the play as "nauseous bombast" and added that it had "nothing of Poetry" and was "often inelegantly familiar, or ridiculously absurd".

Kate Chisholm, in her biography of Fanny Burney, remarks that **"no fewer than sixteen newspapers expressed their concern that the 'author of Evelina' could have produced such a ludicrous tragedy"** [my highlighting]. She states that *The Morning Herald* ridiculed Elgiva's dying scene and the *Morning Post* wrote that the play "was one continued monotonous scene of whining between the two lovers".

Mrs Siddons was the greatest tragedienne of the time. Her portrait by Sir Joshua Reynolds appears on the cover of this book in the role of the Tragic Muse. This did not prevent Mrs Siddons from being laughed off the stage by the audience, such was the poor quality of Fanny Burney's own writing. Mrs Siddons, who took the part of Elgiva, wrote to Mrs Thrale (now Mrs Piozzi): "Oh there never was so wretched a thing as Mrs D'arblaye's Tragedy… the Audience were quite angelic and only laughed where it was *impossible* to avoid it." The other main actor, her brother Mr Kemble, in the end informed the audience that the play was being "withdrawn for alterations", which elicited general applause from the audience. All the reviewers believed that the applause was for the play being withdrawn. It is a measure of Fanny Burney's lack of literary ability that it appears from her journal entry of the time that she genuinely believed that the piece would be altered and then restaged. Here is a sample of the play that is quoted by Kate Chisholm in *Fanny Burney: Her Life*:

Elgiva	O Edwy! lend me courage, – not despair –
Edwy	My Brain turns round – I know not where I am –

	Nor whom – nor what – O kind Distraction
	seize me!
	Merciful Madness! –
Elgiva	Edwy, generous Edwy!
	Repress thy sorrow – for my sake – for me –
	Spare, spare the fleeting moments that
	remain. –
Edwy	I will! – I feel my wrong – Canst thou forgive
	it?

(kneels by her side)

	Can thy pure Spirit – see! I am calm! – forgive
	me?
Elgiva	Forgive? – dear to my Heart! – my noblest
	Edwy! –
	Ah me, I die! – O call forth all thy firmness –
Edwy	I will! believe me – trust – I'll wound no more,
	Expiring Angel! thy seraphic peace! –
Elgiva	Ah – take my last farwell – my tenderest –

Dies

It is possible that the title of this play, *Edwy and Elgiva*, was later satirised by Eliza in one of *Jane Austen's* "Juvenilia" of the 1790s entitled *Frederic and Elfrida*.

Fanny Burney finally left her position at court in the summer of 1791 with a pension of £100 a year granted to her by Queen Charlotte personally. In 1793 Fanny Burney met her husband to be, General d'Arblay, a French exile from the Revolution living in a community of exiles at Juniper Hall in Mickleham, Surrey, near to the estate of Fanny Burney's friends, Mr and Mrs Lock, in the Mole Valley between Leatherhead and Dorking. Juniper Hall is right next to Mickleham Hall, the house belonging to Lady Talbot, who visited Eliza while she was staying in Dorking in 1799. Mickleham is also the village that one had to travel through from Leatherhead (the possible prototype for "Highbury") to go up Box Hill, as did the characters in *Jane Austen's Emma*. Juniper Hall was part of the Juniper Hill Estate, which was owned by a lottery owner called Jenkinson, whose name may have suggested the name of Lady Catherine de Bourgh's humble companion, Mrs Jenkinson, in *Pride and Prejudice*.

It was not until 1796 that the next novel of *Fanny Burney* appeared in print, *Camilla, Or, A Picture of Youth*, the first of the novels to name Frances Burney as its author (the previous two had been published anonymously). This novel is very important to biographers of *Jane Austen* in that it is singled out for admiration more often than any other novel in *Jane Austen's* works. It is also important to Jane Austen biographers in that one of the subscribers to *Camilla* listed at the front of the book is a "Miss J. Austen", as I have previously mentioned.

In style, *Camilla* turns its back on the more skeletal, classical style of *Evelina* and *Cecilia* and looks forward to the richer "romantic" style of *Jane Austen*. It relates the story of three sisters, Camilla, Eugenia and Lavinia, and their various love affairs, as a peg to hang the characters and plot on. The main plot is a love story between Camilla and her respectable lover, Edgar Mandlebert, but the best drawn character in the story is Camilla's uncle, the baronet Sir Hugh Tyrold. Keen on hunting in his youth but low on intelligence and education, he finds through injury in later life he is no longer able to pursue his active interests. He therefore tries unsuccessfully to make up for his early lack of education by hiring a tutor to learn Latin, but he is unsuccessful. He also attempts to compensate for his negligence in allowing Camilla's younger sister, Eugenia, to catch the smallpox, by making her his heir in place of Camilla. Among a strong cast of characters the one that most resembles Eliza is Mrs Arlbery, a witty and independent middle-aged woman of strong character to whom Camilla is attracted against her better judgement. In 1796 Eliza was aged thirty-four and no longer seemed to identify directly with her young heroines. The alternative title *A Picture of Youth* seems to come from a writer who is past her own youth.

In monetary terms, *Camilla* was a remarkable success and the most successful novel of its day, raising £1,000 by subscription and a further £1,000 for the sale of the copyright. *Fanny Burney's* previous two novels had been successful but neither had earned anything like this sum of money for Fanny Burney. Fanny Burney's journal at this time reports an exchange between herself and King George III when in 1796 she brought to him a set of books of *Camilla*. I believe it casts a great deal of light on the authorship of Fanny Burney and Jane Austen:

> "He [the King] laughed – and enquired who corrected my proofs? Only myself I answered. "Why some Authors have told me", cried he, "that they are the last to do that work for themselves. They know by heart what ought to be, that they run on, without seeing what is. They have told me, besides, that a mere plodding head is best and surest for that work, – and that the livelier the imagination, the less it should be trusted to it".

Maybe this is something that should be borne in mind by biographers of Jane Austen and Fanny Burney, who tell us with confidence how in a particular year each was busy with correcting proofs. The king is hinting here that if anyone is correcting proofs it is a sure sign they are not the author. Maybe what Fanny Burney and Jane Austen were able to supply Eliza with was "a mere plodding head... best and surest for that work".

The profits from 'Camilla' went to Fanny Burney and the much larger sum she received for this novel was at last able to provide her with financial security.

Fanny Burney's plays *A Busy Day* and *The Woman Hater* belong to this period from 1799. In contrast to Fanny Burney's "court plays" these were works of great merit, which I believe indicates that they were written by Eliza, with Fanny Burney possibly in the role of secretary. Not performed at the time, they have both been put on recently for the first time. *A Busy Day* was produced in 1993 at the

Hen and Chicken pub in Bristol and *The Woman Hater* in 2007 at the Orange Tree Theatre in Richmond upon Thames; both met with great success and I was privileged to see the latter. It is interesting to note from the letter of Eliza of 29th October 1799 to her cousin, Philadelphia, that she had been staying in Dorking, less than a mile and a half from Fanny Burney's home, for the last six months. She mentions in the letter to her cousin visits from two literary friends, Lady Sophia Burrell and Lady Talbot, but makes no mention of Fanny Burney, supposedly the greatest English novelist of the time. She writes, "I have not found it possible to persevere in my plan of shunning all society, to which I must honestly confess I greatly prefer my Books, my Harp & my Pianoforte."

It would have been very simple for Eliza to have used Fanny Burney as a secretary in the production of these three plays, as they were living less than two miles from each other. The reason why Eliza was staying at home, not revealed to her cousin in her letter, may have been that she was composing these three plays. It is not the first instance where Eliza is being secretive in her letters. Eliza would have known a lot about play writing as she was a keen theatre goer in London and Tunbridge Wells, and took the main parts in amateur theatricals. *The Woman Hater*, written at this time, shows an extensive knowledge of literature on the part of the author, which mirrors Eliza's education.

One very curious fact is mentioned in *Jane Austen's Regency World* Issue 17, September/October 2005, where Maggie Lane writes of Fanny Burney:

"In all the millions of words Fanny committed to her letters and journals, there is no mention of her having read any novel by Jane Austen. This is all the more perplexing given that Fanny was living in Bath, with ready access to bookshops and book gossip, from 1815 to 1818, just the years when Austen's novels were being published and gathering readership. Fanny's half sister, Sarah Harriet

Burney, also a novelist, certainly read and greatly admired *Pride and Prejudice* and *Emma*. (Jane Austen could not return the compliment, since she found the younger Burney's novel *Clarentine* did not bear a third reading)."

It is truly astonishing that the novelist considered the greatest of the late eighteenth century never wrote a single word (among millions) about the novelist considered the greatest of the early nineteenth century, whose novels she influenced so much. The only rational explanation can be that this omission was deliberate because in reality neither were authors.

23.

The Mystery of "The Wanderer"

For those people who uphold the authorship of Fanny Burney of all the works that bear her name, there is one insurmountable problem. This is *Fanny Burney's* final novel *The Wanderer, or Female Difficulties* published in 1814, the year after Eliza's death in 1813. The first edition of 3,000 of *The Wanderer* sold out on the strength of Fanny Burney's reputation but at least half of the copies of the second edition of 1,000 were returned and pulped, as the novel was found by readers to be of such poor quality. To give you a flavour of the writing I choose a passage at random:

"Ellis blushed and paused; but presently, with strengthened resolution, earnestly cried, "If this, sir, is the sum of what you have to say, leave me, I entreat, without further procrastination! Every moment that you persist in staying presents to me the image of Miss Joddrell, breaking from her physicians, and darting, bloody and dying, into the room to surprise you!"

"Pardon, pardon me, that I should have given birth to so dreadful an apprehension! I will relieve you this instant; and omit no possible precaution to avert every danger. But the least reflexion, to a mind delicate as yours, will exculpate me from blame in not remaining at her side, – after the scene of last night – unless I purposed to become her permanent guardian. The tattling world would instantly unite – or calumniate us. But you, who, if you retreat, will be doubted and suspected, You, must, at present, stay, and openly, clearly, and unsought, be seen. Elinor, who breathes but to spur her misery by despair, that she may end it, reserves for me, and for my presence – to astonish, to shock, or to vanquish me, – every horrour she can devise. In my absence, rest assured, no evil will be perpretrated. 'Tis for her, then, for her sake, that you must remain, and that I must depart."

The Wanderer is the story of an émigrée from revolutionary France who comes to England, where she tries to earn her own living in various trades. From what I have just told you, you may imagine that this book is very popular with modern feminist English Literature academics, who sometimes impose a rather contemporary view on the nineteenth century and judge a book solely on how it conforms to this. Surprisingly, Kate Chisholm, in her biography of Fanny Burney, agrees with them and tells how *The Wanderer* deals with "not just 'female difficulties' but also the meaning of existence for both men and women, especially in a society so full of prejudice and inequalities". She also describes *The Wanderer*, incomprehensibly in my opinion, as *Fanny Burney's* "richest and most rewarding book". Critics at the time of the publication of *The Wanderer*, however, were usually educated in the Classics and foreign languages and were therefore better equipped to be judges of literary merit. Almost unanimously they found *The Wanderer* to be an extremely poor novel.

John Wilson Croker, in his review of *The Wanderer* in 1814 (the year of its publication) wrote [my highlighting]:

"but, we regret to say, that The Wanderer, which might be expected to finish and crown her literary labours, is not only inferior to its sister-works, but cannot in our judgment, claim any very decided superiority over the thousand-and-one volumes with which the Minerva Press inundates the shelves of circulating libraries, and increases, instead of diverting the ennui of the loungers at watering-places.

If we had not been assured in the title-page that this work had been produced by the same pen as Cecilia, we should have pronounced Madame D'Arblay [Fanny Burney's married name] to be a feeble imitator of the style and manner of Miss Burney" – we should have admitted the flat fidelity of her copy, but we should have lamented the total want of vigour, vivacity, and originality;"

Croker hit on the truth, that *The Wanderer* was by a different author to the other novels of *Fanny Burney* ("a feeble imitator") and was an unsuccessful attempt by Fanny Burney herself to write in the style of Eliza. Another critic who believed that *The Wanderer* was written by a different author to the rest of the *Fanny Burney* novels was Edward Knatchbull-Hugessen (first Baron Brabourne, who lived from 1829 to 1893). He was the son of Jane Austen's favourite niece, Fanny Knight. He edited in 1884 the first published edition of Jane Austen's letters. In it he wrote in his entry for 1813 [my highlighting but his underlining]:

"I do not know who the Dr. Isham was who was so good as to say that he was "sure that he should not like Madame D'Arblay's new novel half so well" as "Pride and Prejudice," but I imagine that the vast majority of the readers of both books would have agreed with him; for the new novel referred to was "The Wanderer," of which I have already hinted my opinion that the falling off from the previous works of the fair authoress is so very manifest that **it is difficult to suppose that it was written by the same hand to which we are indebted for "Evelina," "Cecilia" and "Camilla."**

Thomas Babington Macaulay, in his essay on Madam d'Arblay of 1843, described *The Wanderer* as "a book which no judicious friend to her memory will attempt to draw from the oblivion into which it has justly fallen". Macaulay was to call the style of *The Wanderer* [my highlighting] **"Madam d'Arblay's later style, the worst style that has ever been known among men"**. He also wrote the following on the style of all Fanny Burney's works published after *Camilla* in 1796 (i.e. all the works that Eliza could not have written) [my highlighting]:

> "It is melancholy to think that the whole fame of Madame D'Arblay rests on what she did during the earlier half of her life, and that everything which she published during the forty-three years which preceded her death [1797 – 1840], lowered her reputation…The truth is, that Madame D'Arblay's style underwent a gradual and most pernicious change, **a change which, in degree at least, we believe to be unexampled in literary history…**
>
> She brought back [from France] a style which we are really at a loss to describe. It is a sort of broken Johnsonese, a barbarous patois, bearing the same relation to the language of Rasselas, [the novel by Dr Johnson] which the gibberish of the negroes of Jamaica bears to the English of the House of Lords. Sometimes it reminds us of the finest, that is to say, the vilest parts, of Mr. Galt's novels; sometimes of the perorations of Exeter Hall; sometimes of the leading articles of the Morning Post. But it most resembles the puffs of Mr. Rowland and Dr. Goss. It matters not what ideas are clothed in such a style. The genius of Shakspeare and Bacon united, would not save a work so written from general derision."

He compared the following passage from *Evelina*:

> "His son seems weaker in his understanding, and more gay in his temper; but his gaiety is that of a foolish overgrown

schoolboy, whose mirth consists in noise and disturbance. He disdains his father for his close attention to business and love of money, though he seems himself to have no talents, spirit or generosity to make him superior to either. His chief delight appears to be in tormenting and ridiculing his sisters, who in reurn most cordially despise him. Miss Branghton, the eldest daughter, is by no means ugly; but looks proud, ill-tempered, and conceited. She hates the city, though without knowing why; for it is easy to discover she has lived nowhere else. Miss Polly Branghton is rather pretty, very foolish, very ignorant, very giddy and, I believe, very good natured."

and the following passage from *Cecilia*:

"It is rather an imaginary than an actual evil, and though a deep wound to pride, no offence to morality. Thus have I laid open to you my whole heart, confessed my perplexities, acknowledged my vainglory, and exposed with equal sincerity the sources of my doubts, and the motives of my decision. But now, indeed, how to proceed I know not. The difficulties which are yet to encounter I fear to enumerate, and the petition I have to urge I have scarce courage to mention. My family, mistaking ambition for honour, and rank for dignity, have long planned a splendid connection for me, to which, though my invariable repugnance has stopped any advances, their wishes and their views immoveably adhere. I am but too certain they will now listen to no other. I dread, therefore, to make a trial where I despair of success. I know not how to risk a prayer with those who may silence me by a command."

with Fanny Burney's "later style" [taken from Fanny Burney's *Memoirs of Doctor Burney* of 1832]:

"He was assaulted, during his precipitated return, by the rudest fierceness of wintry elemental strife; through which, with bad accommodations and innumerable accidents, he became a prey to the merciless pangs of the acutest spasmodic rheumatism, which barely suffered him to reach his home, ere, long and piteously, it confined him, a tortured prisoner, to his bed. Such was the cheek that almost instantly curbed, though it could not subdue, the rising pleasure of his hopes of entering upon a new species of existence—that of an approved man of letters; for it was on the bed of sickness, exchanging the light wines of France, Italy, and Germany, for the black and loathsome potions of the Apothecaries' Hall, writhed by darting stitches, and burning with fiery fever, that he felt the full force of that sublunary equipoise that seems evermore to hang suspended over the attainment of long-sought and uncommon felicity, just as it is ripening to burst forth with enjoyment."

Then he compares the following passage from *Cecilia*:

"Even the imperious Mr. Delvile was more supportable here than in London. Secure in his own castle, he looked round him with a pride of power and possession which softened while it swelled him. His superiority was undisputed: his will was without control. He was not, as in the great capital of the kingdom, surrounded by competitors. No rivalry disturbed his peace; no equality mortified his greatness. All he saw were either vassals of his power, or guests bending to his pleasure. He abated, therefore, considerably the stern gloom of his haughtiness, and soothed his proud mind by the courtesy of condescention."

to a passage from Fanny Burney's *Memoirs of Doctor Burney*:

"If beneficence be judged by the happiness which it diffuses, whose claim, by that proof, shall stand higher than that of Mrs. Montagu, from the munificence with which she celebrated her annual festival for those hapless artificers who perform the most abject offices, of any authorised calling, in being the active guardians of our blazing hearths? Not to vainglory, then, but to kindness of heart, should be adjudged the publicity of that superb charity which made its jetty objects, for one bright morning, cease to consider themselves as degraded outcasts from all society."

He also quotes the following passages from Fanny Burney's "later works":

"The last of men was Doctor Johnson to have abetted squandering the delicacy of integrity by nullifying the labours of talents."

"A similar ebullition of political rancour with that which so difficultly had been conquered for Mr. Canning foamed over the ballot box to the exclusion of Mr. Rogers."

Macaulay continued [with my highlighting]:

"An offence punishable with imprisonment is, in this language, an offence "which produces incarceration." To be starved to death is "to sink from inanition into nonentity." Sir Isaac Newton is "the developer of the skies in their embodied movements"; and Mrs. Thrale, when a party of clever people sat silent, is said to have been "provoked by the dulness of a taciturnity that, in the midst of such renowned interlocutors, produced as narcotic a torpor as could have been caused by a dearth the most barren of all human faculties." In truth, it is impossible to look at any page of Madame D'Arblay's later works without finding flowers of rhetoric like these. Nothing in the language of those jargonists at whom Mr. Gosport laughed, nothing in the language of Sir Sedley Clarendel, approaches this new Euphuism.

It is from no unfriendly feeling to Madame D'Arblay's memory that we have expressed ourselves so strongly on the subject of her style. On the contrary, we conceive that we have really rendered a service to her reputation. **That her later works were complete failures, is a fact too notorious to be dissembled."**

W T Hale also, in 1916, wrote of *The Wanderer* that Fanny Burney's style underwent a "fantastic evolution", that most of the book was rant and that it "lacked entirely a sense of humour". Austin Dobson, in his essay on Fanny Burney of 1903, summed up the general opinion of the literary world at the time of publication of *The Wanderer*, that the novel was unreadable trash:

"The best one can say about The Wanderer; or Female Difficulties, issued in March 1814, is, that it brought grist to the mill. It was not published by subscription like Camilla ; but Mme. D'Arblay herself tells us that 3600 copies were "positively sold and paid for at the "rapacious price" of two guineas each in six months. From a literary point of view the book was an utter failure. It "was apparently never read by anybody," observes Sir Leslie Stephen; and Macaulay says that "no judicious friend to the author's memory will attempt to draw it from the oblivion into which it has justly fallen." Even Mme. D'Arblay's most faithful editor and admirer, Mrs. Ellis, makes open and heartfelt thanksgiving that it is not her duty to read it again. After these discouraging opinions from critics not unfriendly, it is scarcely surprising to learn that The

Wanderer was attacked with unusual severity in the Quarterly for April, 1814; or that Hazlitt should, in the Edinburgh Review for February, 1815, make it the sorry pretext for that admirable survey of the national fiction which he afterwards converted into No. vi. of his Lectures on the English Comic Writers. Hazlitt earned, as has already been told in chapter i., the disapprobation of honest James Burney for his treatment of Mme. D'Arblay's final effort. Yet it is notable that the critic blames The Wanderer not for "decay of talent, but a perversion of it." It is impossible to say as much now. The book, in truth, is wearisome, and its "difficulties" are unreal. The reason for its first success is, we suspect, to be traced to the cause suggested by Mme. D'Arblay herself, namely, the prevailing expectation that its pages would present a picture of contemporary and revolutionary France, where, it was known, the writer had been residing ; and that this led to a number of copies being freely bespoken. When the real nature of its theme — the trivial and improbable adventures, in England, of a female refugee during the reign of Robespierre — was fully appreciated, the sale immediately fell off. Were it not futile, it would be interesting to speculate whether, had The Wanderer taken the place of Evelina in the order of Mme. D'Arblay's productions, it would have succeeded at all, even in the absence of rivals. But it is a curious instance of the irony of circumstance that a book which nobody could read should have brought more than £7000 to somebody in the year in which Miss Edgeworth published Patronage, and Miss Austen, Mansfield Park. It is also more curious still, that in this very year Constable could not see his way to risk more than £700 on the copy-right of an anonymous novel entitled Waverley; or, His Sixty Years Since."

Given the severity of all the above reviews, it is astonishing the number of modern literary critics who take *The Wanderer* seriously as a work of fiction. Some even put it on a par with other works of *Fanny Burney*. Nothing could demonstrate more clearly the total lack of education, literary ability or taste of these modern critics. The reviews of the time demonstrate how the literary world of that time was much more learned, educated and discriminating, and educated reviewers dismissed *The Wanderer* as being completely unworthy of the author of the first three novels of *Fanny Burney*.

The Wanderer was published in 1814, one year after Eliza's death, and was written at a period when Fanny Burney was in some difficulties financially, although this was remedied on the death of her father the same year, when Fanny Burney received more than £5,000 in his will. *The Wanderer* was widely bought by the reading public in expectation of it being of the quality of the three previous *Fanny Burney* books. However, it was generally acknowledged to be so bad that many copies were returned to the publisher and half of the second reprint needed to be pulped.

What could be the explanation for this sudden deterioration in the quality of *Fanny Burney's* writing? There are two possibilities:

1. The writer suddenly lost all her writing ability and style, and started to write like a hack writer in imitation of herself. She suddenly lost the ability to write humorous fiction. She lost the ability to write smoothly and began to write in a verbose, affected and jerky style. The writer in the whole of a long novel was suddenly unable to put together a single sentence reminiscent of her previous style. From being the greatest novelist of the late eighteenth century she suddenly became a writer of unreadable trash.

   Some biographers have unconvincingly put this down to Fanny Burney having written the novel while living in France, from 1802 to 1812. However, Eliza herself spent a lot of time in France and this did not affect her writing style in her own letters. Besides, anyone who speaks a foreign language will know that knowledge of a foreign language enriches, not diminishes, one's abilities in one's own language.

2. The writer of *The Wanderer* was a different writer who was trying to imitate the style of the writer of the previous three novels but had little literary talent herself. In particular, she was trying to imitate the style of *Evelina*.

Some recent biographers have attempted to support the first hypothesis. The less than convincing explanation of one writer, Maggie Lane, is that Fanny Burney had "lost her touch" by the time she wrote *The Wanderer*. Similarly, Claire Harman in her biography of Fanny Burney seeks to explain away the dreadfully poor writing style of *Memoirs of Doctor Burney*, a later work written by Fanny Burney about her father, the only book other than *The Wanderer* written by Fanny Burney after Eliza's death. Claire Harman herself describes it justifiably as an "awful book". However, the explanation she comes up with as to why it is so badly written is not particularly convincing:

> "What were the reasons for Fanny's deplorable performance in the *Memoirs*? Senility is out of the question; she could still write perfectly naturally in her private correspondence long after 1832. Bad taste and bad judgment are part of the answer, as is her residual terror of her father. But it also seems to me significant that the *Memoirs* represent the nether end, almost the logical conclusion, of Fanny's persistent neurosis about authorship. Though it was her last published work, it was in one important respect a long-deferred, long-dreaded *debut*. With the exception of the pamphlet *Brief Reflections*, the dedication to *Camilla* and the preface to *The Wanderer* (all notably stilted), Fanny had always been able to hide her

own voice in fictional forms, whether poetry, novels or plays."

The last sentence of Ms Harman is curious, and does not seem to make logical sense. She states that the reason for the poor quality of writing in *Memoirs of Doctor Burney* is that the writer could not hide her own voice, as she could in her novels. However, Ms Harman ignores the fact that *Fanny Burney's* last novel, *The Wanderer,* is written in the same "notably stilted" style. Harman herself describes the style and language of this novel as "astonishingly awful". If Fanny Burney was able to hide her own voice in the first three novels, what prevented her from doing the same in the fourth, *The Wanderer?*

However, if one examines my initial two hypotheses with a modicum of common sense, the only likely one is the second. This fits in with everything else we know about Eliza and Fanny Burney. Dr Burney, her father, saw writing a novel as a way for Fanny to make money, which indeed it was, as the new book was purchased in large numbers on the reputation of the previous three (although a large number of copies of the second edition of *The Wanderer* were returned and destroyed along with the unsold copies). Since Fanny Burney had been forced to remain in France from 1802 to 1812 and Eliza had died in 1813, the year before publication of *The Wanderer,* Fanny Burney's only recourse had been to write the book herself. One indication that Fanny Burney herself wrote the book is its subject matter, which is the only one of the *Fanny Burney* novels to deal with a heroine who has a life similar to that of Fanny Burney and her family. The heroine, Ellis, is a working woman who, like the people in Fanny Burney's circle, is at different stages a music teacher, seamstress and milliner. This is in contrast to the heroines of all the other *Fanny Burney* novels who, like Eliza, are women of leisure who come from the gentry, who do not work, and are either heiresses or, in the case of Camilla, an ex-heiress, and who marry into rich families of the gentry or nobility.

It is notable that in her novels the author *Jane Austen* referred to

Fanny Burney's Camilla of 1796 more often than any other book, yet she nowhere mentions *The Wanderer*. I at first missed this argument, as *The Wanderer* was only published in 1814, one year after Eliza's death. But if one were to uphold the authorship of Jane Austen, who died in 1817, one would have to explain why she never referred to *The Wanderer* in any of her novels.

One other piece of evidence in support of the hypothesis that there were two authors of the *Fanny Burney* novels, Eliza and Fanny Burney, is the dedication to Queen Charlotte in *Camilla* in 1796, where Fanny Burney for the first time declares herself to be the author. This dedication is written in the same semi-literate sub-Johnsonian style as the whole of *The Wanderer*. Its clumsy, verbose and pompous style contrasts greatly with the elegance of the writing of the novel *Camilla* itself. Even Claire Harman, as I have shown, admits that it is "notably stilted". The dedication in *Camilla* is as follows:

"TO THE

QUEEN

MADAM,

THAT Goodness inspires a confidence, which, by divesting respect of terror, excites attachment to Greatness, the presentation of this little Work to Your Majesty must truly, however humbly, evince; and though a public manifestation of duty and regard from an obscure Individual may betray a proud ambition, it is, I trust, but a venial – I am sure it is a natural one.

In those to whom Your Majesty is known but by exaltation of Rank, it may raise, perhaps, some surprise, that scenes, characters, and incidents, which have reference only to common life, should be brought into so august a presence; but the inhabitant of a retired cottage, who there receives the benign permission which at Your Majesty's feet casts this humble offering, bears in mind recollections which must live there while 'memory holds its seat,' of a benevolence withheld from no condition, and delighting in all ways to speed the progress of Morality, through whatever channel it could flow, to whatever port it might steer. I blush at the inference I seem here to leave open of annexing undue importance to a production of apparently so light a kind – yet if my hope, my view – however fallacious they may eventually prove, extended not beyond whiling away an idle hour, should I dare seek such patronage?

With the deepest gratitude, and most heart-felt respect, I am

MADAM,

YOUR MAJESTY'S

Most obedient, most obliged,
And most dutiful servant,

F. d'ARBLAY.

BOOKHAM,
June 28, 1796"

This verbose and clumsy dedication to the Queen is the only passage in *Fanny Burney's* first three novels to mention Ms Burney as the author.

The Introduction to *The Wanderer* seems to be an attempt by Fanny Burney to clear up discrepancies with regard to the publication of her first novel, *Evelina*, which, to readers at the time, might cast doubt on her authorship. This is in line with Claire

Harman's assertion that much of Fanny Burney's memoirs were later fabrication. Firstly, in the Introduction to *The Wanderer* she tries to clear up doubt as to the dedication to *Evelina* by explaining unnecessarily how it referred to her father, a fact that should have been self-evident; because she talks about the dedication here, it suggests that she knew the dedication was not really to her father.

Secondly, it was widely believed at the time of its publication in 1778 that the author of *Evelina* was of a similar age to the heroine of the book, who was seventeen. The fact that the author in the Preface to *Evelina* asks excuse for her own young age supports this. The author writes to the authors of the *Monthly and Critical Reviews*: "Remember, Gentlemen, you were all young writers once, and the most experienced veteran of your corps, may, by recollecting his first publication, renovate his first terrors, and learn to allow for mine". Fanny Burney herself was twenty-five when *Evelina* was published, which was not an age at this time when women were still regarded as young; for instance Anne Elliott, the heroine of *Jane Austen's Persuasion*, and Elinor Dashwood in *Sense and Sensibility* had reached this age and were considered already to have "lost their bloom".

In order to account for this anomaly in Fanny Burney's age (twenty-five) when *Evelina* was first published, she states for the first time in the Introduction to *The Wanderer* in 1814, that on her fifteenth birthday she burned all her manuscripts in her garden, including an early version of *Evelina* called *Caroline Evelyn*. We have no evidence that any such early version of *Evelina* ever existed; Fanny Burney had had little education at the age of fifteen and would have been totally incapable of writing such an accomplished novel, therefore it seems Fanny Burney made up this story of an earlier version of *Evelina* purely to reconcile the age of herself and its author. Claire Harman notes that Fanny Burney gave various contradictory dates for the time of this bonfire and accuses Fanny Burney's account of her youth, written in later years, of hindsight and wishful thinking. The likelihood Fanny Burney invented this story is reinforced by its appearance alongside the explanation of the dedication of *Evelina* to her father. Claire Harman, in her biography of Fanny Burney, accuses Fanny Burney of many such reinventions of her life and her father's when she edited her diaries and the memoirs of her father later in life. She almost goes so far as to call Fanny Burney an "inveterate liar".

The Wanderer, however, was not a unique example of the sudden decline of Fanny Burney's writing abilities. Between 1801, the date of the unpublished and unperformed play *A Busy Day*, and 6th January 1840, the date of her death, the only books that were published under Fanny Burney's name were *The Wanderer* in 1814 and in 1832 her *Memoirs of Doctor Burney*, a biography of her father. Like all the other works that we can be sure were the product of Fanny Burney's and not Eliza's pen (*The Wanderer* and the "court plays"), this biography of her father had not just a bad but a disastrous reception. Claire Harman describes the biography as "an awful book". She accuses Fanny Burney in the book of the deliberate suppression of many facts and the distortion of others. Baroness Bunsen at the time of its publication wrote "Surely such a quantity of unmixed nonsense never was written before". Maria Edgeworth wrote that "Whenever [she] speaks of herself some false shame, some affectation of humility or timidity or I know not what... spoils her style".

Margaret Ann Doody, in her introduction to *The Wanderer* provides us with an example of the letter writing style of Fanny Burney at around the time of its publication. She quotes a letter of July 1815 from Fanny Burney to her friend, Mary Ann Waddington, objecting to her admiration for Napoleon:

"How is it that my ever dear Mary can thus... be a professed & ardent detester of Tyranny; yet an open & intrepid admirer of a Tyrant? O had you spent, like me, 10 years within the control of his unlimited power, & under the iron rod of its dread, how would you change your language! by a total reverse of sentiment! yet was I, because always inoffensive, never molested: as safe. There, *another* would say, as in London; but you will not say so; the safety of deliberate prudence, or of retiring timidity, is not such as would satisfy a *mind* glowing for freedom like your's: it satisfies, indeed NO mind, it merely suffices for *bodily* security. It was the choice of my Companion, not of my Taste that drew ME to such a residence. PERSONALLY, for the reason I have assigned, I was always well-treated, & personally I was happy: but you know me, I am sure, better than to suppose me such an Egotist as to be really happy, or contented, where Corporal Liberty could only be preserved by Mental forbearance – i.e. subjection."

The dreadful, almost unreadable, writing style of *The Wanderer* is readily visible in this excerpt of her letter in such clumsy sentences as "yet was I, because always inoffensive, never molested: as safe." We can thus be fairly certain that the writer of the above letter, Fanny Burney, is the author of *The Wanderer*. This dreadful writing style of Fanny Burney is really rather unmistakeable. The writing style of *The Wanderer* and of the above letter is in stark contrast to the elegant and witty style of Eliza's letters, closely resembling the style of *Fanny Burney's* first three novels.

Once it is admitted that *The Wanderer* is by a different author from the first three *Fanny Burney* novels, which is hard to argue against, given that this was even the opinion of Jane Austen's great nephew, Edward Knatchbull-Hugessen, we must acknowledge that the true author of the first three novels was not Fanny Burney, and the only likely other author would be Eliza. If Eliza is the author of these novels, it would be highly improbable that she would have given up writing novels at exactly the same time, 1795-6, that Jane Austen started writing them. We can therefore conclude that, because *The Wanderer* is by a different author to the first three *Fanny Burney* novels, this shows that Eliza was the true author of both *Fanny Burney's* and *Jane Austen's* novels.

24.

Stoneleigh Abbey

Of all the properties I have visited in connection with research on this book, the one that I have found puts me most in touch with the works of *Jane Austen* is Stoneleigh Abbey in Warwickshire. It is with some justification that it has been represented as the model for both Northanger Abbey and for Sotherton Court, the residence of Mr Rushworth in *Mansfield Park*.

There is a very interesting guided tour of the house which I took, which gives information on the connections between the property and Jane Austen. The house was owned by cousins of Jane's mother, the Leighs, and was visited by Jane with her mother and sister, Cassandra, in 1806. The reason for their visit was that in 1806, Mrs Austen and her two daughters were visiting the Rev. Thomas Leigh at their estate in Adlestrop in Gloucestershire. While they were there, the Honourable Mary Leigh, who owned Stoneleigh Abbey, died without issue. There was some dispute about the inheritance, but it seemed that she had left the property to Rev. Thomas Leigh of Adlestrop. In order to gain possession of the property as quickly as possible to assert his claim, on hearing the news of the death of Mary, Rev. Thomas Leigh left Adlestrop with Mrs Austen and her two daughters to go directly to Stoneleigh Abbey.

From the letters of Mrs Austen, Jane's mother, describing this visit, it is clear that she and Jane Austen had not visited the property before. Stoneleigh Abbey is a very large and very beautiful country house built in the classical style by a local architect, Francis Smith, in the early eighteenth century, on the site of an old Cistercian abbey, portions of which remain, and the estate had vast quantities of land throughout several counties which produced a massive income of £19,000 a year. In *Jane Austen's Northanger Abbey* the rooms are laid out in a similar way to those of Stoneleigh, as described in a letter of Jane Austen's mother, including the dark wood-panelled rooms and the long gallery. The property is also similar to Northanger Abbey in that it was once an old abbey (a Cistercian abbey) confiscated by Henry VIII during the Reformation in the sixteenth century. Mrs Austen's reaction to the abbey is not dissimilar to that of Catherine Morland when she arrives at Northanger Abbey. Mrs Austen wrote in a letter of 13th August 1806 to Mrs James Austen:

> "I had figured to myself long Avenues dark Rookeries and dismal Yew Trees, but here are no such melancholy things… The Avon runs near the house amidst Green Meadows bounded by large and beautiful Woods, full of delightful walks".

She also wrote:

> "Behind the smaller drawing room is the state Bed Chamber, with a high crimson Velvet Bed: an alarming apartment just fit for a Heroine; the old gallery opens onto it."

The main object of the humour in *Northanger Abbey* is that, although called an abbey, the main part of the property was very modern and comfortable, as was Stoneleigh. However, Northanger Abbey shared similarities with Stoneleigh Abbey in that some of the earlier rooms of the 1720s with their wood panelling had been retained, which was unusual, bearing in mind how out of fashion they would have been at that time. Many sources claim that *Jane Austen* based Northanger Abbey upon Stoneleigh Abbey. The layout of Northanger Abbey seems to correspond with that of Stoneleigh

Abbey and features of Stoneleigh Abbey, such as the above-mentioned wood-panelled rooms and a large old stone porch, bring to mind Catherine Morland's description of Northanger Abbey. Gaye King in her article *The Jane Austen Connection* confirms that the description of the route the heroine Catherine Morland takes through the house in *Northanger Abbey* corresponds in **exact** detail to old drawings of Stoneleigh Abbey. The description of Northanger Abbey in the novel also corresponds to Stoneleigh Abbey as follows:

> "Many were the inquiries she was eager to make of Miss Tilney; but so active were her thoughts, that when these inquiries were answered, she was hardly more assured than before, of Northanger Abbey having been a richly-endowed convent at the time of the Reformation, of its having fallen into the hands of an ancestor of the Tilneys on its dissolution, of a large portion of the ancient building still making a part of the present dwelling although the rest was decayed, or of its standing low in a valley, sheltered from the north and east by rising woods of oak."

The problem that this presents to the authorship of Jane Austen, however, is how Jane Austen would have been able to describe in such detail these interior and exterior features of Stoneleigh Abbey in *Northanger Abbey* (believed to have been written in 1798-9 under the original name of *Susan*, and which we know for certain was sold to the publisher Benjamin Crosby & Co in the spring of 1803) when Jane Austen did not visit Stoneleigh until 1806. Since Jane Austen had at that time not visited Stoneleigh Abbey, she could not have been the author who based Northanger Abbey on the house.

The manner in which Mrs Austen describes Stoneleigh in 1806 confirms it was the first time that she had visited the property. In her letter of 13th August 1806 she writes "The house is larger than I could have supposed... I expected to find everything about the place very fine and all that, but I had no idea of its being so beautiful. I had figured to myself long avenues dark rookeries and dismal yew trees, but here are no such melancholy things." Since she was visiting the property with her daughter, Jane Austen, it must also have been the first time that Jane Austen visited the property, otherwise Jane could have described the property in detail to her mother before their arrival, and her mother would not have been surprised at its appearance in any way. Those who believe Jane Austen to be the author of *Northanger Abbey* cannot even fall back on their usual explanation of last resort, i.e. that Eliza de Feuillide told Jane Austen about Stoneleigh Abbey since, if she had done so, Jane Austen would have described Stoneleigh Abbey to her mother and her mother would not have been surprised at how it looked.

It seems very likely that Stoneleigh Abbey had, however, been visited by Eliza before 1798. Because of the scarcity of the remaining letters of Eliza we have no proof of this. However, it is very likely that Eliza visited Stoneleigh before 1798 for the following reasons:

1. Eliza was a woman of means and much better travelled than Jane Austen, who was dependent upon her parents or relations to pay for the costs of her travel.

2. Eliza was a frequent visitor to her Leigh relations at Adlestrop in Gloucestershire, before 1806 a different branch of the Leigh family to the ones who owned Stoneleigh Abbey. The Leighs who owned the estate in Adlestrop were in fact the senior branch of the Leigh family but were much less wealthy than their Warwickshire relations. The reason for Eliza's frequent visits to them was not, however, a close friendship with this branch of the Leigh family. The reason was that the estate of Adlestrop adjoined the estate of Daylesford (Warren Hastings' estate) and Adlestrop House and Daylesford House were within half a mile of each other. Therefore it would have been very impolite for Eliza not to call on the Leighs at Adlestrop

whenever she visited Warren Hastings at Daylesford, which she did quite frequently. In a letter of 4th August 1797 written from Cheltenham, Eliza records visiting Warren Hastings at Daylesford, and also meeting in the nearby spa town of Cheltenham the Leigh family and their relations, Lord and Lady Saye & Seale.

3. Because of Eliza's friendship with the Leighs of Adlestrop it is likely that she visited their richer cousins at Stoneleigh prior to 1798. She could have done so in 1797 after visiting the Leighs at Adelstrop. It is perhaps more likely that she did not make a special journey but visited Stoneleigh in 1794 en route to visiting her friend, Catherine Egerton, and her husband, the Reverend Charles Egerton, in Washington, County Durham. We know for certain that she visited the Egertons there in 1794, as one of Eliza's letters to Warren Hastings, dated 19th September 1794, is addressed from their house. Eliza's route from London would have been the same that Eliza Bennet took to Derbyshire in *Pride and Prejudice*: through Oxford, Blenheim, Warwick, Kenilworth and Birmingham. This route passed within two miles of Stoneleigh, between Warwick and Kenilworth. As she would have been so close, it would have been a duty, and maybe even a pleasure, for Eliza to call in on her Leigh family relations. Professor Donald Greene in his article (which I cite later) *The Original of Pemberley*, says of Eliza Bennet and Mr and Mrs Gardiner in *Pride and Prejudice* that "Perhaps while the tourists were at Kenilworth they had also visited Stoneleigh Abbey, with its magnificent baroque front, only about a mile away." Eliza de Feuillide's visit to Stoneleigh at this time, combined with her knowledge of gothic fiction and especially of the novels of Ann Radcliffe, would have been her inspiration to write the novel *Northanger Abbey,* which was begun in 1798. Nobody has found any similar inspiration for Jane Austen to have written this novel.

4. In addition, the enthusiastic description of the visit to Bath by the heroine, Catherine Morland, and her lover, Henry Tilney, in *Northanger Abbey* does not fit with Jane Austen's view of Bath at the time. When forced to move there with her family on her father's retirement in 1801 she was extremely despondent. In addition, Jane Austen's Bath is almost a completely different world to the Bath of Jane Austen. *Northanger Abbey* describes the smartest addresses in town, whereas Jane Austen's family resided in the cheaper roads in town, such as Green Park Buildings and Gay Street. The more wealthy Eliza would no doubt have rented rooms in one of the more fashionable streets of Bath. Eliza had visited Bath in early 1792 with her then husband, the Comte, and she enjoyed visiting other spa towns, such as Cheltenham and Tunbridge Wells.

In *Jane Austen's Mansfield Park*, Stoneleigh Abbey is very little disguised in the description in Chapters 8, 9 and 10 of Mr Rushworth's property, Sotherton Court. The description of the chapel especially is exactly like the chapel in Stoneleigh, as I can attest:

> "'Now' said Mrs Rushworth, 'we are coming to the chapel, which properly we ought to enter from above, and look down upon; but as we are quite among friends, I will take you in this way, if you will excuse me'... Fanny's imagination had prepared her for something grander than a mere spacious, oblong room, fitted up for the purpose of devotion – with nothing more striking or more solemn than a profusion of mahogany, and the crimson velvet cushions appearing over the ledge of the family gallery above".

The chapel still survives with its red cushions and a very fine organ from the Leighs' relative, the Duke of Chandos, taken from his London house, "Cannons", where once Handel had been director of music. When Mrs Rushworth says in the novel that prayers have been left off in the chapel by Mr Rushworth's father, this in fact has a double meaning. It does not necessarily mean that the family had become less religious, as Mary Crawford believes (and appears to approve of). The reason that the chapel was built at Stoneleigh was probably so that prayers could be said for the Stuarts, which was not possible in the local church where prayers had to be said for the ruling dynasty, the Hanoverians. The fact that the elder Mr Rushworth no longer wished to pray for the Stuarts indicated that he saw it as advantageous for political and social reasons for his family to change and to support the Hanoverian dynasty. The local church at Stoneleigh is, as in Sotherton, the place that the family are buried and where the banners and monuments are to be found, while the chapel is simple and almost without decoration.

Eliza's Stuart and Catholic leanings may be attributed to her links with the Leigh family, in addition to her French connections. During the English Civil War the Leighs had given refuge to Charles I when the gates of Warwick had been barred to him. Later, in 1745, Charles Edward Stuart (Bonnie Prince Charlie) visited the house, the furthest south in England that he was to come before his army returned to Scotland (not Derby as is widely believed). Portraits in the panelled rooms of Bonnie Prince Charlie and Mary Queen of Scots attest the family's historic support of the Stuarts, although the Leighs were not a Catholic family. I have mentioned elsewhere Eliza's support of the Stuarts demonstrated by her support for Mary Queen of Scots in *Jane Austen's The History of England* and references to her Catholic leanings in her letters.

Mr Rushworth's estate of Sotherton is also similar to Stoneleigh in that the Sotherton grounds are being "improved". In the case of Stoneleigh the grounds were improved by the famous landscape gardener Humphrey Repton, whose book of plans is on show in the house. His ambitious plans included diverting the River Avon to create the illusion of a lake next to the house. Mr Rushworth was also planning to use Repton to improve his estate, as Repton had successfully improved the estate of his friend, Smith. In Chapter 6 he says "Smith's place is the admiration of all the country; and it was a mere nothing before Repton took it in hand. I think I shall have Repton."

There has been dispute as to where *Jane Austen* found the names for her characters but it is believed by those at Stoneleigh that the majority of *Jane Austen's* names come from her Leigh relations; for instance, Wentworth, Woodhouse, Darcy, Fitzwilliam, Brandon, Middleton, Willoughby, Ferrers, Watson.

The most striking resemblance of a character in *Jane Austen's* works to the Leighs is in the plot of *Persuasion*. The widowed Mrs Robert Lord, who at one time owned Stoneleigh, did not wish her daughter, Elizabeth, to marry her poor lover, Lieutenant Wentworth, but they married in secret. Soon afterwards Lieutenant Wentworth went off to France to fight in the army. In the meantime Elizabeth refused all the suitors put forward by her mother. However, when Lieutenant Wentworth later returned from France as a wealthy Lieutenant General, both he and Elizabeth were forgiven by Mrs Lord. This story, combined with a visit by Eliza to Bath and Lyme Regis in 1804, no doubt formed the basis for the characters and plot of *Jane Austen's Persuasion*. Since from the style and geographical background of the novel it appears that *Persuasion* was written about 1804, this would have been too early for Jane Austen to have learned this story from her Leigh relations at Stoneleigh, and therefore she cannot have been the author of *Persuasion*.

25.

A Digression - On Which Town was "Lambton" Based in "Pride and Prejudice"

I will here describe an interesting diversion which I stumbled upon in the research for this book, which should be of interest to all *Jane Austen* scholars and especially lovers of *Pride and Prejudice*. Although this chapter is not strictly relevant to the theme of my book, I thought it would be interesting as an example of the poor quality of much previous research on *Jane Austen*. It shows how mistakes and erroneous facts have been copied from one writer on *Jane Austen* to another, and new writers have done little to correct this through original research. It also shows how writers have not read *Pride and Prejudice* itself properly, otherwise they would not have made such errors.

In *Pride and Prejudice* Elizabeth Bennet is on a tour of Derbyshire in the north of England with her aunt and uncle, Mr and Mrs Gardiner. After seeing the main attractions of Derbyshire they decide to visit a town in the county where Mrs Gardiner had spent many years in her youth, and where she still has friends. This town is called "Lambton" in the book but no town of such a name exists in Derbyshire. In *Pride and Prejudice* the town is described as being five miles from Pemberley, Mr Darcy's house in Derbyshire.

Many biographers of Jane Austen agree that Pemberley was based on Chatsworth House in Derbyshire, the home of the Duke and Duchess of Devonshire, a magnificent stately home which of course still exists and is visited by many thousands each year. I believe that the mother of the present owner, the Dowager Duchess of Devonshire, is of the opinion that Pemberley as described in the book was based on Chatsworth at the time. In locating Lambton I am agreeing with her conclusion.

Traditionally Lambton has been identified as the town of Bakewell, now a lovely picturesque old town on the River Wye near to Chatsworth House. This is reiterated in local tourist information in Bakewell. At the time of the novel Bakewell was, however, a town at the forefront of the Industrial Revolution; Richard Arkwright, the early industrialist who came from Preston in Lancashire and who had invented the water frame, built one of the earliest cotton spinning mills in Bakewell in 1777. It was therefore at this time a busy industrial town and not a "small market town" as Lambton is described in the novel. However, Bakewell is now much quieter and is most famous in Derbyshire for its Original Bakewell Puddings and throughout the world for that culinary parvenu, the Bakewell Tart. One inn there, the Rutland Arms Hotel, used to make the extraordinary claim that Jane Austen stayed there in 1811, even identifying the room in which she slept; according to them it was the one on the first floor looking out over Rutland Square and Matlock Street. I do not know if this claim is still made, however.

Bakewell, however, cannot be Lambton. One of the main reasons for this is that Bakewell is only two miles from Chatsworth, whereas Lambton is described as being five miles from Pemberley. The identification of Bakewell as Lambton, however, was probably based on a misreading of the book. In the novel Mr Gardiner, while staying at Bakewell, plans the route to Lambton that he, his wife and Eliza Bennet will take the next day. It is decided (once Elizabeth Bennet has had confirmation from the staff at the inn that Mr Darcy is not at Pemberley) that they will visit Pemberley en route to Lambton. They set off from Bakewell to Lambton and on the way Elizabeth and Mr and Mrs Gardiner visit Pemberley. However, Mr Darcy arrives at Pemberley unexpectedly, where he meets Elizabeth. She explains to him "that his arrival had been very unexpected – 'for your housekeeper', she added, 'informed us that you would certainly not be here till tomorrow; and indeed, **before we left Bakewell,** [my highlighting] we understood that you were not immediately expected in the country.'"

This reference to Bakewell has been taken to be a mistake by *Jane Austen*, where she forgot to write "Lambton" instead. However, this is incorrect. The author is generally meticulously accurate in her descriptions of place. Elizabeth and Mr and Mrs Gardiner left Bakewell that morning and were intending to travel to Lambton. They had decided to make a short detour from their route in order to visit Pemberley, which Mr Gardiner describes as being "not in their direct road; nor more than a mile or two out of it." In this respect it corresponds to a visit to Chatsworth if they are heading eastwards from Bakewell in the direction of Chesterfield, which also requires a diversion of one or two miles. After leaving Pemberley/Chatsworth, they fairly soon arrive at Lambton, which suggests the road to Lambton is a well maintained one, probably a turnpike road, which was a road which charged tolls for its upkeep. We can be completely sure that Lambton is not Bakewell, however. This is because when Mrs Gardiner arrives at Lambton the book makes it clear that it is the first time that she is arriving there; she is not returning to Bakewell, which she left the same morning:

> "Mrs Gardiner was surprised and concerned; but as they were now approaching the scene of her former pleasures, every idea gave way to the charm of recollection; and she was too much engaged in pointing out to her husband all the interesting spots in its environs, to think of anything else. Fatigued as she had been by the morning's walk, they had no sooner dined than she set off again in quest of her former acquaintance, and the evening was spent in the satisfactions of an intercourse renewed after many years discontinuance."

If Bakewell is not Lambton, is there another candidate? If one examines the map for a likely town for Lambton to be based upon, there is one obvious candidate, which is the present day Old Brampton, known at that time simply as Brampton. Not only are the names extremely similar, but Old Brampton is five miles from Chatsworth, just as Lambton is five miles from Pemberley. Old Brampton has a beautiful mediaeval church and it had numerous inns at the time of *Jane Austen* for travellers on the road between Chesterfield and the Peak District of Derbyshire. At present there is an inn there called "The George and Dragon" opposite the church. In *Jane Austen's* time Brampton lay to the east of Chatsworth along the main turnpike road from Baslow to Chesterfield, which was built in 1759. There is a fine description of this turnpike road on the website "GENUKI: Baslow, Derbyshire – Golden Gates for the Duke, or Baslow in the 1820s".

"The first Turnpike connecting Baslow to Chesterfield, built in 1759, passed up through The Park [Chatsworth Park], crossed the Heathy Lea Brook just before reaching Robin Hood and continuing to Wigley and Old Brampton.

The eastern part of the Turnpike over the moors – the old road – must have become inadequate for the traffic which would have included heavy industrial goods. In 1812 a diversion was built starting from the bridge below the Robin Hood. It continued for a kilometre on the south bank of the Heathy Lea Brook, often at stream level, up the narrow steep sided valley until it reached open moorland at the junction of the Umberly and Blackleach Brooks. It then followed a new route (the present A619), across the moors to Wadshelf and Chesterfield."

Elizabeth and Mr and Mrs Bennet would have followed the route of the 1759 turnpike, leaving Chatsworth Park on the route described above. Continuing along this turnpike road would have led them gradually uphill and then along a long ridge to the small town of Brampton, the model for the small market town of Lambton. Since the turnpike was a toll road and well maintained, it would have been possible, as outlined in the book, for Mr Darcy and his sister to visit the town after breakfast the day after Eliza's visit to Pemberley. Average speeds on good roads at this time were seven miles an hour, and so Brampton would probably have not been more than an hour or two away by carriage from Chatsworth. Assuming this corresponds with Lambton and Pemberley in *Pride and Prejudice*, it would have taken only a short time for Mr and Mrs Gardiner to visit Pemberley again, as they do in *Pride and Prejudice*.

For those who wish to look at this in more detail, I recommend them to study the Ordnance Survey OS Explorer Map 0L24. The route of the turnpike road follows the present A619 from Baslow to Chesterfield, takes the B6050 to the left at Robin Hood Farm and takes a right turning from the B6050 at Cornerstone Farm. The road then proceeds straight to Old Brampton, passing through the village of Wigley. I can assure you that this is a very beautiful route to take, with views from the ridge and avoiding the modern main road to Chesterfield which passes through the bleak moors below.

Deirdre Le Faye is more astute than most writers on *Jane Austen*, however, as she states that Lambton is based on a village near Bakewell, not Bakewell itself. She suggests as the model for Lambton a village near Tideswell, which is a lovely old stone village, still well preserved, to the west of Bakewell, with an enormous church known as "The Cathedral of the Peak". However, Tideswell and nearby villages are further than five miles from Chatsworth and would have taken longer to reach than it took to travel from Pemberley to Lambton in *Pride and Prejudice*. Tideswell and any surrounding villages are also in the wrong direction if Mr and Mrs Gardiner wished to end their tour of Derbyshire here before returning to London. It would have been logical for them to end their tour in Brampton, as this is on their way east to Chesterfield, where they would have regained the main road to London. In *Pride and Prejudice* it is made clear that Mr and Mrs Gardiner and Eliza

Bennet only visit Lambton after completing their tour of Derbyshire. They would have left this visit till last only if Lambton was on the route of their return journey. The author writes:

"To the little town of Lambton, the scene of Mrs. Gardiner's former residence, and where she had lately learned some acquaintance still remained, they bent their steps, after having seen all the principal wonders of the country."

One curious fact about the town of Old Brampton is that a large number of its inhabitants had the surname "Hancock" (fifty-nine deaths are recorded for people of this surname, the largest of any surname). This could indicate some family connection to Eliza's father although, as the surname is very common, this is not necessarily the case. Perhaps Eliza just noticed the beauty of the town as she passed through it herself on her journey to the north. She would also have noted its close proximity to Chatsworth and how Eliza Bennet could conveniently stay here while visiting Darcy. Another curious fact is that a town named Brampton is mentioned in *Jane Austen's Catharine, or the Bower*, although this was written before 1794.

The identification of Lambton with Old Brampton suggests that the author of *Pride and Prejudice* had visited the area herself and had personal knowledge of it, and had probably passed through Bakewell and Brampton herself. As Old Brampton is such a small town, it is unlikely that the author would have based a town in the book on it, unless she had visited it herself. The author also unconsciously shows an especial love of the incomparable county of Derbyshire, the beauty of which could only have been appreciated by someone who had visited it. She, like Mr and Mrs Gardiner and Elizabeth, probably visited Dovedale, Matlock, and possibly Buxton and the Castleton area. The author seems to have been acquainted anyway with the reputation of the town of Castleton, the only area in the world that contains the beautiful yellow and blue fluorspar crystals known as "Blue John", which were used to make jewellery and ornamental vases. She refers to these crystals as "petrified spars":

> "With the mention of Derbyshire, there were many ideas connected. It was impossible for her to see the word without thinking of Pemberley and its owner. 'But surely', said she, 'I may enter his county with impunity, and rob it of a few petrified spars without his perceiving me.'"

Eliza would probably have known about this also from the shops in Matlock and Bakewell which sold such minerals.

It seems most unlikely that Jane Austen visited Derbyshire herself, given her restricted financial situation. Most biographers of Jane Austen agree that she never went so far north. Deirdre Le Faye confidently affirms that she never travelled further north than Staffordshire. However, it is extremely likely that Eliza visited Derbyshire in 1794, as she would have passed through it on her way to visit her close friend, Catherine Egerton, and her husband, Reverend Charles Egerton, who lived in Washington, County Durham. Washington is a town just south of Newcastle upon Tyne in the far north east of England; it is Newcastle to which Wickham and Lydia move at the end of *Pride and Prejudice*. What is more, Eliza probably followed the same route through Derbyshire as Eliza Bennet does in *Pride and Prejudice*. My wife has drawn a map to illustrate this route.

Eliza's route from London to Washington would have begun in the same way as Eliza Bennet's in *Pride and Prejudice*: "Oxford, Blenheim, Warwick, Kenilworth, Birmingham, etc." From Birmingham she would likely have made her way via Lichfield to Ashbourne in Derbyshire, near to which she would have viewed the famous tourist spot of Dovedale, which is a picturesque river valley. A likely route would then have been to travel to the popular spa town of Matlock and thence to Chatsworth, which, like Pemberley, could be viewed by well-bred members of the general public. If she did this, she would probably have stayed overnight at an inn at Bakewell first, as Eliza Bennet does (in *Pride and Prejudice* Elizabeth Bennet seems to have taken the same route; she discusses with Mr Darcy when she meets him unexpectedly at Pemberley how she has visited Dovedale and Matlock. On her road to Pemberley, Eliza Bennet would have travelled from Ashbourne and Dovedale to Matlock and then to Bakewell, visiting Pemberley and from there to Lambton). To proceed further on her journey north to Washington after visiting Chatsworth, Eliza would have taken the turnpike road mentioned above from Chatsworth to Chesterfield, passing through Brampton on the way. She would no doubt have at least stopped at Brampton for rest and refreshment, as it was the largest town on the turnpike road between Chatsworth and Chesterfield. Eliza Bennet would also have taken the same route from Pemberley to Lambton. When Eliza Bennet and her uncle and aunt had to return unexpectedly to London, they would have continued eastwards along this road to swiftly regain the main road to London at Chesterfield.

If Eliza de Feuillide had taken this route through Derbyshire, it would have only been a short diversion from her direct route northwards, which otherwise would have been a direct route from Ashbourne to Chesterfield, which would have been far less interesting. It is quite likely therefore that Eliza would have taken this diversion, as it would have been early summer when she was travelling and she was not under any time constraint. We also know from one of her previous letters that Eliza had visited the stately home of Blenheim near Oxford, and it is highly likely therefore that she would have been curious to visit its even more magnificent counterpart in the north of England, Chatsworth House. This short diversion would also have taken in the two other main tourist attractions of Derbyshire at this time, Dovedale and Matlock (for those unacquainted with Derbyshire, Dovedale is the beautiful valley of the River Dove and Matlock was a spa town also famous for its spectacular cliffs). The sights of Dovedale and Matlock were at this time a major tourist attraction. Their wild cliffs offered a view of the picturesque which could no longer be easily obtained by travelling on the continent, due to the restrictions on travel caused by the Revolution in France.

It seems that Eliza Bennet, while in the Peak District, may also have visited other areas, as the author informs us that she and Mr and Mrs Gardiner made their way to Lambton after seeing the principal wonders of the county of Derbyshire. These "seven wonders" had been listed by Charles Cotton in his book, *The Wonders of the Peak*, of 1681. They were as follows: Peak Cavern at Castleton (also known less politely as "The Devil's Arse"); the "shivering" hill of Mam Tor near Castleton; Poole's Cavern and the hot spring of St Anne's Well in Buxton; Eldon Hole; the Ebbing and Flowing Well; and, finally, Chatsworth House, also known as "The Palace of the Peak". It is likely, therefore, that she and Mr and Mrs Gardiner travelled to Buxton and Castleton from Bakewell to see these wonders and then returned to Bakewell, which is when we pick up the story again.

Eliza de Feuillide may also have visited these wonders if she had time, or she may have just stopped in Bakewell and visited Chatsworth the next day. In addition to viewing these picturesque areas of Derbyshire, Eliza would have passed through an area which was at that time at the cutting edge of the Industrial Revolution. Her route would have taken her through Cromford, where Richard Arkwright built his first cotton spinning mill in 1771, and through Matlock and Bakewell, where two further mills were in operation. Thus Eliza would have been well informed about the Industrial Revolution then going on in England. This contradicts what others have written about the author *Jane Austen*, that because she was based in the south of England she was unaware of the changes being brought about in the north of England by the Industrial Revolution. This shows that the author made a conscious decision in her books not to write directly about this aspect of life. However, there are hints as to the industrial north, which is the unspoken source of wealth of both Mr Bingley and Mr Darcy in *Pride and Prejudice*.

In her letter to Warren Hastings dated 19th September 1794 written from Washington, County Durham, Eliza states that she arrived there at the house of her friend Catherine Egerton in July 1794. The letter also relates how Eliza had agreed to stay there till after Christmas. Therefore it is likely that Eliza returned to London early in 1795. This fits in very well with the time that Eliza began to write the first version of *Pride and Prejudice*, which was first written under the title of *First Impressions*. Deirdre Le Faye, in *Jane Austen: The World of her Novels* writes that this was "written between October 1796 and August 1797. The action covers fifteen months, from the autumn of one year to the Christmas of the next; she probably envisaged it as happening in 1794-5."

The time of the action of 1794-5 would coincide exactly with Eliza's visit to Derbyshire at this time. But this is not the most important thing. I believe that this gives us a clue as to where the idea for *Pride and Prejudice* was conceived. I believe that the novel must have been inspired by Eliza's visit to Chatsworth. Her impressions of Chatsworth would have been fresh in her mind and inspired the idea of a love affair of an ordinary woman like herself with one of the greatest personages of the land. We know from her own letters that Eliza may have been considering looking for a more wealthy husband than Henry Austen. In a letter of 3rd July 1797 to her cousin Phylly she made enquiries to her about a certain George Courthope, writing "I want to know something about his fortune." Those who affirm that Jane Austen was the author, on the other hand, are not able to say where her inspiration for *Pride and Prejudice* came from, other than from the author's vivid imagination.

This was also a time of great happiness for Eliza, which is reflected in the brightness and optimism of *Pride and Prejudice*. The cause of her happiness was not a conventional one; in March 1794 she had learned that her husband, the Comte de Feuillide, had been sentenced to death by guillotine in Paris. He had been executed on

22nd February 1794. This took from Eliza the great burden of her marriage of convenience to the Comte de Feuillide and gave her the unexpected opportunity to marry for love. As she wrote in her letters, she had not lost a husband but regained her liberty. Her courtship of her cousin, Henry Austen, took place during this period, culminating in their marriage on 31st December 1797. *First Impressions*, the first version of *Pride and Prejudice*, was completed by 1st November 1797, when it was unsuccessfully offered to the London publisher Thomas Cadell, who had earlier published *Fanny Burney's Cecilia* and *Camilla*.

One interesting conclusion that can be drawn from what I have written above is that Chatsworth House was without a doubt the model for Pemberley, Mr Darcy's house in *Pride and Prejudice*, as has often been suggested. It has often been remarked how the description of Pemberley in *Pride and Prejudice* accords with how Chatsworth House appears in a painting at Chatsworth of 1770 by William Marlow of the west view of Chatsworth House, which shows the house as it would have been at the time of *Jane Austen*, before its later enlargement. The approach to Pemberley in *Pride and Prejudice* is described as follows:

"They gradually ascended for half a mile, and then found themselves at the top of a considerable eminence, where the wood ceased, and the eye was instantly caught by Pemberley House, situated on the opposite side of a valley, into which the road with some abruptness wound. It was a large, handsome, stone building, standing well on rising ground, and backed by a ridge of high woody hills; – and in front, a stream of some natural importance was swelled into greater, but without any artificial appearance. Its banks were neither formal nor falsely adorned. Elizabeth was delighted. She had never seen a place for which nature had done more, or where natural beauty had been so little counteracted by an awkward taste. They were all of them warm in their admiration; and at that moment she felt that to be mistress of Pemberley might be something!

They descended the hill, crossed the bridge, and drove to the door."

There are other correspondences too: on his arrival at Pemberley, Mr Darcy leads his horse to the stables, which are at the rear of the house, as are those at Chatsworth. The description of the walk in the grounds of Pemberley is also like Chatsworth. The river in front of the house, as at Chatsworth, is enlarged to accommodate an imposing bridge, and Elizabeth and her aunt and uncle walk from here down the river for about a mile before crossing it at its narrowest point by a simple bridge (at Chatsworth this is called the "One Arch Bridge"). Here, as at Chatsworth, the river continues through a copse and meander, but, as Mrs Gardiner is tired, they ignore this and walk back to the house, as one can at Chatsworth, along the opposite bank of the river. This detailed knowledge of Chatworth could only have been gained at first hand by Eliza; such factual detail could not have been known to Jane Austen, however imaginative she was or however many prints of old houses she looked at.

There is no doubt from where Eliza took the name of Lambton. There was at the time only one place in England of this name, the village of Lambton near Chester le Street, very close to Washington, County Durham (now known as "New Lambton"). As I have described above, Eliza travelled through Derbyshire in 1794 on her way to visit her friend, Catherine Egerton, at her house in Washington, County Durham (now in the county of Tyne & Wear). It cannot be coincidence that the author should use the name of this small village, close to Washington, where Eliza was staying at the exact time period (1794-5) on which *Pride and Prejudice* was based. The village was named after the Lambton family, large landowners who had lived for centuries at Lambton Hall nearby, and who later became Earls of Durham (the Sixth Earl of Durham, Antony

Lambton, became briefly well known under the name of Lord Lambton, the Conservative politician who resigned over a sex scandal in 1973). Lambton Hall was demolished in 1797 and a new building, known as Lambton Castle, was built for the family on the opposite side of the River Wear in the same year. Lambton Castle was designed by the architect Joseph Bonomi and his son Ignatius, and it is notable that the architect Bonomi is mentioned by *Jane Austen* in *Sense and Sensibility*. Lambton Castle was erected on the site of the existing Harraton Hall, which was the ancestral seat of the D'Arcy family. Perhaps this was where Eliza took the surname for the hero of *Pride and Prejudice*.

Basing the town in *Pride and Prejudice* on Brampton, Eliza was looking for a similar name for it to use in the novel and, as she was staying at the time very close to Lambton, this would have been an obvious choice of name for her (an alternative spelling for Lambton at this time was "Lampton").

Not far from the village of Lambton in County Durham was the famous Lambton Hall, the seat of the Lambton family, who became rich from the large deposits of coal under their land. This house was famous for the old County Durham folk tale of the Lambton Worm, a sort of giant snake that terrorised the North East in mediaeval times. The tale deals with John Lambton of Lambton Hall, who when young caught a small worm when he was fishing, which he threw into a well. He went on the crusades and when he returned it had grown into a giant reptile which was eating people and terrorising the area. He went to seek the advice of the local wise woman, who told him to fight the reptile wearing a suit of armour with spikes on it. But she said that, after killing it, he must kill the first living thing that emerged from the threshold of his house. Otherwise his descendants would not die in their beds. So he arranged with his steward for his dog to be let out to meet him after he returned from fighting the reptile. With his special suit of armour, he succeeded in killing the monster but when he returned home, in the excitement his father ran out of the house to meet him.

Unwilling to kill his father, he then asked for his dog to be let free and he killed the dog. But it was too late, and succeeding generations of Lambtons met untimely deaths.

Those who affirm that Jane Austen was the writer of *Pride and Prejudice* have no explanation as to where the author took the name "Lambton" from (unless it is their usual explanation, i.e. that Eliza de Feuillide told Jane Austen about it).

I have written the above independently and solely through my own research, as it was possible for me to research the matter at first hand after moving house from Surrey to an area near Derbyshire. However, since writing it, I have been highly gratified to discover an article which reaches the same conclusions independently and I believe completely supports my arguments. This article is *The Original of Pemberley* by Professor Donald Greene of the University of Southern California. I would recommend those who wish to find more detail on this matter to read the whole of this thoroughly researched article. Professor Greene is an astute scholar and agrees with me that Lambton is a very thinly disguised version of the real town of Brampton. He writes:

> "If Jane Austen didn't bother to disguise the name of Bakewell, she took little more pains to disguise the original of Lambton. Five miles east of what I shall argue is Pemberley, what do we find? The town of Brampton, now part of the urban sprawl of Chesterfield, but then a separate community".

However, not living in the area, it seems he has slightly misidentified 'Lambton' as the modern New Brampton, a suburb of Chesterfield, instead of Old Brampton, which is a separate village a few miles west of Chesterfield lying on the turnpike road which existed in 1794. In 1794 Old Brampton was known as just "Brampton". The *Cassini Historical Map Old Series* of 1837 to 1842 identifies the modern Old Brampton in large type as simply "Brampton", while New

282

Brampton is named as such and shown in very small type as a tiny suburb of Chesterfield. New Brampton only began to be called simply "Brampton" at a much later date, as it became a larger and a growing suburb. Old Brampton, like Lambton, is five miles from Chatsworth/Pemberley, whereas New Brampton is six or seven miles from it. Professor Greene's misidentification of New Brampton as Lambton in this article is slightly odd, since in an earlier article entitled *Pemberley Revisited* he correctly identifies Lambton as Old Brampton and as being five miles from Chatsworth.

Professor Greene is also adamant that Pemberley corresponds almost exactly with Chatsworth. He identifies the road that Eliza Bennet took from Bakewell through the villages of Rowsley and Beeley, entering Chatsworth Park at Beeley Lodge (named on the above historical map as Blue Moors Lodge); this lodge still stands next to the stone wall enclosing Chatsworth Park, and is, like the entrance to Pemberley in the novel, at one of the lowest points of the park. He shows in his article how the route of Eliza Bennet from this lodge to the house at Pemberley corresponds exactly with the route from Beeley Lodge to Chatsworth House, even supplying maps to show the corresponding points. The above historical map shows how the road climbing from the lodge was wooded at this time, and how, as in the novel, the trees ended once the road reached a high eminence from which Chatsworth House came into view.

He shows how the layout of the guided tour of Eliza Bennet and the Gardiners around Pemberley House corresponds exactly with Chatsworth House at the time. He also agrees with me that the walk Eliza Bennet and Mr and Mrs Gardiner take around the Pemberley estate corresponds in its details exactly to Chatsworth Park and shows this also on a detailed map. He notes how particular details correspond, for instance how the land near the simple bridge across the River Derwent that they cross on foot is "contracted into a glen" both in the book and in reality. The River Derwent at the time, like the river at Pemberley, was a fishing stream in which both trout and grayling could be caught. Like myself, Professor Greene dismisses the idea that the author could possibly have gained all of these details solely from looking at prints of the house, and is insistent that the author must have visited Chatsworth in real life. He writes:

> "Photographs of the views from various places on the route, or, better, following it on foot with a copy of *Pride and Prejudice* in one's hand, will reinforce the impression that Pemberley is Chatsworth. But even with no better aid than a map, the reader must be impressed by the number of correspondences in detail. At some time or other, one feels, Jane Austen must have visited Chatsworth herself; in those pre-photographic days, only her own sharp eyes could have carried away so much vivid and authentic detail. One argument against this thesis is that, if Pemberley is Chatsworth, Jane Austen could have obtained enough information for her description from an engraving in one of the many books about the great English country houses available in her time – Miss [Elizabeth] Jenkins reproduces one of Chatsworth in her report. It is true that such an engraving and its accompanying description could furnish the general appearance of the place – the situation overlooking a stream and the wooded hills behind it. But could it have furnished such precise details as the ascent of the road from the south during its first half-mile, the sudden view of the house across the stream when one emerges from the woods on the "considerable eminence", the steep descent of the road to the bridge, the view from a west-facing window of the house, the fact that the road from the stables would bring someone following it to the spot where a visitor emerges from the entrance hall of the house, the exact topography of the walks on both sides of the river? It seems unlikely."

Here he is somewhat at a loss, as he admits there is no evidence Jane Austen visited Chatsworth. In stating that the author definitely visited Chatsworth House, he is putting himself in opposition to nearly all other biographers of Jane Austen, who believe that she never travelled further north than Staffordshire. Desperately he seeks an explanation for this anomaly. The only time he can find Jane Austen anywhere near Derbyshire is when she, her mother and her sister visited Stoneleigh Abbey in Warwickshire in 1806, as previously mentioned. On 13th August 1806, they travelled from there to Hamstall Ridware in Staffordshire where they stayed for five weeks with Mrs Austen's nephew, Reverend Edward Cooper, just north of Lichfield. (Reverend Edward Cooper has been seen by some biographers as the model for Mr William Collins in *Pride and Prejudice*. It is likely that Eliza also stayed with Reverend Cooper on her way north in 1794, as her route would have passed through Lichfield, as mentioned above.) Professor Greene puts forward the idea that there could have been a trip by Jane Austen, her sister and her mother from Hamstall Ridware to visit Chatsworth, which was thirty-five miles away.

However, I believe it would be very unlikely that such a long trip would have been undertaken at their relatives' expense during such a short stay. There is also the problem of chronology. The original version of *Pride and Prejudice*, entitled *First Impressions*, was submitted to the publisher, Cadell, in November 1797, long before 1806. As the estate of Pemberley is so central to the novel, it is highly likely that Pemberley was described in *First Impressions*. The central plot of *First Impressions* and *Pride and Prejudice*, as I have written previously, can only have come to the author after visiting Chatsworth, as it concerns the love of an ordinary woman for one of the greatest personages in the land, whose estate is in Derbyshire. Since Jane Austen did not visit Chatsworth before 1797, if at all, therefore, it must be conceded that Jane Austen is not the author of *Pride and Prejudice*, and Eliza almost certainly is.

Professor Greene in his article also mentions objections to the identification of Chatsworth as Pemberley. After dealing with these, he is still strongly of the opinion that Pemberley is based on Chatsworth. One interesting argument of Elizabeth Jenkins that he deals with is that the income from Chatsworth was much more than the £10,000 a year that Pemberley provides. However, he shows that in the novel, when Mr Wickham describes Mr Darcy's income he calls it "a *clear* ten thousand a year", by which he means £10,000 after all expenses and mortgages have been paid on all the family's several large homes, therefore in reality a much larger sum.

Our digression on the subject of Lambton, which began as an interesting diversion to correct its erroneous identification with Bakewell, has changed its nature in the writing of it. Through logical argument, often a stranger to writers on *Jane Austen*, we have reached the conclusions after taking each logical step, that 1. Pemberley is almost certainly based on Chatsworth House and 2. Jane Austen was almost certainly not the author of *Pride and Prejudice* and Eliza de Feuillide almost certainly was.

While we are on the subject of the setting of *Pride and Prejudice*, I mentioned at the beginning of this book that it is also possible to identify the real house which was the model for "Longbourn", the home of Mr and Mrs Bennet and the heroine, Elizabeth Bennet, in the novel. This is in fact a subject which has been explored previously, though without success. While previous investigators have come to erroneous conclusions, their research on this matter has helped me to identify the house, which still stands.

Deirdre Le Faye, in *Jane Austen: the World of her Novels* writes that in the novel Longbourn lies one mile south of a small market town named Meryton and also close to another market town, which the author does not name. In the novel, Longbourn is both the name of the village and of the house belonging to the Bennet family. Ms Le Faye also correctly states that we learn in Chapter 46 of the novel that Longbourn is situated within ten miles of the Great North Road, which is now known as the A1000. We know this from the following extract from the first letter that Elizabeth Bennet receives from her sister, Jane, while she is in Lambton. In this letter, Jane is under the mistaken impression that Wickham and Lydia have eloped and travelled from London to Gretna Green in Scotland in order to get married:

> "They were off Saturday night about twelve, as is conjectured, but were not missed till yesterday morning at eight. The express was sent off directly. My dear Lizzy, they must have passed within ten miles of us."

Therefore, according to Ms Le Faye, if the towns of Meryton and the unnamed town lie to the west of this road, they are probably Hemel Hempstead and Watford; if they lie to the east, they are probably Hertford and Ware. Ms Le Faye then goes on to say that from further clues later in the book, it is possible to deduce that the towns lie to the east of the road and that therefore Meryton equates to Hertford and the unnamed town to Ware. The problem with this is that Ms Le Faye does not state whereabouts in the novel it is suggested that the towns lie to the east of the Great North Road, and to my knowledge nobody else has ever been able to locate any such clue in the novel.

In addition, Meryton is described in the novel as a "small market town" about a mile north of Longbourn. As mentioned previously, Lambton is described in the same way, and it is based on the real town of Brampton, which we would now describe as a small village. We must assume therefore that Meryton was the equivalent of what we would now call a small village. Therefore Hertford, a large county town (the town after which the county of Hertfordshire was named) cannot be Meryton. Written records confirm that in 1839 Hertford had a population of at least 5,000.

The other author who attempts to identify the original of Longbourn is Dr Kenneth Smith, Senior Lecturer in Criminology in the Faculty of Humanities and Social Sciences, Buckinghamshire Chilterns University College, in an article entitled *The Probable*

Location of "Longbourn" in Jane Austen's Pride and Prejudice, which can be viewed on the internet. His article is worth reading in full, but the salient conclusions he draws from reading the novel are as follows:

1. Meryton is "a small market town".

2. Sir William Lucas's house, Lucas Lodge, is "within a short walk of Longbourn".

3. Lucas Lodge is only "about a mile" from Meryton.

4. Therefore Meryton is about a mile from Longbourn.

5. Netherfield Park, the large house that Mr Bingley rents, is "only three miles" from Longbourn. When Elizabeth walks from Longbourn to Netherfield Park, Kitty and Lydia accompany her for the first mile into Meryton and then Elizabeth walks a further two miles across fields to Netherfield Park. Thus Netherfield Park is about two miles from Meryton.

6. Meryton must be to the north of Longbourn because when Lydia and Wickham travel to Longbourn from London they do not pass through Meryton.

7. Longbourn is "only twenty-four miles" from Gracechurch Street, the London street in which lies the home of Mr and Mrs Gardiner; the street is close to the present day Bank of England. I believe that at the time of the novel, such a measurement would refer to the length of the journey by road, rather than as the crow flies.

Dr Smith then goes on to identify the town of Harpenden in Hertfordshire as being Meryton. However, Harpenden is not one of the options mentioned by Ms Le Faye.

When searching for Longbourn, it is logical to search for a house in Hertfordshire with connections to Eliza de Feuillide, or at least to her family. As I mentioned at the beginning of my book, the principal connection of Eliza's family to Hertfordshire was through members of the Freeman family, who were maternal cousins who lived in Hertfordshire; Eliza's mother and father were always grateful for the generosity shown in particular by John Cope Freeman to Eliza's mother when she was young (it is possible she lived in his house at some point) and they remained lifelong friends. John Cope Freeman was also one of the godparents to Jane Austen's brother Charles at his public christening on 30th July 1779 at Steventon.

On his retirement in the 1770s Sir John Cope Freeman built for himself a fine house in Abbots Langley in Hertfordshire, which he named "Langley House". It still exists but has been converted into luxury flats and now bears the name of Breakspear Place; a photo of this beautiful house can be viewed on the internet. Sir John Cope Freeman later became County Sheriff of Hertfordshire but he was also the owner of a large slave plantation in Jamaica, no doubt the source of much of his wealth. Could Langley House then be the model for "Longbourn"? There are many indications that this is the case.

Firstly, there is the name. "Lang" is old English for "long" and so there is a striking similarity in the names of the houses.

Secondly, just as Longbourn is the name of both the house and the village, Langley House also bears the name of the village of Abbots Langley (Eliza always referred to Abbots Langley in her letters as merely 'Langley'). When you visit Abbots Langley, you can still imagine how it was in Eliza's time; the large Langley House and a few other beautiful old houses still cluster round the small church and village green.

Thirdly, when we look at its geographical situation, it seems to fit in perfectly with that of Longbourn. The unnamed town in the novel corresponds well with Watford, while Meryton seems to correspond with Kings Langley, which is a mile north west of Langley House and which, like Meryton, would have been the size of "a small market town".

Likewise, a two mile walk west across the fields from Kings Langley ("Meryton") would lead to the village of Chipperfield, corresponding geographically to Netherfield Park and sharing a similarity of names.

Fortunately we can identify the original of Netherfield Park. This is Chipperfield Manor, a Queen Anne house later updated during the time the novel was written. It has been owned by the actor and comedian Peter Sellers. It is a very large, long, low, red brick building with the windows of its attics bricked up. We can identify it as Netherfield Park, as it is the only house for miles around which was surrounded by its own large park at the time of the novel, as can be seen on eighteenth century maps of Hertfordshire. This large park was donated to the public during the nineteenth century by the then owner, Mr Blackwell of Crosse & Blackwell fame, and it is now known as Chipperfield Common. Plantings of many large foreign trees show how it was once part of the estate of the house.

The walk from the church in Meryton/Kings Langley to Netherfield Park/Chipperfield Manor still remains almost the same as it was in Eliza's day, and is a beautiful walk of two miles across several fields, just as described in the novel.

Andrew Davies, the screenwriter for the famous BBC production of *Pride and Prejudice*, seems to agree with me on the real location of Longbourn, as he gives the following speech to Mr Collins:

"I shall travel as far as the turnpike in my own modest equipage, where I hope to catch the Bromley Post at thirty-five minutes past ten, and thence to Watford, from whence I shall engage a hired carriage to Longbourn."

26.

The Character of Warren Hastings

Perhaps the most important man in Eliza's life was her natural father, Warren Hastings, who was born on 6th December 1732. Indeed it is difficult not to see a reflection of him, or an idealised version of him, in the heroes of *Fanny Burney* and *Jane Austen*. The relationship between Eliza and her natural father was to be a key element in her life. From the dedication to *Fanny Burney's Evelina* we can see that Eliza was attempting to live up to his reputation and the outstanding education he had provided her with. The poem of dedication to him at the beginning of *Evelina* also shows us that she was aware that Warren Hastings was her natural father, even at the age of sixteen.

Eliza herself seems to have almost worshipped Hastings. In her letter from France of 25th July 1785 to Philadelphia Walter she wrote "The Public News must long ere have acquainted You with Mr. Hastings' arrival in England, a circumstance which gives great Satisfaction to his Friends, that is to say a very extensive circle, for who that is neither blinded by interest nor biassed by Party can possibly refuse Esteem & Admiration to a Character too much the ornament of the present Age not to be consigned in the Records of succeeding ones". Opinions about him tend to be starkly at odds. To me the legend of Warren Hastings as a noble and incorruptible reformer hardly bears examination. Eliza's precise relationship with Warren Hastings is something of an enigma. At first it seems that he was unaware that Eliza was the author of the *Fanny Burney* and *Jane Austen* novels. However, on consideration, this seems to be an unrealistic view. Eliza kept in touch with Warren Hastings on his return to England and they visited each other on several occasions, and corresponded.

The author Sydney C Grier (the pen name of Hilda Caroline Gregg), in her *Letters of Warren Hastings to his Wife* of 1905 states that Warren Hastings was a huge admirer of the novels of *Fanny Burney*. Hastings was on the list of subscribers to *Fanny Burney's* third novel *Camilla* in 1796. Grier also mentions the well known letter of Jane Austen which refers to her pleasure at his admiration for the copy of *Pride and Prejudice* that had been sent to him by the Austens. Reading Grier's book, one can see recreated a picture of the society around Warren Hastings at the time. She mentions Warren Hastings meeting Lord Mansfield, who she describes as Hastings' old friend. Warren Hastings had met Lord Mansfield and later he corresponded with the law lord to ask his advice about implementing Hindoo and Muslim laws in Bengal.

Both Warren Hastings and Lord Mansfield were literary friends of Lady Sophia Burrell. Warren Hastings and Lady Sophia Burrrell wrote to each other and exchanged poems, while Lord Mansfield had been a poet praised by both Pope and Cowper, and Lord Mansfield was a friend of Lady Sophia Burrell also. Lady Sophia Burrell wrote poems dedicated to Hastings, Lord Mansfield and Eliza. Thus one can see that Eliza must have been a member of their literary circle. It would not have been difficult for Hastings to have kept her secret, a man whose whole life had been hidden behind a veil of secrecy. Considering Hastings' wide literary connections (he had also been a friend of Samuel Johnson) it is extraordinary that he, like Lady Sophia Burrell, did not include Fanny Burney in his literary circle and this tends to show that he knew she was not the real author and that he was aware of the true author's identity. When Warren Hastings and Eliza met, they would no doubt have talked much about life in India. It would have been from these conversations that Eliza would have gained the background knowledge of the life and literature in India which she demonstrates, as I shall show later, in *Elizabeth Hamilton's Translations of the Letters of a Hindoo Rajah*. It is unlikely that she could have remembered much of her life there as a little girl. Eliza satirises her own wide knowledge of life in India in *Sense and Sensibility* in the discussion about Colonel Brandon between Elinor, Marianne and Willoughby:

"'My protegé, as you call him, is a sensible man; and sense will always have attractions for me. Yes, Marianne, even in a man between thirty and forty. He has seen a great deal of the world; has been abroad; has read, and has a thinking mind. I have found him capable of giving me much information on various subjects, and he has always answered my inquiries with the readiness of good-breeding and good nature.'

'That is to say,' cried Marianne contemptuously, 'he has told you that in the East Indies the climate is hot, and the mosquitoes are troublesome.'

'He would have told me so, I doubt not, had I made any such inquiries, but they happened to be points on which I had been previously informed.'

'Perhaps,' said Willoughby, 'his observations may have extended to the existence of nabobs, gold mohrs, and palanquins.'"

[Nabobs were alternatively Indian princes or the English who got rich in India, gold mohrs were gold coins, and palanquins were a sort of Indian sedan chair]

Clive Caplan in his article *The source for Emma's William Larkins* identifies William Larkins, the bailiff of Mr Knightley in *Emma*, with the faithful William Larkins, the East India Company's accountant-general in Calcutta, who testified in Warren Hastings' defence at his trial for corruption in Parliament. There are other connections in the names of *Jane Austen's* novels with surnames of Hastings' acquaintances in India, such as Price, Palmer, Middleton and

Gardiner (Fanny Price is the heroine of *Mansfield Park*, Mr Palmer and Sir John Middleton are friends of the Dashwood family in *Sense and Sensibility* and Mr and Mrs Gardiner are Eliza Bennet's uncle and aunt in *Pride and Prejudice*). Sydney C Grier in *The Letters of Warren Hastings to his wife* writes that, "Captain Joseph Price was a very faithful and trouble-some adherent of Hastings. He appears first in the Correspondence as taking charge of his money matters on [Tysoe Saul] Hancock's death, although, like Hancock, he was generally in pecuniary difficulties himself." Hastings appointed Major William Palmer as his military secretary in 1776 and in 1784 as his special agent in Lucknow at the court of the Nawab of Oudh. Nathaniel Middleton was Hastings' Resident in Lucknow. A relative of Hastings, William Gardiner, was killed in the storming of Lahar, and Hastings paid for his son Billy to be educated at Westminster School in London.

27.

"Imhoff Indienfahrer" (Imhoff, Traveller in India)

A remarkable book has recently been published in Germany which gives us one of the best pictures of Warren Hastings. It is *Imhoff Indienfahrer, Ein Reisebericht aus dem 18. Jahrhundert in Briefen und Bildern* (*Imhoff, Traveller in India, a Travel Guide from the 18th century in letters and pictures*), a collection of excerpts from the journal of Christoph Adam Carl von Imhoff, edited and with an introduction by Gerhard Koch, Professor of English and German Philology at the Munich Fachhochschule. Imhoff was the common law husband of Anna Maria Apollonia Chapuset, who was later to become Warren Hastings' second wife, Marian. The journal is written in the form of letters. This book has only been published in German and I have not seen it mentioned in any previous biographies of *Jane Austen*. However, the journal of Imhoff throws a lot of light on society in England and India at the time of *Jane Austen*. It deserves to be translated into English.

Christoph Adam Carl von Imhoff was a very accomplished German miniaturist and portrait painter, and a soldier in the service of the Duke of Württemberg. Born on 7th October 1734 in Mörlach in Germany, he came to London in 1767 with his common law wife to try to make his fortune there as a painter. Imhoff discovered that the prices he could get for his paintings were much higher in London than in Germany, but unfortunately the cost of living in London was even higher. In his letters Imhoff describes London of the time vividly but, more importantly, he describes the economics of trying to make a living in such an expensive city. Remarkably, one of his first commissions was to paint Queen Charlotte, who comes across from his letters as a remarkably friendly and unconceited woman. The painting pleased the queen and was exhibited at the Society of Artists in London on 28th April 1768. By a strange quirk of fate, Imhoff and his wife became close friends with Mme Schwellenberg, Queen Charlotte's principal lady-in-waiting. She was the same lady who was the tyrant with whom Fanny Burney was forced to spend many hours in her position at court as Second Keeper of the Robes. Fanny Burney had said of Mme Schwellenberg that in her "Harshness, tyranny, dissension and even insult seemed personified". Perhaps because of their shared nationality, however, the Imhoffs got on very well with Mme Schwellenberg, although all the time Imhoff was in fear of it being discovered that his wife and himself were not legally married. This was a complication due to his position as an officer in the army of the Duke of Württemberg, which forbade officers to marry.

Later, on her return to England as Marian Hastings, the wife of Warren Hastings, the former Anna Maria Chapuset wrote in affectionate terms to Mme Schwellenberg on 29th September 1784, sympathising with her ill health. The letter's unconventional spelling shows that even by that time she had not lost her German accent. In October 1786, when Marian Hastings met the German novelist Sophie von la Roche, Marian Hastings said of Mme Schwellenberg:

"Ich werde nie vergessen, daß Miß Schwellenberg meine Wohlthäterin war, und mir bei meiner Abreise nach Ostindien Kleider und Weißzeug schenkte."

"I will never forget that Miss Schwellenberg was my benefactor and on my journey to India she sent me clothes and linen."

Since he could no longer afford to live in London, through various contacts, including Miss Schwellenberg and William James of the East India Company, and in spite of his nationality, Imhoff managed to secure a position as a cadet with the army of the East India Company. No doubt his military experience helped. He, his wife and his infant son Carl set sail for India in 1769 on the same ship (the *Duke of Grafton*) as Warren Hastings, who was returning to India on the instructions of the East India Company. Warren Hastings had been appointed one of the members of their Council in Madras and Deputy Governor of Fort St George in Madras. On the way to India, a relationship developed between Imhoff's "wife" Anna Maria Chapuset and Warren Hastings, while Warren Hastings remained friends with Imhoff.

This is curiously similar to Hastings' earlier relationship with Eliza's mother while remaining on good terms with her husband, Tysoe Hancock. It seems Hastings was a rather heartless and ruthless man, who destroyed the happiness of two loving husbands, and behaved coldly by denying his natural daughter, Eliza, even after her death. Hastings' "civilised" behaviour and continuing friendship towards both Hancock and Imhoff after stealing their wives is seen as a sign of his good character by many biographers. However, to myself it shows an extreme cold-heartedness which was later borne out by his refusal to acknowledge Eliza as his daughter, while still meeting and corresponding with her in a "civilised" manner. Perhaps some anger or recrimination towards his former friends or daughter would indicate a more human personality. It has often been remarked on how even Hastings' letters to his wife Marian seem formal and stiff.

Any claims of lack of corruption by Warren Hastings are laughable. Imhoff describes the huge sums that the Governor General was able to return home with on his final return from India. In fact Imhoff says that Hastings returned home with only £80,000. However, given Hastings' expenditure on his return, e.g. his purchase of the large mansion of Beaumont Lodge in Old Windsor, Berkshire and his later purchase and renovation of his family estate at Daylesford in Gloucestershire, and the massive legal fees he spent on his trial, it seems this was only the sum he declared which was taxed. That a huge amount was spent by Hastings on his newly bought back family estate at Daylesford is shown by Eliza's letter to Phylly Walter of 4th August 1797:

"They [Mr and Mrs Hastings] have got a place called Daylesford, which is one of the most beautiful I ever saw I will not wrong it by endeavoring to give a description of it and it shall therefore suffice to say that the Park and Grounds are really a little Paradise, and that the House is fitted up with a degree of Taste & Magnificence seldom to be met with –"

The normal way to avoid tax, Imhoff says, was to bring back the rest of the money in the form of diamonds. This method was indeed used by Tysoe Saul Hancock. One has only to view the magnificent porcelain service belonging to Hastings, half of which was exhibited until recently at Chatsworth House in Derbyshire, to see how immensely wealthy he had made himself. In addition to bearing the legal costs of his trial in Parliament of more than £70,000 he also built himself a grand house at his old family estate in Daylesford, which he had repurchased at twice its real value. The new house was built by the architect Samuel Pepys Cockerell. A truer figure of the amount of money Hastings returned to England with was probably the £500,000 quoted by the Franckfurter Staats-Ristretto of the time, even though this paper was something of a scandal sheet and not terrifically reliable. The same paper reported on 14th April 1788 his wife Mrs Hastings causing unpopularity by wearing a dress with jewels on it worth £40,000 which would have been too expensive for even Queen Charlotte to afford. Mrs Hastings indeed caused a lot of controversy by the expense of the clothes she wore, which did not help Hastings in his endeavours to counter claims of corruption in India.

We know that Warren Hastings was in fact extremely secretive about his financial affairs, and especially about the original source of his wealth. In *Echoes from Belvedere: Home of National Library, Kolkata* P. Thankappan Nair investigated Hastings's acquisition of the Belvedere estate in Alipore near Calcutta, and concluded that he had solved this mystery. He writes, "We are tempted to assert that Warren Hastings got the undivided Belvedere Estate from Mir Jafar as a free gift and was in actual possession of the Belvedere Mansion since 1763." He also writes "Hastings' own assertion that he 'purchased the house occupied by his predecessors Mr Verelst and Mr Cartier, called Belvidere, for the sum of 60,000 Sicca Rupees, and is in actual possession of it' is open to question." The house had in fact been owned by Hastings since 1763 and was merely let out by him after this date to Mr Verelst and Mr Cartier. To hide how he acquired the Belvedere Estate, Hastings then pretended to purchase it from his tenants, Mr Verelst and Mr Cartier.

It seems that the initial source of Hastings' wealth was his support for the Nawab Mir Jafar Ali Khan, who had been deposed from the Musnud of Moorshebad by the British Governer, Henry Vansittart, in 1760 and whose reinstatement to the throne as Nawab Nazim of Bengal was aided by Hastings, who was then a member of the governing Supreme Council of the East India Company. The Nawab had come to live in Alipore, a suburb of Calcutta, after his deposition and he made a free gift of the major part of his property in Alipore to Hastings. He did this in return for Hastings' support in his restoration. This was considered even at the time as a corrupt practice. As evidence of this, the Bengal Obituary of 1848, in its eulogy of Warren Hastings, states "While his colleagues were making large fortunes by pulling down one Nabob and setting up another, he was never suspected of having received any thing." The fact that Warren Hastings later used subterfuge to suggest that he had himself purchased his estate at Alipore, when it already belonged to him, shows that he knew he was involved in a corrupt practice. It confirmed Warren Hastings to be somebody who liked to keep his financial and personal dealings hidden from the outside world.

On arrival in Madras on 2nd September 1769 the Imhoffs lived together with Warren Hastings. Here Mr Imhoff was able to paint some portraits of the residents and at least one of the Indian princes, or "Nabobs", from whom he received £400 and a ring worth £80. Although not one of the top miniature painters of the time, the quality of his work was very good. After painting many of the residents of Madras, Imhoff then wished to proceed to Calcutta, which he described as the richest and pleasantest place in India, where he would be able to paint the portraits of the residents and several of the Indian princes. He writes in his journal that he expected to make much more money from his paintings in Calcutta than in Madras.

Ironically, in September 1770 Warren Hastings wrote from Madras to Eliza's father, Tysoe Saul Hancock, who was in Calcutta, further north up the coast, to facilitate the removal of Imhoff from Madras to Calcutta, while Imhoff's wife was to stay behind in Madras with Hastings:

> "In my last I desired you to take the trouble to enquire for a lodging for Mr Imhoff, who proposes to try his fortune as a miniature painter in Bengal. Mr Imhoff is a shipmate of mine, an officer of some rank in the German service, sent hither with great expectations as a cadet with a family, and must have starved had he not, happily, been qualified to seek a livelihood in a more profitable employment. He has had some success here, having taken off the heads of half the settlement, but he must soon be aground."

Imhoff found a ship to take him to Calcutta and arrived there by himself on 1st November 1770. His wife remained in Madras, living with Warren Hastings, on the rather spurious grounds that it was too unhealthy for her in Calcutta. It was ironic that Imhoff stayed on his arrival in Calcutta with Hancock, when both of them had lost their wives to Hastings. Hancock did not seem to be very enamoured of Imhoff, who he described as "truely a German". Imhoff arrived in Calcutta, however, at a terrible time in the history of Bengal, in the middle of the terrible famine of 1770. It was estimated at the time that one and a half million Indians died of starvation due to crop failure in the rice, which was their staple food. Imhoff describes in his journal terrible scenes of Hindus calmly lying down in the street and resigning themselves to their fate, and of thousands of bodies lying there being eaten by dogs and vultures. He says that a few of the English had tried to help the natives, including Dr Hancock, who distributed £5 to £10 daily to the poor, but Hancock was forced to stop after his house became besieged.

In April or May 1771, Imhoff was ill for several days, but recovered after he was treated by Dr Hancock; presumably he had been suffering from malaria. It may have been this illness which led ultimately to his ill health and premature death after his return to Germany. Imhoff travelled up the Ganges river after this to Mootigil, in order to find more comfortable weather during Calcutta's wet season. On his return to Calcutta in October 1771 he learned that Hastings was to become Governor in Madras the next year and had hopes of becoming Governor of Bengal in Calcutta. Imhoff described the Calcutta post as an astounding position where one could easily earn £100,000 in only two or three years. It was confirmed on 1st November 1771 that Hastings had been made Governor of Bengal. Hastings was in fact to be Governor of Bengal from 1771 to 1785. Assuming Imhoff to be correct, we can estimate that as Governor of Bengal during this period Hastings earned for himself a fortune of between £500,000 and £700,000 in addition to the property he already possessed.

In December 1771 Imhoff's wife, who had been staying in Madras with Warren Hastings, arrived in Calcutta from Madras with their son on the ironically named *Success Galley* after a dangerous sea journey in which she had almost lost her life. On 13th February 1772 Imhoff and Hancock both went to meet Hastings himself on his arrival in Calcutta. On 19th April 1772 Tysoe Hancock wrote to Eliza's mother:

"In a former Letter I promised to give You some Account of Mr. Hastings;… There is a Lady by name Mrs. Imhoff who is his principal favorite among the Ladies. She came to India on Board the same Ship with Mr. Hastings, is the Wife of a Gentleman who has been an Officer in the German Service & came out a Cadet to Madras, finding it impossible to maintain his family by the Sword and having a turn to Miniature painting. He quitted the sword and betook himself to the latter profession. After having painted all who chose to be painted at Madras, He came to Bengal the latter end of the Year 1770, she remained at Madras and lived in Mr. Hastings's House at the Mount chiefly I believe. She is about twenty six Years old has a good person & has been very Pretty, is sensible, lively and wants only to be a greater Misstress of the English Language to prove she has a great share of Wit. She came to Calcutta last October. They do not make a part of Mr. Hastings's Family, but are often of his private Parties. The Husband is truely a German. I should not have mentioned Mr. Imhoff but I know every thing relative to Mr. Hastings is greatly Interesting to You."

No doubt Mr Hancock relished the opportunity of underlining to Eliza's mother that she had been supplanted as the favourite of Hastings. Meanwhile, the directors of the East India Company had caught up with Imhoff, who they accused of coming to India under false pretences and not to take up his commission as an officer in the army. On 25th March 1772 the directorate of the East India Compay in London wrote to the Presidency in Madras:

"The reasons assigned by Messrs Scott, Imhoff & Dupuy

for declining to accept Commissions sufficiently prove that they have been guilty of an artful & deliberate design to impose upon the Company. And although their application was prior to your receipt of our orders of 23rd March 1770 to send home such Cadets as should not conform to a military life, yet our sense of the conduct of such persons was too fully expressed for you to be justified in permitting them to remain in India. – It was reasonable to suppose you would immediately inform Messrs. Scott, Imhoff, and Dupuy of our pleasure respecting Cadets, after you had received our Commands, & if they had then hesitated to fulfil their engagements to the Company you ought to have sent them home forthwith – and as we are determined totally to discountenance and prevent this practice we do hereby direct that if Messrs. Scott, Imhoff, and Dupuy do still refuse to serve in the Military that you send them home by the first Ship which may sail from your Presidency for Europe & if Mr. Imhoff should have proceeded to Bengal you are to send a copy of this our order to the Governor and Council of that Presidency who are in such case to conform to our Commands above signified."

On 15th January 1773, Imhoff wrote to the Directorate of the East India Company that he had resolved not to take up his commission in the East India Company Army and he requested a ship back to England. It would seem that he had made as much money as he could in India from his portrait painting. He hoped to return to India later, however, and was travelling to England to get permission from the East India Company for this. He wanted to return to India, where he hoped to take up a position in the service of one of the Indian princes, the fourteen-year-old Mubarak-ud-daula. The young Indian prince had been extremely pleased with the portrait Imhoff had painted of him, and had offered Imhoff a position in his service in Kasimbazar. Mubarak-ud-daula had become Nawab of Bengal, Bihar and Orissa in 1765 on the death of Mir Jafar, the prince I have mentioned previously who had been restored to his throne by Warren Hastings. It is possible that Warren Hastings himself, as Governor General of Bengal, may have had the power to grant to Imhoff permission to remain in India, but pretended he did not in order to make sure that Imhoff left India without his "wife". In this regard Tysoe Saul Hancock wrote again ironically to his wife Philadelphia, Eliza's mother, on 27th February 1773, from Calcutta:

"Mr. Imhoff is going to England. I shall give Him a Letter of Introduction to you: his Lady stays here, As – He intends returning in the Service."

Mr Hancock wrote again to her on 2nd March 1773:

"Dear Phila,
This will be delivered to you by Mr Imhoff whose son I recommended to your care. I mentioned this Gentleman to you in former Letters, it is very needless to say more, than to request you will receive Him as an Acquaintance."

On 5th March 1773 Imhoff returned to England aboard the *Marquis of Rockingham* without his wife, but accompanied by three native servants, a chameleon and a few small mammals. We do not know the fate of this menagerie, but Imhoff later returned to Germany with the servants. On his return to Germany, Imhoff was to use the money he earned in India to build himself a new house and gardens at the family estate in Mörlach, a project which was later to ruin him financially. The house, built in the rococo style, still stands and is very beautiful, and it can be viewed on the internet.

The first we hear of Imhoff after his return to Europe is from the secret journal of Moritz von Imhoff, his brother. In November

304

1774 he writes that Imhoff has just revealed to him that he had never been married to Anna Maria Chapuset and that his two sons were therefore illegitimate. He also told him that Anna Maria was not returning from India. He was therefore free to find a wife and was looking for one. Imhoff lost no time in his search. He spent the winter of 1774 to 1775 in Gotha, where he met Louisa von Schardt. They became publicly engaged on 16th January 1775 and married soon after. The fact that he did not divorce Marian before this marriage shows that he and Marian were never legally married. Louisa von Schardt was the sister of Charlotte von Stein, a lady-in-waiting at the court of Weimar and a close friend of the writers Friedrich Schiller and Johann Wolfgang von Goethe. Charlotte was a strong influence on Goethe's writing. Imhoff himself was also a friend of Karl Ludwig von Knebel, who was a close friend of Goethe's. Thus, curiously, the link between Schiller, Goethe and *Jane Austen* was not very distant. The daughter of Imhoff and Louisa, Amalie, who was born soon afterwards, was to become a well known writer herself as Amalie von Helvig.

A declaration of the divorce of Imhoff and Anna Maria Chapuset was obtained in Calcutta from Carl August Duke of Saxony. This document is somewhat ambiguous as to whether they had ever been formally married, or only lived together as man and wife. However, it was this document that was used by Hastings to obtain permission for his marriage to his beloved Marian in Calcutta on 8th August 1777.

Hastings continued in India amid growing political troubles. The *Franckfurter Staats-Ristretto* reported on 31st August 1784 that Marian Hastings had returned to England (believed to be because of ill health) and had brought back with her a personal fortune of £1 million and a large number of precious stones. It also reported that Hastings had made a present of a ring worth £2,000 to the captain of the ship on which she returned. They also reported on 4th December 1784 the presentation from Mrs Hastings to Queen Charlotte of an ivory Indian bed worth £40,000. This gift was later to be satirised during Hastings' trial by the author of a satirical poem called "The Rolliad".

By this time the financial affairs of Imhoff were in disarray. The building of a new house at his family estate at Mörlach in Germany had cost more than he had anticipated, and he decided that the only way out of his troubles was to seek a visit to Marian Hastings in London to repair his fortunes. So he and his new wife travelled to London. His new wife, Louisa, met Mrs Hastings several times and they became friends. Although Mrs Hastings got on well with Imhoff's new wife, at first she refused to see Imhoff himself. However, she eventually agreed to an emotional reunion with Imhoff in which he broke down in tears. Imhoff's wife, Louisa, wrote in a letter from Mörlach in Germany to Knebel on 9th May 1785:

"Wir setzten uns also im Wagen und fuhren nach dem Park. Ich sprach ihm Mut ein und mußte wirklich über seine Verzagtheit lachen und freute mich schon zum voraus, ihm bald heiterer und ruhiger zu sehen. Kaum waren wir im Park, so sah ich schon die gute Hastings von weiten kommen. Sie verdoppelte ihre Schritte, wie sie uns sah. Sie nahm mich gleich bei der Hand und sagte: "Guten Morgen, wie geht's Ihnen zusammen?" Sie sah ganz freundlich darzu den I. an, doch wurde sie stark rot, und er wurde blaß wie eine Leiche. Darauf nahm ich seine Hand und legte sie in ihre Hand und drückte sie beide zusammen. Sie waren beide stumm, und es hätte beinahe not getan, ich wär beider Souffleur gewesen, denn jedes hatte seine Rolle vergessen."

"We sat down in the coach and drove to the park. I tried to give him [Imhoff] courage and had to laugh at his concern, and looked forward to seeing him better and calmer. Scarcely were we in the park than I saw the good Lady Hastings coming from a distance. She doubled her steps when she saw us. She took me by the hand and said "Good morning, how are you both? She looked at Imhoff in a friendly way but she became bright red and he turned as white as a sheet. So I took his hand and laid it in hers and pressed them together. They were both struck dumb and it was almost necessary for me to prompt them, as each had forgotten their lines."

However, back in Germany, Imhoff's affairs were in too much trouble already and by June 1785 he was forced to sell the family estate in Mörlach and move to Weimar. His visit to Marian Hastings did not prove as productive financially as Imhoff had hoped. While Hastings was happy to support Mrs Hastings' two sons financially and in furthering their careers, he offered no substantial financial help to Imhoff himself. In any case, Hastings was soon to have many demands on his own finances including the legal costs of his trial for corruption in India which began in Parliament in 1788. Hastings had arrived in London on 15th June 1785 with, according to the *Franckfurter Staats-Ristretto* of 25th June 1785, a reported £500,000 and many presents for the royal family.

Back in Germany, Imhoff himself had suffered badly with his health, and his character had become increasingly bad tempered, probably due to his ill health and financial misfortunes. He had also by now become estranged from his wife, Louisa. He died on 9th August 1788, perhaps from the result of illnesses contracted in India. Henriette von Knebel had written of him on 4th November 1787 in a letter to her brother Carl Ludwig:

> *"Max sagt mir, daß Imhoff so elend aussähe, daß es unmöglich mehr lang mit ihm währen könnte…. Er ist ein unglücklicher Mensch."*

"Max tells me that Imhoff looked so miserable, that it was impossible for him to last much longer… He is an unhappy and unlucky man."

The early death of Imhoff broken down by disease and unhappiness can only recall the similar fate of Tysoe Saul Hancock. Certainly it would seem that life might have been better for both if they had never met Warren Hastings.

In 1795 Hastings was acquitted in his trial in Parliament but had to pay his own legal costs, estimated to be at least £150,000. This expense was however mitigated to a large degree by a payment to him from the East India Company of £71,000 and a pension of £5,000 a year. His combined income from the pension and lump sum would have covered the legal costs almost entirely and left Hastings still a rich man. If these figures are correct, it would seem that Warren Hastings was far from ruined by the trial.

Eliza's relationship with Warren Hastings was, in many ways, the most important relationship in her life, apart from her relationship with her mother. This of course would only be natural, as it is our parents to whom we have the closest bonds, as even our spouse is not related to us by blood. Certainly Eliza seems to have felt much closer to Warren Hastings than to Tysoe Hancock, who lived apart from her most of her life and to whom she seldom wrote and who, in any case, died when she was only thirteen years old. However, what Eliza recognised above all was that her unique gifts as a writer came to her "genetically" from her biological father, Warren Hastings; he was the "author of her being". She knew that her mother was not gifted intellectually and she regarded her mother with the affection of a daughter, rather than with admiration. In this respect her views of her parents mirrored those of Eliza Bennet in *Pride and Prejudice*.

The German novelist Sophie von la Roche, in her diary of a trip through Holland and England, met Hastings and his wife at their then home in Beaumont Lodge, Old Windsor in October 1786. She wrote of Hastings:

"Ich bemerkte noch mehr, als das erstemal, daß dieser Mann die zwei vortreffliche Eigenschaften des Verstandes und der Sprache vereint besitzt; Kürze und Feinheit des Ausdrucks, und nie eine

Sylbe zu viel, nie eine zu wenig – immer den edelsten Ton und Form der Ideen findet."

"I noticed even more than the first time that in this man were united the two most excellent qualities of understanding and speech; brevity and subtlety of expression, and never a syllable too many, nor one two few – with always the most noble tone and form of ideas."

Such a compliment could be equally applied to the author *Jane Austen*.

The tragedy of Eliza's life was her desire for recognition by her father, which she was never able to achieve. In many ways she was "in denial" about her need for her father's love. Although she visited Hastings on many occasions and he returned her visits when he was in London, it was never mentioned between them that there was this special relationship. As I have written, she must have discussed literary matters with him and their mutual friend, the poet Lady Sophia Burrell. We know from Jane Austen's letter dated 15th September 1813, that Hastings admired *Jane Austen's Pride and Prejudice* when Jane Austen wrote "And Mr. Hastings! I am quite delighted with what such a man writes about it."

It is very sad to read the final letter that survives from Eliza, which she wrote in her late forties in 1807 or 1809 to Warren Hastings. Even at this age she was behaving less like a mature woman and more like a young girl anxious for her father's love, a love which was always denied to her:

"I have taken the liberty of sending you a breakfast cup & Saucer, which I have had much pleasure in painting and gilding for you. They are not worthy your acceptance, but as the work of my hands I trust you will kindly receive them, and also grant my earnest request that you will make daily use of my imperfect performance; by which means I shall have the pleasure of knowing that once in every twenty four hours you probably bestow a thought on, your much obliged and truly affectionate God daughter, Eliza: Austen."

After Hastings' death, this cup and saucer appeared in the inventory in the bedroom of his wife Marian. The last entry in Hastings' diary for Eliza is for August 1808, when Eliza and Henry called on him at Daylesford. Henry visited Warren Hastings shortly after Eliza's death in 1813. However, Hastings did not note Eliza's death in his diary or show any particular interest to Eliza's husband, Henry, about her death. Jane Austen, normally a sympathetic writer, seems to have been greatly shocked at this and wrote in a letter of 15th September 1813, "Mr Hastings never <u>hinted</u> at Eliza in the smallest degree". What was the reason for Warren Hastings' treatment of Eliza? On the one hand he provided for her handsomely in a material sense with his trust fund of £10,000, but emotionally he was always distant from her. Did he fear that Eliza and each of her husbands would take advantage of him and that she was only interested in benefiting from the connection financially? It seems that to some extent Eliza had hoped to benefit from their relationship, for example by calling her son "Hastings", and it may be that Henry Austen may also have tried too bluntly to gain an advantage from the connection, especially in asking for financial support at the beginning of his banking career.

It may also be that, since Hastings had no other surviving children of his own but provided for the two (illegitimate) sons of his wife Marian, he feared that Eliza or her husband might have had some financial or legal claim on his estate which he did not wish to acknowledge. We know that he intended to leave his estate after the death of his wife to the eldest of Marian's two sons, Charles Imhoff. Hastings, who was no lawyer and relied on expert advice in any legal matters, may have been uncertain about this and unwilling to consult a lawyer about this very personal matter. He may have been very fearful about a legal claim on his estate from Eliza if she was acknowledged as his only child still living. We know from correspondence of Hastings that he had no legal training and relied on others for legal advice. After the death of her mother and husband, Eliza had written to one of the trustees, Mr Woodman, to request that the trust fund set up by Warren Hastings be dissolved and that she receive all the monies in it. Mr Woodman wrote to Warren Hastings who replied on 6th July 1797:

"Dear Brother, You have set a case to me, which I am not qualified to solve; nor can I with propriety take the opinion of Counsel upon it, or take any other steps regarding it."

Hastings must have worried about the damage to his reputation that would be caused if the story leaked out that he had an illegitimate daughter (the reference to "propriety" in the above letter may refer to this). He had been exposed to ridicule enough over his relationship with his second wife, and revelations over an earlier affair with a married woman could damage his reputation irreparably. His marriage to Marian Imhoff had already made him the subject of much ridicule in England. In a satirical poem of the time, "The Rolliad", Hastings' private life was used to mock him and to denigrate his political career in India:

"The poet then hints at a most ingenious proposal for the embellishment of the India-bench, according to the new plan of Parliamentary Reform; not by fitting it up like the Treasury-bench, with velvet cushions, but by erecting for the accommodation of the Leadenhall worthies, the ivory bed, which was lately presented to her Majesty by Mrs. Hastings.

O that for you, in Oriental state,
At ease reclin'd to watch the long debate,
Beneath the gallery's pillar'd height were spread
(With the QUEEN's leave) your WARREN's ivory bed!

The pannels [!] of the gallery too, over the canopy of the bed, are to be ornamented with suitable paintings.

Above, in colours warm with mimic life
The German husband of your WARREN's wife
His rival's deeds should blazon; and display,
In his blest rule the glories of your sway.

What singular propriety, what striking beauty must the reader of taste immediately perceive in this choice of a painter to execute the author's design! It cannot be doubted but Mrs. Hastings would exert all her own private and all Major Scott's public influence with every branch of the Legislature, to obtain so illustrious a job for the man to whose affection, or to whose want of affection, she owes her present fortunes. The name of this artist is Imhoff; but though he was once honoured with Royal Patronage, he is now best remembered from the circumstance, by which our author has distinguished him, of his former relation to Mrs. Hastings.

Then follow the subjects of the paintings, which are selected with the usual judgment of our poet.

Here might the tribes of ROHILCUND expire,
And quench with blood their towns, that sink in fire;
The BEGUMS there, of pow'r, of wealth forlorn,
With female cries, their hapless fortune mourn
Here hardly rescu'd from his guard, CHEYT SING
Aghast should fly; there NUNDCOMAR should swing;
Happy for him! if he had borne to see
His country beggar'd of the last rupee;
Nor call'd those laws, O HASTINGS, on thy head,
Which, mock'd by thee, thy slaves alone should dread.

These stories, we presume, are too public to require any explanation."

Rohilcund was a province in North West Hindustan besieged by the Afghan Rohilla tribe. Hastings was paid £400,000 by the Nawab of Oudh to provide an East India Company army to defeat them. The subsequent cruel treatment of the Rohillas by the native soldiers of the East India Company was one of the main accusations against Hastings at his trial in Parliament.

Hastings had extorted as much money and troops as he was able to from the Begums, which led them to rebel. Cheyt Singh, Raja of Benares, already paid tribute money to the East India Company. Hastings tried to extract a large amount of further money from him and, when he refused, he was arrested. This led to riots in which Cheyt Singh escaped. Hastings subsequently defeated his army and overthrew him, replacing him with a puppet ruler, who was an underage nephew of the Raja.

Nundcomar was the Raja of Hugli who opposed Hastings and as a result ended up being accused of forgery. On the insistence of Hastings and a judiciary friendly to him, Nundcomar was hanged for this offence, despite powerful objections and some convincing legal arguments that forgery was not a capital offence in India, as it was in England at that time.

There were further satires of the time attacking Warren Hastings. *The Daily Universal Register* of 27th March 1787 wrote:

"A caricature of a well-known person delivering up his wife to her second husband, was some years since handed about at Calcutta, and gave great offence; – it contained this laconic inscription, I'M – OFF!"

We can see from the ridicule Hastings suffered about his marriage to Marian, that Eliza was trying to protect Hastings from similar mistreatment. When she wrote in the preface of *Evelina* that she

313

"would not sink thy fame" she was specifically promising to protect Hastings from the ridicule which could befall him if it became known that she was the author of *Evelina* and his illegitimate daughter. However, it seems to me that Hastings did not appreciate that Eliza was far more concerned to have an emotional than a financial connection to her father. Hastings seemed somehow blind to the virtues in Eliza that others saw in her, and we have no record of him praising her in any way.

28.

Postscript - Other Possible Pseudonyms of Eliza

Once we have established from the preceding chapters that Eliza was an author who published in the late eighteenth century and early nineteenth century, either anonymously or under pseudonyms, we are faced with a great problem. Because we have shown that two authors of this period were in fact pseudonyms used by Eliza, what is to stop there being further pseudonymous authors whose names she used?

From a stylistic review of authors of this period, there are several candidates whose works, or some of whose works, may have been written by Eliza. I do not pursue this matter further here, but it is likely that a major re-examination of the authorship of works of this period may need to be undertaken to ascertain if any other authors were pseudonyms of Eliza. The whole question of pseudonymous authorship in eighteenth and early nineteenth century women's literature has been largely swept under the carpet by academics and literary critics, who are simple souls who prefer to take authorship as stated at the front of books at face value. It saves work and after all, "the play's the thing" and it doesn't matter who wrote literature in any case. I understand that this is a prevalent view in academic circles but those who are of a more humanistic tendency, like myself, prefer our authors to be creatures of flesh and blood.

There is one work in particular, which appeared in 1796, which strongly suggests that it was written by Eliza. This is *Translations of the Letters of a Hindoo Rajah* by *Elizabeth Hamilton*. This work was published in 1796, the same year as *Fanny Burney's Camilla*, which was to be such a successful novel that it would raise the sum of £2,000 for Fanny Burney. *Translations of the Letters of a Hindoo Rajah* is a work of satire which takes as its premise the visit of a Hindoo Rajah to England from India. He has come to see for himself how the English live and especially how they base their lives on their Bible, as he is led to believe that they do. The book is a purported "translation" of his letters.

The name of the Hindoo Rajah is Zaarmilla, an obvious reference to *Camilla*, since the letter "Z" does not occur in Hindu languages and so the name is entirely fictitious. In fact it appears to be the combination of "Camilla" with the Indian name of Mirza, which has a Persian origin. The appearance of the book in 1796, in the same year as *Camilla* was published, can only lend credence to it being a reference to *Camilla*. The book is extravagently dedicated to Warren Hastings in his role as "patron" of the translation of Sanskrit and Persian Literature. Given his literary abilities and his knowledge of Sanskrit and Persian, it is possible that Warren Hastings' role as "patron" may also have included his translating and publishing some of this literature himself under a pseudonym, as it may not have been possible for him to have published under his own name, given his position in society. I have discussed earlier Hastings' view of himself as primarily a literary intellectual, which is reflected in the two portraits of him by Sir Joshua Reynolds as a young man and, in old age, by Sir William Beechey. Lady Sophia Burrell also dedicated a poem to Hastings on reading one of his odes.

An anonymous publication of the time urging the creation of a chair of Persian at Oxford University is widely believed to have been written by Hastings. It must be remembered that at this time Persian was the language of the ruling elite in India, who had originally come from Persia. Hastings was also the first President of the Asiatic Society in Calcutta, a society founded in 1784 by the famous linguist Sir William Jones, the Supreme Court Judge in Bengal. The society was devoted to the translation of Indian texts and Hastings' friend Charles Hamilton was an important member of it. Charles

316

Hamilton had translated the Indian classic *The Hedaya: or Guide, A Commentary on the Mussulman Laws*, which was a guide to Muslim law in India. Warren Hastings had been corresponding with Lord Mansfield to ask his advice about implementing Hindoo and Muslim laws in Bengal and it seems that Charles Hamilton was central to Hastings' project.

Elizabeth Hamilton's book is purportedly a translation by Elizabeth Hamilton, Charles Hamilton's sister, of the letters of a Hindoo Rajah, although this is plainly a fiction for satirical purposes. Charles Hamilton had died in 1792 and his sister, Elizabeth, born in 1758 and unmarried, was left financially unsupported. In fact Elizabeth Hamilton's situation was strikingly similar to that of Jane Austen, as both were unmarried women of limited financial resources, who lived with their sisters. In view of its Indian theme, if Eliza had written this work it was likely that it would therefore be Elizabeth Hamilton to whom it would have been attributed, and the profit from the book would also have provided financial support for her. I find it highly unlikely that Elizabeth Hamilton could have written this work, partly because of her lack of education but also because, although she was already in middle-age, Hamilton had made no previous important literary contributions, and also for the following reasons:

1. The satirical and humorous tone of the work ill accords with the work of somebody who has just lost their most important and beloved relative, as she had just lost her brother Charles, and presumably faced the difficult life of a single woman short of money and unable to earn a living.

2. The author implies in the preliminary dissertation to the book that she is a student of Greek and Latin, as she compares her lack of knowledge of the Indian authors to the familiarity she has had since a young age with Greek and Latin authors. Elizabeth Hamilton had no such knowledge as she had not been educated in Greek and Latin.

3. There are frequent references in the book to English society of the time. The chief object of the satire is English society and such instutions as the Church of England. The satire is centred on London especially. While Eliza lived for most of her life in London, Elizabeth Hamilton had spent nearly all her life in Scotland and only lived in London between 1788 and 1792. Scotland, Elizabeth Hamilton's native country, is hardly mentioned in the book at all, other than to refer to the family pride of the Scottish being even greater than that of the English, a prejudice more likely to be held by an English person. Indeed, in *Jane Austen*'s "Juvenilia" the author makes fun of the family pride of the Scottish in a similar way.

4. Reference is made to Elizabeth Hamilton towards the end of the book when the character of Mr Denbeigh advises the heroine, Charlotte Percy, that she should temper her sorrow on the death of her relative and not give way to the overreaction of "sensibility":

    "Such a one has Miss Percy experienced in the father of Denbeigh. He has already convinced her that the indulgence of melancholy, instead of being an amiable weakness, rather deserving of admiration than censure, is, in reality, equally selfish and sinful – It is, he says, the height of ingratitude to the Giver of all good, peevishly to refuse the enjoyment of the many blessings that are left us, because we are deprived of a few, which were in their very natures perishable. – 'But alas!' replied Miss Percy, 'what is left to those whose earliest and dearest friends have been snatched from them by the hand of death?' 'Much is left to all,' replied Mr Denbeigh. 'No one, who enjoys the blessings of health, and a peaceful conscience, can, without ingratitude, repine. The proper discharge of the duties of life is a source of happiness to every well regulated mind.'"

This is written very much from the point of view of an outsider advising Elizabeth Hamilton. Critics of the book have identified the character of Charlotte Percy as being a representation of Elizabeth Hamilton herself. The above passage is very much in tune with what we know of the opinion of "sensibility" in the works of *Fanny Burney* and *Jane Austen*. It would be rather absurd for Elizabeth Hamilton to write of herself in the third person here and advise herself about her own grief. It is more likely to be Eliza's advice towards Elizabeth Hamilton. One character in the book, Lady Grey, gives the opinion of the author towards sensibility, which reflects a similar standpoint to the author of the novels of *Jane Austen* and *Fanny Burney*:

"'Sensibility, my dear niece', said Lady Grey, 'is but too often another word for selfishness. Believe me, that sensibility which turns with disgust from the sight of misery it has the power to relieve, is not of the right kind. To weep at the imaginary tale of sorrow exhibited in a Novel or a Tragedy, is to indulge a feeling, in which there is neither vice nor virtue: but when the compassion which touches the heart, leads the hands to afford relief, and benevolence becomes a principle of action; it is then, and then only, that it is truly commendable... I have taken them [my principles] from the doctrines of Jesus Christ and his Apostles.'"

The use of the name of Elizabeth Hamilton is only used as the fictional translator of the letters of the Rajah and she is nowhere named as the author of the book. Therefore her role in the book is entirely fictional.

The style and humour of the book is identical to that of *Fanny Burney* and *Jane Austen*. As evidence that this is not just my personal opinion but was also believed at the time, when *Jane Austen's Sense and Sensibility* first appeared it was believed in Cheltenham to be the work of Elizabeth Hamilton.

Translations of the Letters of a Hindoo Rajah is indeed very entertaining and amusing and I would recommend anyone to read it for pleasure, especially those who enjoy the novels of *Jane Austen*. As an example of the style of this book I enclose the following comments on contemporary female education in England from the Hindoo Rajah:

"Another indispensable part in the education of females of every Cast, of every rank, and in every situation, is the knowledge of the language spoken in their neighbouring nation. I was for some time at a great loss to know what reason could be assigned for so strange a custom, and after many conjectures, I rested in the belief, that as the French nation was frequently at war with the English, it might either be customary to send the women as Hircarrahs, into the camp of the enemy, or, in case of defeat, to employ them in procuring terms of peace, which from the remarkable complaisance of their adversaries to the female sex, it might be supposed, would be negociated by the Bibbys with peculiar advantage to their country. I was, however, forced to give up this conclusion, on being assured, that after years spent in the study of the language, as it is taught at these excellent Seminaries, few are capable of reading, and still fewer of conversing, with any degree of fluency in this tongue: and that the only real advantage resulting from it was, that by what they knew of it, they were enabled to understand the peculiar terms belonging to the articles of dress imported from that country, which had an acknowledged right of imposing its fashions on the other nations of Europe.

Dress is, indeed, one science in which full scope is given to the faculties of these females: and the love of it, is at the great Schools of the Christians, so successfully inculcated, that it remains indelible to the latest period of life. Nor is the mode of education I speak of confined solely to the children of higher Casts, it extends to all, even to the daughters of the tradesmen, and mechanics, who are employed, during the years of improvement, exactly in the manner I have described. All of the difference is, that at the inferior Schools, where inferior masters are employed, the girls do not, perhaps, arrive at the art of running their fingers over the bits of wood, called Keys of a Harpsichord, with an equal degree of velocity; they make rather more execrable copies, of more wretched pictures, and the knowledge they acquire of the French language does not, perhaps, enable them to run over the names of the new fashions, with an equal degree of volubility; but as to making any attempt at instructing the daughters of Christians, in any thing useful to themselves, or society, the idea would be deemed equally ridiculous in Seminaries of every class."

Eliza, as a fluent French speaker, is lamenting the poor teaching of French which has always been a tradition in English schools. (I am proud to say that this tradition of poor teaching of modern languages has been successfully re-established in English schools despite a shocking lapse in the 1960s and 1970s. I understand that A grade A levels in modern languages are now handed out like sweets to students, only required to memorise by heart the words of an oral "exam" from a script written in advance for them by their teacher. Students are also not required to translate, nor to read a single novel in the language they are studying, the strain of which would no doubt be a form of "child abuse" likely to bring on serious psychiatric consequences as well as the tragedy of "low self esteem" in the event of failure, a consequence to be avoided at all costs.) Eliza would be proud to know that 200 years later, after five years spent in the study of a modern language, as it is taught at our excellent Seminaries, few are capable of reading, and still fewer of conversing, with any degree of fluency.

Similar criticisms of female education can be found frequently in the novels of *Jane Austen* and *Fanny Burney*. The description of French fashions reminds us of Eliza's comments about French fashions in her letters, especially those written from Paris. The passage reflects Eliza's own perfect knowledge of French and her criticism of female education in the fashionable London schools for women, which is made throughout the novels of *Jane Austen*. In her private life, Eliza would feel the same about the fashionable school attended by Elizabeth Austen, the wife of Jane Austen's brother, Edward.

Another example of humour reminiscent of *Jane Austen* and of Eliza's view of marriage, is when the Hindoo Rajah describes how the Hindoo woman may throw herself onto her husband's funeral pyre to enter paradise with him, but even "her admission into Paradise, depends on her husband's title to an entrance into that state of felicity". In contrast, the Rajah notes "Christian women are more fortunate; they may enjoy Heaven without the company of their husbands!" Only somebody who had been married, like Eliza, but unlike Elizabeth Hamilton, would write these words.

Indeed, Elizabeth Hamilton herself did not urge her claims of authorship very strongly. She sent a copy of the book to her friend Mrs Gregory, hinting it was not her own book, by referring to it as her "black baby":

> "I am afraid to enquire what you will say to my black baby: I had no sooner given it out of my hands, than I passed sentence of condemnation on it myself, and was almost ashamed at having exposed it even to your eye; but there is one thing of which I must beg leave to assure you, and that is, I have so little of authorship about me, that there is no occasion for the smallest piece of delicacy in pointing out its defects, or, indeed, in condemning in toto, any child of my brain, towards whom I am so unnatural a parent, that I have hitherto seen them smothered without remorse."

One of the most striking pieces of evidence that the work is by

Eliza is the poem in the book, which has been seen as being to Elizabeth Hamilton's uncle as her guardian, where she describes him as more than a father to her and as the inspiration for her literary work. This is not logical for Elizabeth Hamilton, as Elizabeth Hamilton had to devote much of her life unwillingly towards looking after her uncle, and any literary inspiration would not have been received from him, but from her brother Charles. However, the poem, included in the book for no obvious reason, fits very well as a eulogy of Warren Hastings, which is not surprising given that the book is dedicated to him. Strikingly, the poem is in the same metre and style as the dedication to *Fanny Burney's Evelina*, quoted previously, which is also a eulogy to Warren Hastings. The poem in *Elizabeth Hamilton's* novel includes the stanzas [my highlighting]:

If e'er my breast with love of virtue glow'd
Or ardent sought the Muses hallow'd shrine,
To thee my dawning taste its culture owed;
Each high-born sentiment, dear shade, was thine.

Oh! if thy sainted spirit hovers near,
With smiles benign my filial vows approve;
Vows like thy conduct, artless, and sincere,
Pure as thy faith, and spotless as thy love.

But see! Where comes my venerable sire,
With cheerful air, and looks serenely gay:
He comes to lead me to the social fire,
To warn me of the dews of parting day.

I come, my more than father! Best of friends!
Dear, good old man; how good, how dear to me?
Beyond thy life, for me no hope extends.
My comfort, and my peace, expire with thee.

The lines:

"If e'er my breast with love of virtue glow'd
Or ardent sought the Muse's sacred shrine"

remind one of the lines in the dedication to *Fanny Burney's Evelina* shown earlier in this book:

"If in my heart the love of Virtue glows,"

The line "Or ardent sought the Muse's sacred shrine" seems to be quite obvious in meaning. Since "ardent" means "burning" it must refer to Eliza previously seeking the Muse's sacred shrine (i.e. writing a book) under the name of "ardent", a pun on "Burney", and once again Eliza is implying that Warren Hastings is the inspiration for her literary efforts.

In addition, it may be noted that the next stanza begins "Oh! if". If we look back at the dedication of *Evelina*, this is identical to the first two words of the first and third lines and forms an acrostic downwards from the initial letters of lines 1, 3, 5 and 7. As explained before, the letters "OHIF" could stand in Latin for "*Ouarren Hastings ipse fecit*" translated from the Latin as "Warren Hastings himself made me". All these stylistic similarities are indicative of the author of both poems being the same. The line "I come my more than father! Best of friends!" is also reminiscent of *Fanny Burney's* original first line of the dedication to *Evelina*, which was "Friend of my Soul, & Parent of my Heart".

The year 1796, when *Translations of the Letters of a Hindoo Rajah* was published, was an important time for Warren Hastings and for Eliza, since the year previously Warren Hastings had been acquitted in his trial in Parliament of crimes he was accused of commiting in India. It is no surprise then that, in *Translations of the Letters of a Hindoo Rajah*, much of the book is dedicated to exonerating Hastings from any wrongdoing in India. The author is very well acquainted with the arguments used against Warren Hastings in his trial. However, Hastings is praised by the fictitious Hindoo Rajah as an honourable gentleman and the liberator of the Hindoos from the oppressive rule of the Muslim rulers of Northern India.

The author lays special emphasis on exonerating Hastings from any crimes in Rohilkund, one of the main accusations of his accusers in Parliament, such as Edmund Burke. Here the East India Company was paid £400,000 by the Nawab of Oudh to attack the Muslim Afghan Rohillas and it was alleged this was merely done to earn money for the East India Company, and not for any proper political purpose. The subsequent brutality of the East India Company's native troops against the Rohillas went unchecked by Hastings. *Translations of the Letters of a Hindoo Rajah* includes many references to the trial of Warren Hastings, supports the arguments for his conduct and puts the arguments of his chief accuser, Burke, into a bad light. Burke's arguments against Hastings, especially in connection with the Rohilla wars, are put to the Hindoo Rajah who says he does not agree with them in the slightest and says he has the "most profound respect" for the Governor General.

If Elizabeth Hamilton had been the true author, it is unlikely that the book would have placed quite so much emphasis on exonerating Hastings and would have been so wholly in his favour. In *The Analytical Review*, volume 24, (October 1796): 429-31 the reviewer at the time expressed the opinion that "the compliments which are paid by our author to governor Hastings" were not strictly objective but "the grateful language of private obligation or friendship."

The themes of the book are similar to the themes in Eliza's other works. Sensibility is discussed and lamented as an overreaction to ill fortune, and a practical approach to ill fortune is advised instead to Charlotte Percy (who represents Elizabeth Hamilton) by Mr Denbeigh in the later stages of the book.

The form of religion supported by the author is one of practical good works and a lack of "enthusiasm" or religious fanaticism. The basic premise of the book is that the Rajah is an ingénu who naively expects English society to be governed by the rules of the Christian religion. When he finds this is not so, he assumes that there must be one volume of the Bible with which he is not acquainted, "A New Revelation" which he has not seen. The author also detests "the Poojah of cards" (a Poojah in Calcutta is a religious ceremony) and loud assemblies ("routs"). Eliza's cousin, Philadelphia Walter, wrote from Tunbridge Wells of Eliza and her mother in a letter to her brother of 19th September 1787 that "My aunt and cousin never touch a card". There would have been two reasons for this, firstly that Eliza was careful with money (in *Fanny Burney's Camilla*, a character called Mrs Berlinton loses all her money through playing cards). Secondly, it would appear that Eliza "preferred her books" as she wrote in her letter from Dorking. In the works of *Jane Austen* the writer does not condemn cards directly. However, it is characteristic of *Jane Austen* that she condemns by giving the love of cards to the most stupid of her characters, such as Mr Hurst and Mrs Bennet in *Pride and Prejudice*. Any reader of *Jane Austen* will recognise the author's strong antipathy towards cards, and this love of cards is satirised as above mentioned in *Translations of the Letters of a Hindoo Rajah*. As can be seen from the excerpt quoted, the book also satirises and laments the poor quality of education that was the fate of most women of the time.

Interestingly, the author is deeply opposed to the slave trade as being against the principles of Christianity, and she also criticises the severe game laws of the time, as well as the criminalisation of the poor. We can surmise that Eliza opposed the slave trade, since her friend Lady Sophia Burrell was a close friend of Lord Mansfield and praised him in her poems in high tones for his famous ruling in *Somerset's Case* of 1772, which had the result of outlawing slavery in England. In this case Lord Mansfield had confirmed his own hatred of slavery in his verdict:

"On the part of Somerset, the case which we gave notice

should be decided, this day, the Court now proceeds to give its opinion. The state of slavery is of such a nature, that it is incapable of being introduced on any reasons, moral or political; but only positive law, which preserves its force long after the reasons, occasion, and time itself from whence it was created, is erased from memory: it's so odious, that nothing can be suffered to support it but positive law. Whatever inconveniences, therefore, may follow from a decision, I cannot say this case is allowed or approved by the law of England; and therefore the black must be discharged."

Lord Mansfield's objection to slavery was not just theoretical; his nephew, John Lindsay, had had an illegitimate daughter with a black slave and this daughter, Dido Elizabeth Belle, lived with Lord Mansfield at Kenwood House, his mansion in Hampstead in North London. Her position in the household somewhat resembled that of Fanny Price in *Mansfield Park* as, though she lived in comfort and was loved and treated kindly, she was never accorded the same status as Elizabeth, Lord Mansfield's other great niece, who was both white and legitimate. The title of *Jane Austen's Mansfield Park* could be seen as an ironic description of England as a park where black slaves are safe under Lord Mansfield's ruling, but from where they are exploited at a distance by rich English plantation owners such as Sir Thomas Bertram. It is likely that those who had lived in India, such as Warren Hastings, a man with a high respect not only for Indian civilisation but also for the ordinary Hindoo, regarded the slave owners of the West Indies with the same disgust as did his friend Lord Mansfield. The author of 'Emma' also shows her contempt towards Mrs Elton and the connection of her family to the slave trade in Bristol.

The author of *Translations of the Letters of a Hindoo Rajah*, like Hastings, shows a sympathy towards the Hindus as being a civilised but vulnerable race dominated by the more warlike Muslims. She also shows a deep interest in the Hindu literature and culture of

India, no doubt an interest which Eliza picked up from her conversations with Warren Hastings. Warren Hastings had great respect for Indian culture and considered Indian literature – especially the Mahabharata, the ancient epic poem written in Sanskrit – to be the greatest in the world. Many of the Indian terms used in the book are explained by the author at the beginning.

The same sense of humour and style evident in *Fanny Burney's* and *Jane Austen's* works is present in this work of *Elizabeth Hamilton*. There is an interesting reference to Elizabeth Hamilton in a letter from Jane Austen to her sister Cassandra, dated 6th November 1813, which was shortly after Eliza's death. The "Eliza" referred to in the letter below is therefore not Henry's wife. In it Jane Austen writes the following about the second edition of *Sense and Sensibility* or *Pride and Prejudice*:

> "Since I wrote last, my 2nd edit. has stared me in the face. Mary tells me that Eliza means to buy it. I wish she may. It can hardly depend upon any more Fyfield Estates. I cannot help hoping that *many* will feel themselves obliged to buy it. I shall not mind imagining it a disagreeable duty to them, so as they do it. Mary heard before she left home that it was very much admired at Cheltenham, and that it was given to Miss Hamilton. It is pleasant to have such a respectable writer named. I cannot tire you, I am sure, on this subject, or I would apologise."

Jane Austen first says that she is desperate for more people to purchase the book to increase her income. However, in spite of this the book was given free to Elizabeth Hamilton. It seems unlikely that Elizabeth Hamilton would have been able to afford a copy. No doubt she was given it because of her connection with Eliza. This is hinted at in the final sentence above which is extremely cryptic ("I cannot tire you, I am sure on this subject") and once again Jane Austen is sharing an in-joke with her sister Cassandra.

29.

The Source of Jane Austen's "Emma"

In all my reading of biographies of Jane Austen, I have never been able to find reference to the original source of *Jane Austen's Emma*. We have the sources of *Sense and Sensibility* and *Pride and Prejudice* which were *Elinor and Marianne* and *First Impressions*, both started in the late 1790s. However, I believe I have found the source of *Emma* in a section of *Elizabeth Hamilton's Translations of the Letters of a Hindoo Rajah* of 1796. In one of the final chapters of the book, the Hindoo Rajah, Zaarmilla, visits a Mr Denbeigh who has a young daughter called Emma. This daughter is the same age as *Jane Austen's* Emma, twenty, and indeed the author lays great stress on Emma being twenty as an age where she is old enough to choose a suitable life partner for herself, in contrast to Indian women who are married at a much younger age (compare Elizabeth Bennet in *Pride and Prejudice* who is also twenty).

Emma Denbeigh is shortly to be married to a Mr Darnley (a cross between Mr Darcy and Mr Knightley?). Mr Darnley bears a striking resemblance to the hero of *Emma*, Mr Knightley. Mr Darnley is described as being very nearly twice Emma's age, i.e. thirty-eight or thirty-nine. In *Jane Austen's Emma* Mr Knightley is also thirty-eight or thirty-nine years old. Mr Darnley's character is also very similar to that of Mr Knightley. They are both neighbouring landowners and squires rather than aristocrats, keen on agricultural improvement and both prefer literature and the improvement of the mind to hunting. They are both shown to be caring landlords towards their tenants, in spite of their interest in agricultural progress, and both are highly educated and experienced men who are able to improve the minds of their younger fiancées. Mr Darnley in *Translations of the Letters of a Hindoo Rajah* is described as follows:

"He was soon discovered to be a very strange, whimsical sort of a creature, by the neighbouring 'Squires. – The sufferings of a poor timorous animal, harassed by fatigue, and tortured by the agonizing sensations of excessive fear, were not necessary for his amusement. He could enjoy much pleasure in walking over a fine country, without being the butcher of either hare or partridge: and take delight in rambling by the side of our river, though his heart never felt the triumph of beholding the dying struggles of a poor trout, or exulted in its writhing agony while tearing the barbed dart from its lacerated entrails. His mind sought for other objects of gratification. The study of Mineralogy and Botany, and exquisite relish for the beauties of nature, refined by an acquaintance with the sister arts of Poetry and Painting, gave sufficient interest to the rural scenery, without any aid from the misery of inoffensive animals. To the amusements of elegant Literature, he has added those of Agricultural improvement... He found her [Emma's] mind more cultivated than is common with girls of that age, and took delight in improving her already formed taste. His conversation was far superior, in point of elegance and information, to that of any person she had ever met with: besides, it must be confessed, that there is a charm in the manners of a man who has seen something of the world, and been accustomed to move in the upper circles of life, which is very captivating to a delicate mind."

It is true that there is not very much happening between Mr Darnley and Emma in *Translations of the Letters of a Hindoo Rajah* but this has often been remarked on as being true of *Jane Austen's Emma* as well. Even the publisher of *Emma*, John Murray, wrote to Walter Scott on 25th December 1815 "It wants incident and romance does it not?"

There is also a possible geographical connection between Emma Denbeigh and Emma Woodhouse. Once again, this centres on the Mole Valley in Surrey. The connection is that her surname of "Denbeigh" could be taken from the Denbies Estate near Dorking, spelled "Denbighs" at that time, which is roughly in the same geographical location as the fictional house of Emma Woodhouse, Hartfield. They both lie in the Mole Valley between Leatherhead and Dorking. Denbies is famous in the present time for being the largest vineyard in England (and one of the best).

The area where Emma Denbeigh lives is similar to the area around Dorking, being covered in beech woods. This area was well known to Eliza, who had visited her friend Lady Sophia Burrell at her house at The Deepdene, near to Dorking. Another connection is that the estate of Denbighs was the only other large estate in Dorking apart from The Deepdene, and it must have therefore been well known to Eliza. At that time it was owned by a Mr Denison, a man well known in the town of Dorking for his popularity and his charitable works. Since he lived at Denbighs and his name was Denison, it is likely he may be the model for Mr Denbeigh in the book. Like Mr Woodhouse in *Jane Austen's Emma*, Mr Denbeigh would give joints of meat to the needy. Mr Darnley also resembles to a degree Sir William Burrell, the husband of Eliza's literary friend, Lady Sophia Burrell, who had lived at The Deepdene in Dorking. He married his wife when he was about forty and she about twenty, and he was interested in science and local history as well as poetry and painting, commissioning the painting of many local scenes by the professional Swiss artist Samuel Hieronymus Grimm.

We can see how *Emma* developed from this short extract into *Jane Austen's* unpublished novel *The Watsons*, written about 1803 and set in Dorking. This was written shortly after Eliza herself had been living in Dorking. The heroine is Emma Watson, who resembles Emma

Woodhouse somewhat in character as well as in name. There is also a strong resemblance between Emma Watson's father and Mr Woodhouse, as both are rather selfish hypochondriacs/valetudinarians. The comparison between *Emma* and *The Watsons* has been supported by the famous critic Q D Leavis in *A Critical Theory of Jane Austen's Writings*.

If this is correct, then the origin of *Jane Austen's* novel *Emma* goes back further than has been previously thought. It also suggests that the novel *Emma* was begun considerably earlier than 1814, when Jane's sister Cassandra stated it was begun.

One connection between *Jane Austen's Emma* and Eliza's life is the situation of Frank Churchill's aunt, Mrs Churchill, in the novel, who is sent to stay at Richmond upon Thames from London. She "has been recommended to the medical skill of an eminent person there." There are similarities between this and the removal of Eliza's friend, Lady Sophia Burrell, to Richmond in 1802, when her health was in a deplorable state, according to Eliza. Eliza wrote to Warren Hastings in March 1802 that Lady Sophia Burrell was directed to stay in Richmond by one of the eminent physicians of the time, Sir Lucas Pepys (this Sir Lucas Pepys lived in Mickleham in Surrey and is buried in Mickleham Church, the same church in which Fanny Burney was married, which lies opposite Mickleham Hall where Eliza's friend, Lady Talbot, lived). Sir Lucas Pepys had been created a baronet during his lifetime and he and his family were on close terms with Fanny Burney, who mentions them on several occasions in her diary. Sir Lucas Pepys was presumably also well known to Lady Sophia Burrell's husband, as both were Fellows of the Society of Antiquaries. Eliza wrote of Lady Sophia Burrell in her letter to Warren Hastings that "the nature of her complaint which appears to be a confirmed decline, leaves but little hope of her restoration to the many friends who love and esteem her."

Being a resident of Surrey myself, I would like to make a few comments on the setting of *Emma*. The setting seems to be a cross between Guildford, Great Bookham, Leatherhead, Dorking, and

Cobham, all towns in Surrey well known to myself and to Eliza. The two houses of Hartfield and Donwell, where Emma and Mr Knightley live respectively, could have been based on the two country houses of Hatchlands and Clandon near Guildford. Hartfield is similar to Hatchlands in being close to the town and almost part of the grounds of Clandon. Hatchlands was owned by Mrs Frances Boscawen, the widow of Admiral Boscawen. She had literary interests and was known as a member of London literary society of the time, known informally as "the bluestockings". She was also one of the ladies to whom the novel *Camilla* was dedicated by *Fanny Burney*.

It is easy to see how the name of Donwell Abbey could have been drawn from Clandon and Stoneleigh Abbey, which I have mentioned earlier. The "Don" in Donwell Abbey is no doubt pronounced as "dun" or "done", as is the "don" in real life Clandon. Thus Mr Knightley's house is ironically named "done well", i.e. the house and especially its gardens live up to the ideals of the age (as does Mr Knightley). By contrast, Mr Knightley describes Emma's actions in mocking Miss Bates at the picnic on Box Hill as "Badly done!" In the novel *Emma*, as in real life, Donwell/Clandon is a slightly larger and grander house than the neighbouring Hartfield/Hatchlands.

Another possible model for Hartfield is Thorncroft Manor in Leatherhead, which resembles Hartfield in being so close to the town it was almost part of it. This house would no doubt have been visited by Eliza, since it was owned by Henry Boulton and his wife, Juliana Raymond, the sister of Eliza's literary friend, Lady Sophia Burrell. Deirdre Le Faye in *Jane Austen: The World of her Novels* includes a photograph of Thorncroft Manor, which she sees as being of the correct age and size to be a model for Hartfield. The property can also be viewed on the internet.

Thorncroft Manor is described by Peter Brandon in *A History of Surrey* as a *"ferme ornée"*, which he calls an "(ornamental or villa farm) which was not so much a business as an essay in the Picturesque. In the *ferme ornée* the farm offices were often joined to the house and the grounds were laid out with a view to utility as well as to beauty."

Another coincidence of names, in *Jane Austen's Mansfield Park*, is that the living of Thornton Lacey in *Mansfield* Park seems to take its name from two neighbouring estates in Surrey's Mole Valley, Thorncroft and Polesden Lacey.

Critics often warn us that we must always beware of finding direct connections between real places and the places mentioned in the works of *Jane Austen*, as they are an amalgam of different places. However, elements of real places do appear in her books and the author does not choose names at random, but seems to enjoy leaving clues to real places in the fictional names she employs. Her choice of names often reflects her love of wordplay. John Halperin, in his very interesting article *Inside Pride and Prejudice*, argues that the real house of Chevening Park in Kent corresponds in detail to Rosings, and that the character of Lady Catherine de Bourgh was inspired by the mother of the owner, the Dowager Lady Stanhope, the name being drawn from her mother in law, Catherine Burghill. Indeed, such close connections have been found in the *Jane Austen* novels between Pemberley and the real Chatsworth, Rosings and the real Chevening, and Northanger Abbey and the real Stoneleigh Abbey that critics should re-examine the idea of *Jane Austen's* houses as being merely "composites".

Of all her books, however, *Emma* is the one which is most rooted in its location, Surrey, which Mrs Elton rather erroneously describes as "the garden of England". The author seems much more familiar with this location than those of other novels and indeed Eliza was well acquainted with this area. In the novel, Mr Weston has a house called Randalls, and indeed there was at that time a house called Randalls near Leatherhead, the seat of the baronet, Sir John Coghill. Nearby Mickleham, where Eliza's friend Lady Talbot lived (she was the wife of the baronet Sir Charles-Henry Talbot) is also mentioned in the novel. Box Hill is visible from the estate of Eliza's friend, Lady Sophia Burrell, The Deepdene, which lies just below it to the south. As an inhabitant of Surrey for most of my life, I know the geography of this area particularly well. The author of *Emma* was, I judge, also very well acquainted with the area in real life. This area, in the valley of the River Mole, consisted in the eighteenth century of several estates belonging mostly to rich Londoners. Their estates therefore did not need to yield an income from agriculture, and so were often designed for pleasure and heavily planted with trees. The area could, with justification, be described *in toto* as the largest landscape garden in England. Many are still deceived by its "natural" beauty.

The town of Leatherhead, in its website, claims to be the model for Highbury in *Emma*. As mentioned, some places in Leatherhead, such as Randalls, are specifically mentioned in the novel and the website claims that Highbury society was a satire on Leatherhead society of the time. Highbury's location, like Leatherhead, is also close to Box Hill. Leatherhead is also the only town in the area set high above the surrounding towns, hence the name "Highbury". However, Jacqueline Banerjee, in her book *Literary Surrey*, also puts forward the case for nearby Cobham, details of which are similar to Highbury. Leatherhead is also close to the estate of Norbury Park, which belonged to Fanny Burney's friends, William and Frederica Lock, on whose estate Fanny Burney's cottage in West Humble was built. This area is also notable for the presence of Juniper Hall in Mickleham, at the foot of Box Hill, whose inhabitants were exiles from the French Revolution, including the writer Mme de Stael, and General D'Arblay, a French Army officer who Fanny Burney married. Bearing in mind that Eliza's first husband was also a French exile and Eliza spoke fluent French, it is possible she could have visited this house while she was living nearby, but we have no evidence for this.

One final comment upon *Emma*. For an Englishman from Surrey, one of the most affecting passages is when the author describes the view from Mr Knightley's estate of Donwell Abbey:

"It was a sweet view – sweet to the eye and the mind.

English verdure, English culture, English comfort, seen under a sun bright, without being oppressive."

It has often struck me how only somebody who had travelled abroad would be able to write this. The author seems to be contrasting England with another country. As they say, "What do they know of England, who only England know?" Jane Austen herself never left England. The author is contrasting the warm sun of the south of England with the heat of another country, no doubt the South of France where Eliza had lived, where the oppressive sun had driven her indoors but had brought out her natural dark complexion.

30.

Memoirs of Modern Philosophers

In spite of its title, *Memoirs of Modern Philosophers*, Elizabeth Hamilton's follow-up to *Translations of the Letters of a Hindoo Rajah*, published in 1800, is in fact a comic novel, and it is a novel which continues the attack of *Translations of the Letters of a Hindoo Rajah* on the modern philosophers of the time such as William Godwin and Mary Wollstonecroft. It supports traditional Christian values as a more sensible basis for life. It develops this theme from *Translations of the Letters of a Hindoo Rajah*, where the subject is only a short segment of the book. It has three heroines: Bridgetina Botherim appears to be a parody of the philosopher Mary Hays who follows the Jacobin philosophy, the philosophy of the revolutionaries in France. She irrationally believes the hero, Henry Sydney, to be in love with her, in spite of all evidence to the contrary. Following her philosophy, she wishes to emigrate with him to lead the life of a noble savage with the Hottentots in Africa. This may have been a dig by Eliza at her husband, Henry Austen, who had, according to Deirdre Le Faye, once considered joining the 86th Regiment of the regular army who were to spend three years at the Cape of Good Hope in Africa before transferring to India.

The second heroine, Julia Delmont, is a young lady of good character who is seduced by a hairdresser, Vallaton, who uses the beliefs of the new philosophy, such as that marriage is not necessary, in order to seduce her. Vallaton later shares the fate of Eliza's first husband in being executed by guillotine in Paris. However, the real heroine of the book is Harriet Orwell, who returns the love of the hero, Henry Sydney, and who counters the new philosophy by living

337

in accordance with the principles of her simple Christian faith. In 1798, just before the publication of the book, Eliza and Henry were living in Ipswich in Suffolk, which lies on the estuary of the River Orwell, and no doubt Eliza took Harriet's surname from this river. She would not be the last person to use this river as a literary surname.

There is also another interesting connection in this book with the author *Jane Austen*. The character and name of the hero, Henry Sydney, remind us of the clergymen hero, Henry Tilney, in *Jane Austen's Northanger Abbey*, who is often believed to have been based on the witty real life clergyman, Sydney Smith. Certain aspects of Henry Tilney, such as his exposition on the word "nice", echo similar writings by Sydney Smith. A passage in *Northanger Abbey* reads as follows:

> '"But now really, do not you think Udolpho the nicest book in the world?' 'The nicest; – by which I suppose you mean the neatest. That must depend upon the binding.' 'Henry,' said Miss Tilney, 'you are very impertinent. Miss Morland, he is treating you exactly as he does his sister. He is for ever finding fault with me, for some incorrectness of language, and now he is taking the same liberty with you. The word "nicest", as you used it, did not suit him; and you had better change it as soon as you can, or we shall be overpowered with Johnson and Blair all the rest of the way.' 'I am sure,' cried Catherine, 'I did not mean to say any thing wrong; but it is a nice book, and why should not I call it so?' 'Very true,' said Henry, 'and this is a very nice day, and we are taking a very nice walk, and you are two very nice young ladies. Oh! it is a very nice word indeed! – it does for every thing. Originally perhaps it was applied only to express neatness, propriety, delicacy, or refinement; – people were nice in their dress, in their sentiments, or their choice. But now every commendation on every subject is comprised in

that one word.' 'While, in fact,' cried his sister, 'it ought only to be applied to you, without any commendation at all. You are more nice than wise.'"

Sydney Smith himself wrote:

"A nice person is neither too tall nor too short, looks clean and cheerful, has no prominent feature, makes no difficulties, is never misplaced, sits bodkin, is never foolishly affronted, and is void of affectations.

A nice person helps you well at dinner, understands you, is always gratefully received by young and old, Whig and Tory, grave and gay.

There is something in the very air of a nice person which inspires you with confidence, makes you talk, and talk without fear of malicious misrepresentation; you feel that you are reposing upon a nature which God has made kind, and created for the benefit and happiness of society. It has the effect upon the mind which soft air and a fine climate has upon the body.

A nice person is clear of little, trumpery passions, acknowledges superiority, delights in talent, shelters humility, pardons adversity, forgives deficiency, respects all men's rights, never stops the bottle, is never long and never wrong, always knows the day of the month, the name of every body at table, and never gives pain to any human being.

If any body is wanted for a party, a nice person is the first thought of; when the child is christened, when the daughter is married – all the joys of life are communicated to nice people; the hand of the dying man is always held out to a nice person.

A nice person never knocks over wine or melted butter, does not tread upon the dog's foot, or molest the family cat, eats soup without noise, laughs in the right place, and has a watchful and attentive eye."

Jane Austen biographers have suggested that it was possible that she actually met Smith on one of her visits to Bath or Cheltenham, or perhaps in London. However, there is a much closer connection between Sydney Smith and Eliza. Eliza's husband, Henry Austen, was an exact contemporary of Sydney Smith at Winchester College (the public school) where Smith's academic excellence led to him being made captain of the school. Like Henry Austen, Smith also subsequently studied at Oxford University. Smith would therefore have been a well known figure to Henry Austen, and it is likely that he could have introduced him to Eliza. One can see how the name of Sydney Smith has mutated to Henry Sydney in *Memoirs of Modern Philosophers* (perhaps by his character being mixed with that of Henry Austen) and from there to Henry Tilney in *Northanger Abbey* (the surname "Tylney" was also used by *Fanny Burney* in the play *A Busy Day* written at the same period).

Eliza seems to have been a great admirer of Sydney Smith, as their writing styles share a lot of similarities. It is not difficult, moreover, to see reflections of Sydney Smith in *Jane Austen's* most famous hero, Mr Darcy, in *Pride and Prejudice*. While his humour is rather drier, Mr Darcy shares the same irreverent wit as Henry Tilney. Certain passages in the essays of Sydney Smith remind us of key passages in *Pride and Prejudice*. In his essay on Female Education, from *The Edinburgh Review* of 1810 (*Pride and Prejudice* was only published in 1813) Sydney Smith writes:

"A great deal is said in favour of the social nature of the fine arts. Music gives pleasure to others. Drawing is an art, the amusement of which does not centre in him who exercises it, but is diffused among the rest of the world. This is true; but there is nothing, after all, so social as a cultivated mind. We do not mean to speak slightingly of the fine arts, or to depreciate the good humour with which they are sometimes exhibited, but we appeal to any man, whether a little spirited and sensible conversation – displaying modestly, useful acquirements – and evincing rational curiosity, is not well worth the highest exertions of musical or graphical skill. A woman of accomplishments may entertain those who have the pleasure of knowing her for half an hour with great brilliancy; but a mind full of ideas and with that elastic spring which the love of knowledge only can convey, is a perpetual source of exhilaration and amusement to all that come within its reach; – not collecting its force into single and insulated achievements, like the efforts made in the fine arts – but diffusing, equally over the whole of existence, a calm pleasure – better loved as it is longer felt – and suitable to every variety and every period of life. Therefore, instead of hanging the understanding of a woman upon walls, or hearing it vibrate upon strings, – instead of seeing it in clouds or hearing it in the wind, we would make it the first spring and ornament of society, by enriching it with attainments upon which alone such power depends."

It is very likely that Eliza would have read *The Edinburgh Review* as it was one of the major literary publications of the time. The above piece of course reminds us of the following passage from *Pride and Prejudice*:

"'It is amazing to me,' said Bingley, 'how young ladies can have patience to be so very accomplished as they all are.'

'All young ladies accomplished! My dear Charles, what do you mean?'

'Yes, all of them, I think. They all paint tables, cover screens, and net purses. I scarcely know anyone who cannot do all this, and I am sure I never heard a young lady spoken of for the first time, without being informed that she was very accomplished.'

'Your list of the common extent of accomplishments,' said Darcy, 'has too much truth. The word is applied to many a woman who deserves it no otherwise than by netting a purse or covering a screen. But I am very far from agreeing with you in your estimation of ladies in general. I cannot boast of knowing more than half-a-dozen, in the whole range of my acquaintance, that are really accomplished.'

'Nor I, I am sure,' said Miss Bingley.

'Then,' observed Elizabeth, 'you must comprehend a great deal in your idea of an accomplished woman.'

'Yes, I do comprehend a great deal in it.'

'Oh! certainly,' cried his faithful assistant, 'no one can be really esteemed accomplished who does not greatly surpass what is usually met with. A woman must have a thorough knowledge of music, singing, drawing, dancing, and the modern languages, to deserve the word; and besides all this, she must possess a certain something in her air and manner of walking, the tone of her voice, her address and expressions, or the word will be but half-deserved.'

'All this she must possess,' added Darcy, 'and to all this she must yet add something more substantial, in the improvement of her mind by extensive reading.'

'I am no longer surprised at your knowing only six accomplished women. I rather wonder now at your knowing any.'

'Are you so severe upon your own sex as to doubt the possibility of all this?'

'I never saw such a woman. I never saw such capacity, and taste, and application, and elegance, as you describe united.'"

Memoirs of Modern Philosophers reflects Eliza's anti-Jacobin and somewhat conservative view of society. It also reflects her rejection of modern philosophers, such as Godwin, in favour of putting into practice the practical teachings of the Bible and especially the New Testament. Socially she was conservative and believed strongly in marriage, even if her own experience of the institution had not been entirely happy.

31.

Conclusion

Dopo l'orrore d'un Ciel turbato
Più vago e bello appare il dì

When once the storm and dark is blown away
More beautiful and lovely shines the day

(Handel, Ottone)

We have grown accustomed to the myth of Jane Austen, the spinster, writing her delicately crafted portraits of provincial families on her little piece of ivory, turning out "little gems" of Georgette Heyer-esque romance for the edification of middle-aged, middle-brow women. This is Austen for American quilters, English muffin eaters, National Trust visitors, tea towel collectors. Then we have had the revolt of the academics, reassessing Jane Austen; behind the respectable pince-nez there lurked a savage sarcastic mind, ready to coruscate the follies of the age and its patriarchal brutalities, poking fun at masculine pretensions, yet at the same time unforgivably skating over the social realities of the slave trade and the Napoleonic wars. Lately we have seen the emergence of chick-flick Austen; the swooning over her heroes and the fantasising of the Bridget Jones generation. Recently, in a bizarre further twist, writers and film makers have started to concentrate on inventing a complex love life for Jane Austen where none existed, "as the writer of such novels of passion must have experienced love in her own life."

How are these outlooks on *Jane Austen* changed by the realisation that it was her cousin Eliza who wrote these novels? Does it make the books themselves easier to like if we know that the author was writing from experience and had led a full and satisfying life (including a full and satisfying sex life)? As far as sexual matters are concerned, *Jane Austen* has a completely unjustified reputation as a prude, perhaps because it was believed the author was unmarried and had remained a virgin. Although it is true of the author, as Henry Austen wrote in his *Biographical Notice of the Author* prefacing *Northanger Abbey* that "without the slightest affectation she recoiled from everything gross", this does not detract from the fact that sexual attraction is the central theme of all her novels. Her attitude to sex would probably be summed up in the poem by the German humorist, Wilhelm Busch, "Pst!":

Es gibt ja leider Sachen und Geschichten,
Die reizend und pikant,
Nur werden sie von Tanten und von Nichten
Niemals genannt.

Verehrter Freund, so sei denn nicht vermessen,
Sei zart und schweig auch du.
Bedenk: Man liebt den Käse wohl, indessen
Man deckt ihn zu.

There are things and stories in this world
To shock us and entrance
But never are they mentioned
By nieces or by aunts

My dearest friend, don't be so bold
Stay quiet as a pup
It doesn't mean you don't love cheese
If you keep it covered up.

The reader's enjoyment of *Jane Austen* is not improved by the knowledge that Eliza was the author, but the reader's understanding of the text is. We are none the happier, but we are better informed. Perhaps no author has been so defined by her sex as has *Jane Austen*. Any admiration society will be found to be preponderantly made up of women. This is very ironic, as Eliza herself, as an heiress of independent means with intellectual pursuits, all but led the life of an eighteenth century gentleman. As a man writing about *Jane Austen* one has the feeling of "encroaching" on female territory, that there is something not quite right about a man enjoying these novels. This "feminisation" of *Jane Austen* has of course devalued the novels no end. Being a woman and writing on themes of love, *Jane Austen* suffers an awful lot of criticism about the simplicity of the plots of her novels.

We also have to reassess *Jane Austen* as being a "one trick pony", only capable of writing the same kind of books, romances based on the middle class society of the time. It has been said of the novels of *Jane Austen* that they all have the same story, it is only the names of the houses that change. The works of *Elizabeth Hamilton* display a more direct satirical polemic, a steady Christian faith, and an interest in politics; the novels of *Fanny Burney* demonstrate a more youthful but less genteel side of the author's nature. What has been most surprising to myself is that some of the plays of *Fanny Burney* show Eliza to have been an extremely accomplished playwright, whose plays deserve to be in the repertoire. It is likely that we are dealing with a prolific author for whom the works of *Jane Austen* were just one aspect of her oeuvre. We are dealing with a master of prose, capable of writing in any genre.

One major result of my book that would give me great pleasure would be for more people to read the novels of *Fanny Burney* (apart from *The Wanderer!*) which I believe are a treasure house and will give them as much pleasure as those written under the name of *Jane Austen*. In spite of their length, they are very easy to read. Readers would also greatly enjoy the humour of *Elizabeth Hamilton's*

Translations of the Letters of a Hindoo Rajah. Critics satisfied with the existing *Jane Austen* novels will now have to cope with the reassessment of the author's additional works under the names of *Fanny Burney* and *Elizabeth Hamilton* and how these fit in with our view of the author. In view of Eliza's use of these pseudonyms, it would also be highly unlikely that she did not use others. Critics have always thought of *Jane Austen* as a writer of few books, whereas I have a suspicion, in view of the apparent freedom with which she wrote, that Eliza was an extremely prolific author. We may have to totally re-evaluate the history of late eighteenth and early nineteenth century fiction, as there is a very real possibility that some other names, maybe even some "great names" of the period were merely pseudonyms for Eliza. It is highly likely that such an accomplished writer would have written in several different genres, each requiring a different pseudonym.

There is interesting evidence to back up the use of pseudonyms at that time, in the Introduction to Sir Walter Scott's *Ivanhoe*, published in 1820. The author here endorses the belief I have expressed above, that a great writer would not confine himself to one genre:

> "Nothing can be more dangerous for the fame of a professor of the fine arts, than to permit (if he can possibly prevent it) the character of a mannerist to be attached to him, or that he [be] supposed capable of success only in a particular and limited style. The public are, in general, very ready to adopt the opinion, that he who has pleased them in one peculiar mode of composition, is, by means of that very talent, rendered incapable of venturing upon other subjects. The effect of this disinclination, on the part of the public, towards the artificers of their pleasures, when they attempt to enlarge their means of amusing, may be seen in the censures usually passed by vulgar criticism upon actors or artists who venture to change the character of their

efforts, that, in so doing, they may enlarge the scale of their art.

There is some justice in this opinion, as there always is in such as attain general currency. It may often happen on the stage, that an actor, by possessing in a pre-eminent degree the external qualities necessary to give effect to comedy, may be deprived of the right to aspire to tragic excellence; and in painting or literary composition, an artist or poet may be master exclusively of modes of thought, and powers of expression, which confine him to a single course of subjects. But much more frequently the same capacity which carries a man to popularity in one department will obtain for him success in another, and that must be more particularly the case in literary composition, than either in acting or painting, because the adventurer in that department is not impeded in his exertions by any particularity of features, or confirmation of person, proper for particular parts, or, by any peculiar mechanical habits of using the pencil, limited to a particular class of subjects."

What is more interesting is that, in the same Introduction, Sir Walter Scott proposes that an author writing in different genres should use different pseudonyms for each. After completing the set of novels known as the "Waverley novels" (the first of them was *Waverley*), which were all set in Scotland, the author changed subject matter and wrote *Ivanhoe*, a historical novel set in England, and decided, as the subject matter was different, that he should publish it under a different name:

"It is not, perhaps, necessary to enumerate so many reasons why the author of the Scottish Novels, as they were then exclusively termed, should be desirous to make an experiment on a subject purely English. It was his purpose, at the same time, to have rendered the experiment as complete as possible, by bringing the intended work before the public as the effort of a new candidate for their favour, in order that no degree of prejudice, whether favourable or the reverse, might attach to it, as a new production of the author of Waverley."

As I have shown, *Jane Austen* was a much more learned author than has been admitted to date, being educated in Latin and Greek and completely fluent in the French language. As a result, respect for her literary status, especially among the general population of men, has not been as great as it has deserved to be. The fact that she wears her learning lightly is all the more indicative of her huge intellect. The authorship of Eliza Austen tends to confirm what common sense would indicate to us, that great works of literature are produced by people of a very high intellect with very original minds and a very high standard of education. If we view *Jane Austen's* novels as the creation of Eliza Austen, we look at the author aright, as writing from the sphere of intellectual society. The world of Eliza Austen is the world of judges and thinkers such as Lord Mansfield and Sir William Jones, the world of poets such as Pope and Cowper, the world of writers such as Dr Johnson and Goethe, the world of the composers Mozart and Handel.

No doubt Eliza Austen inherited her extremely high intelligence and originality from her remarkable father, Warren Hastings, who was undoubtedly one of the most educated, intelligent and learned people in eighteenth century England and who, on his retirement, devoted himself entirely to reading and writing literature. After studying the life of Eliza Austen we find that at the centre of her life was the enigmatic character of Warren Hastings. It was the fact of Eliza's illegitimacy which was a disgrace to the Austen family and which they were determined to cover up after Eliza's death, and for which the myth of Jane Austen's authorship was invented at that time. Warren Hastings' love as her father remained, however, an unattainable ideal for Eliza.

Bibliography

Auerbach, Emily – *Searching for Jane Austen* – University of Wisconsin Press, 2004

Austen, Caroline – *My Aunt, Jane Austen: a Memoir*, Jane Austen Society, 1952

Austen, Henry – *Biographical Notice of the Author* – prefaced to Northanger Abbey – John Murray, 1818

Austen, Henry – *Memoir of Miss Austen* – prefaced to *Sense and Sensibility* – London, Richard Bentley, 1833

Austen, James – *To Miss Jane Austen the reputed Author of "Sense and Sensibility"* – By kind permission of David Gilson and the Provost and scholars of King's College, Cambridge

Austen, James – *Venta Within Thy Sacred Fane* – By permission of the Warden and Scholars of Winchester College

Austen, James et al. – *The Loiterer* – London, 1789-90

Austen, Jane – *Emma* – Penguin Classics, 1966

Austen, Jane – *Mansfield Park* – Everyman's Library, 1906

Austen, Jane – *Mansfield Park* – Fontana, 1983

Austen, Jane – *Mansfield Park* – Wordsworth Editions Limited, 1992

Austen, Jane – *The Minor Works*, vol. 6 of *The Works of Jane Austen*, ed. R.W. Chapman (Oxford: Clarendon Press, 1954)

Austen, Jane – *Northanger Abbey* – Everyman's Library, 1906

Austen, Jane – *Persuasion* – Everyman's Library, 1906

Austen, Jane – *Pride and Prejudice* – Everyman's Library, 1906

Austen, Jane – *Pride and Prejudice* – Penguin Classics, 1966

Austen, Jane – *Sanditon and Other Stories* – Everyman's Library, 1996

Austen, Jane – *Sense and Sensibility* – Everyman's Library, 1906

Austen, Jane, edited Deirdre Le Faye – *Jane Austen's Letters* – Oxford Paperbacks, 3rd edition, 1997

Austen, Jane – *Letters of Jane Austen: selected from the compilation of her Great Nephew, Lord Brabourne* – Roberts Bros, 1892

Austen-Leigh, James Edward – *A Memoir of Jane Austen* – Oxford University Press, 2002

Austen-Leigh, Richard – *Austen Papers, 1704-1856* – London, 1942 reprinted Routledge/Thoemmes 1995

Barbauld, Anna Letitia – *The British Novelists* – vol. 38 (London, 1810) i-iii

Banerjee, Jacqueline – *Literary Surrey* – John Owen Smith, 2005

Barrett, Charlotte – *Diary and Letters of Madame d'Arblay* – Henry Colburn, 1842-46

Beechey, Henry William – *The Literary Works of Sir Joshua Reynolds: first President of the Royal Academy* – Henry G Bohn, London 1852

Bence-Jones, Mark – *Clive of India* – Constable, London 1974

Benger, Elizabeth – *Memoirs of the late Mrs. Elizabeth Hamilton* – London: Longman, Hurst, Rees, Orme and Brown, 1818

Bernstein, Jeremy – *Dawning of the Raj: The Life & Trials of Warren Hastings* – Aurum Press Ltd, 2001

Blanc, Olivier Blanc and Sheridan, A – *Last Letters: Prisons and Prisoners of the French Revolution* – Farrar Straus & Giroux (T), August 1987

Brandon, Peter – *A History of Surrey* – Phillimore & Co. Ltd © Peter Brandon, 1998

British Library – Oriental and India Office Collections/Madras Dispatches/E/4/864/S.452f.

British Library – The Warren Hastings Papers

Burney, Dr Charles, from his memorandum book, quoted in *The Atheneum*, 1832, by James Silk Buckingham, page 739

Burney, Fanny – *A Busy Day* (adapted by Alan Coveney) – Oberon Books Ltd, 2000

Burney, Fanny – *Camilla* – Oxford World's Classics, Oxford University Press, 1999

Burney, Fanny – *Cecilia* – Virago Press, 1986

Burney, Fanny – *The Early Journals and Letters of Fanny Burney, edited by Lars E Troide and Stewart J Cooke* – 3 volumes. Oxford [Oxfordshire] Clarendon Press, Oxford; New York: Oxford University Press, 1987-94

Burney, Fanny – *The Journals and Letters of Fanny Burney*, edited by Joyce Hemlow, Curtis D Cecil, Althea Douglas, Patricia Boutilier, Edward A Bloom, Lillian D Bloom, Peter Hughes, Patricia Hawkins and Warren Derry. 12 volumes – Oxford: Clarendon Press, 1972-84

Burney, Frances – *Evelina* – Penguin Classics, 1994

Burney, Frances – *Evelina* – W.W. Norton & Company, Inc. , 1998

Burney, Frances – *Journals and Letters* – Penguin Classics, 2001

Burney, Fanny – *The Wanderer* – The World's Classics – Oxford University Press, 1991 Excerpt (187 words) from Introduction by Doody MA from *The Wanderer* by Burney F (1991) by permission of Oxford University Press

Burney, Frances – *The Witlings* and *The Woman Hater* – Broadview Press Ltd, 2002

Burney, Frances – *The Complete Plays of Frances Burney* – Pickering & Chatto (Publishers) Limited, London, 1995

Burrell, Lady Sophia – *Poems* – London, Leigh & Sotheby, 1793

Busch, Wilhelm – *Zu guter Letzt* – Munchen: Bassermann, 1904

Butler, Samuel – *The Way of All Flesh* – 1903

Caplan, Clive – *The Source for Emma's William Larkins* – Jane Austen Society of North America magazine *Persuasions: The Jane Austen Journal* vol. 21, no. 2, (Summer 2000)

Cecil, Lord David – *A Portrait of Jane Austen* – London, Book Club Associates, 1978

Chisholm, Kate – *from Fanny Burney: Her Life 1752-1840* by Kate Chisholm, published by Chatto & Windus. Reprinted by permission of The Random House Group Limited

Church, Alfred John and Brodribb, William Jackson – *Tacitus* – London Macmillan, 1882

Croker, John Wilson – *Review of The Wanderer, by Frances Burney* – *Quarterly Review* 11, April 1814, 123-4

d'Arblay, Madame – *Memoirs of Doctor Burney* – Edward Moxon, 1832

De Alemeida, Hermione and Gilpin, George H – *Indian Renaissance: British Romantic Art and the Prospect of India* – Ashgate Publishing, 2006

DeForest, Mary – *Jane Austen: Closet Classicist* – Jane Austen Society of North America magazine *Persuasions: The Jane Austen Journal* vol. 22, 2000

de Feuillide, Eliza – *Letters to Phylly Walter*; originals in Austen-Leigh family archive, with microfilm copies in Hampshire Record Office; part-published in *Austen Papers*. One letter owned by the Jane Austen Memorial Trust, Chawton

Derry, Stephen – *The Two Georgianas: The Duchess of Devonshire and Jane Austen's Miss Darcy* – Jane Austen Society of North America magazine *Persuasions: The Jane Austen Journal* #11, 1989, pp. 15-16

Devert, Michel – *La Dame du Marais de Gabarret et de Barbotan, Eliz Capot de Feuillide, 1761-1813* – *Bulletin de la Société de Borda* No 411, 1998

Dillon, Brian – *Circumventing the Biographical Subject: Jane Austen and the Critics* – *Rocky Mountain Review of Language and Literature* Vol. 46, No. 4 (1992), pp. 213-21 (article consists of nine pages). Published by: Rocky Mountain Modern Language Association Stable URL: http://www.jstor.org/stable/1347131

Dobson, Austin – *Essay on Fanny Burney* – London, MacMillan & Co 1903

Donovan, Robert Alan – *The Mind of Jane Austen* – *Jane Austen Today*. Ed. Joel Weinsheimer. Athens: U of Georgia P, 1975. 109-27.

Ennos, Dr Roland – *Statistical and Data Handling Skills in Biology* – Prentice Hall, 2nd edition, 13 December 2006

l'Estrange, Reverend A G (ed.) – *A Life of Mary Russell Mitford, related in a selection of letters to her friends* – London, 1870

Farrant, John H – *The Family Circle and Career of William Burrell, antiquary* – Sussex Archaeological Collections 139, 2001 (169-185)

Fergus, Jan – *The Professional Woman Writer* – from *Cambridge Companion to Jane Austen* – Ed. Edward Copeland and Juliet McMaster – © Cambridge University Press, 1997, reproduced with permission

Fleming, Lindsay – *Sanditon and Bognor* – from *The Jane Austen Society Report for the Year 1960*

Flynn, Carol Houlihan – *The Letters* – from *Cambridge Companion to Jane Austen* – Ed. Edward Copeland and Juliet McMaster – © Cambridge University Press, 1997, reproduced with permission

Forster, E. M. *Miss Austen and Jane Austen* – *TLS* (10 November 1932) 821-22. Rpt. in "Jane Austen." *Abinger Harvest*. New York: Harcourt, 1936. 148-64. Ext. *NCE 2*. 359-65.

Franckfurter Staats-Ristretto, Frankfurt am Main 1772-1818

Garrod, H. W. – *Jane Austen: A Depreciation* – Lecture, Royal Society of Literature, 1928. *Essays by Divers Hands. Transactions of the Royal Society of Literature*, NS 8. London: Oxford UP, 1928. 21-40

GENUKI: *Baslow, Derbyshire* – *Golden Gates for the Duke, or Baslow in the 1820s*
www.genuki.org.uk/big/eng/DBY/Baslow/Baslow1820s.html

Germanisches Nationalmuseem – Archiv – Bestand Schloβarchiv Imhoff-Hohenstein

Abt. Familiensachen, Fasz. 32 (letters of Christoph Adam Carl von Imhoff and Louisa von Imhoff)

Green, Georgina – *Sir Charles Raymond of Valentines*

Green, Georgina – *Lady Sophia Burrell (1753 – 1802)*

Greene, Donald (1988) – *The Original of Pemberley* – Eighteenth-Century Fiction: Vol. 1, Iss. 1, Article 2. Available at: http://digitalcommons.mcmaster.ca/ecf/vol1/iss1/2

Greene, Donald – *Pemberley Revisited* – Pages 12, 14 in the Jane Austen Society of North America magazine *Persuasions: The Jane Austen Journal* #1, 1979

Grier, Sidney C – *The Letters of Warren Hastings to his Wife* – William Blackwood and Sons, Edinburgh and London, 1905

Goldsmith, Oliver – *History of England* – 1764

Halperin, John – *Inside Pride and Prejudice* – Jane Austen Society of North America magazine *Persuasions: The Jane Austen Journal* #11, 1989, pages 37-45

Hamilton, Elizabeth – *Memoirs of Modern Philosphers*, edited Claire Grogan – Broadview Press Ltd, 2000

Hamilton, Elizabeth – *Translations of the Letters of a Hindoo Rajah*, edited Pamela Perkins and Shannon Russell – Broadview Press, 1999

Hancock, Tysoe Saul – *Letterbook*, preserved among the Hastings Papers, British Library Add MS 29,236. Part-published in *Austen Papers*

Harman, Claire – *Fanny Burney, A Biography* – Reprinted by permission of HarperCollins Publishers Ltd. © (Claire Harman) (2000)

Hastings, Warren – *Hastings Papers* – British Library: letters, accounts, diaries – Add MS 29,125 – 41,608

Hawkridge, Audrey – *Jane Austen and Hampshire* – Hampshire County Council, 1995

Honan, Park – *Jane Austen, Her Life* – George Weidenfeld & Nicolson Ltd, 1987

Howard, Maurice – *The Vyne, Hampshire* – The National Trust, 2002

Hughes, Charles, contrib.. by Hester Lynch Piozzi – *Mrs. Piozzi's Thraliana: With Numerous Extracts Hitherto Unpublished* (London: Simpkin, Marshall, Hamilton, Kent and Co., 1913),

von Imhoff, Christoph Adam Carl, edited by Gerard Koch – *Imhoff Indienfahrer: Ein Reisebericht aus dem 18. Jahrhundert in Briefen und Bildern* – Wallstein Verlag, Goettingen, 2001

Jenkins, Elizabeth – *Birth of a Legend* – from *The Jane Austen Society Report for the Year 1965*

King, Gaye – *The Jane Austen Connection* – from *Stoneleigh Abbey The House, Its Owners, Its Lands* – published in 2004 by Stoneleigh Abbey Limited in association with The Shakespeare Birthplace Trust

Knatchbull, Lady (Fanny Knight) – *Diaries 1804-72* – Centre for Kentish Studies, Maidstone

Lane, Maggie – *Jane Austen's World* – Carlton Books Ltd 1996

Lane, Maggie – *Fanny Burney: Jane Austen's literary Godmother* – *Jane Austen's Regency World* Issue 17, September/October 2005

Laski, Marghanita – *Jane Austen* – Thames and Hudson, 1969 and 1975

Leavis, Q D – *The Watsons and Emma* – Scrutiny, 10 (1941-42)

Le Faye, Deirdre – *Jane Austen and her Hancock Relatives* – *The Review of English Studies*, New Series, Vol.30, No. 117 (Feb., 1979), pp. 12-27 – Oxford University Press

Le Faye, Deirdre – *Jane Austen's Outlandish Cousin: The Life and Letters of Eliza de Feuillide* – The British Library, London, 2002

Le Faye, Deirdre – *Jane Austen: The World of her Novels* – © Frances Lincoln Ltd, 2002

Le Faye, Deirdre – *A Family Record* – Cambridge University Press, 1989:2004

Lewes, George Henry – *The Novels of Jane Austen* – *Littell's Living Age* 62 (1859), 424-436 [*Blackwood's Edinburgh Magazine* 86 (1859) 99-113] [Gilson M106]

Lewes, George Henry – *The Lady Novelists* – *Westminster Review*, 58 (July 1852), 134

Macaulay, Thomas Babington – *The Diary and Letters of Mme D'Arblay* – Edinburgh Review, 76, January 1843, pp 561-2

Macaulay, Thomas Babington – *Essay on Madame d'Arblay* – 1843

Milward, Richard – *The Tombstone Inscriptions at Hampstead to 21.11.1881.* London Borough of Camden Central Library

Myer, Valerie Grosvenor – *Jane Austen, Obstinate Heart* – Michael O'Mara Books Ltd, 1997

Nair, P Thankappan – *Echoes from Belvedere: Home of the National Library, Kolkata* – Associated Book Agency, Kolkata, 2004

National Portrait Gallery, London – *A File of Correspondence between R W Chapman and Henry Hake*, 1932-48

Nicolson, Harold. Rev. of *Jane Austen's Letters to Her Sister Cassandra and Others*. Ed. R. W. Chapman. *New Statesman* (1932): 659.

Nicolson, Nigel – *The World of Jane Austen* – George Weidenfeld and Nicolson, 1991

Nokes, David – *Jane Austen – A Life* – Fourth Estate Ltd, 1997

Piggott, Patrick – *The Innocent Diversion: a study of music in the life and writings of Jane Austen* – Douglas Cleverdon, London, 1979

Pinion, F B – *A Jane Austen Companion* – The MacMillan Press Ltd, 1973

von la Roche, Sophie – *Tagebuch einer Reise durch Holland und England von der Verfasserin von Rosaliens Briefen* – Offenbach/Main 1788

Rogers, Pat – *Sposi in Surrey: Links between Jane Austen and Fanny Burney* – *Times Literary Supplement*, 4873, 23 August 1996

Scott, Sir Walter – *Ivanhoe* – Everyman's Library, edited by Ernest Rhys, 1906

Selwyn, David – *The Poetry of Jane Austen and the Austen family* – University of Iowa Press, 1997

Shields, Carol – *Jane Austen*, Weidenfeld & Nicholson 2001

Smith, Dr Kenneth – *The Probable Location of "Longbourn" in Jane Austen's Pride and Prejudice* – Jane Austen Society of North America magazine *Persuasions: The Jane Austen Journal* #27

Smith, Sydney – *The Selected Writings of Sydney Smith,* ed. with an introduction by W.H. Auden. New York: Farrar, Straus and Cudahy, 1956.

Southam, Brian – *Jane Austen's Literary Manuscripts* – The Athlone Press, 2001

Spence, Jon – *Becoming Jane Austen* – Hambledon and London, 2003, Continuum, an imprint of Bloomsbury Publishing Plc.

Spenser, Edmund – *The Faerie Queene* – Penguin Classics, 1987

Stepankowsky, Paula L – *British Library Newspaper Library News* No. 28 Summer 2000

Stepankowsky, Paula L – *British Library Newspaper Library News* No. 30 Summer 2001

Sutherland, J & Le Faye, D – *So You Think you know Jane Austen* – Oxford University Press, 2005

Tomalin, Claire: *Jane Austen – a Life* – © Viking, 1997 – Reproduced by permission of Penguin Books Ltd – pages 18-19, 54, 124, 252

Tucker, George Holbert – *Jane Austen, The Woman* – St Martin's Press

Inc., 1994 reproduced with permission of Palgrave Macmillan

von Straβburg, Gottfried, edited A T Hatto – *Tristan* – Penguin Classics, 1960

von Straβburg, Gottfried – *Tristan* – Philipp Reclam jun. GmbH & Co., Stuttgart, 1980, 1983

Wilks, Brian – *The Life and Times of Jane Austen* – Hamlyn, 1978

Willoughby, Rupert – *Sherborne St John & The Vyne in the time of Jane Austen*, Rupert Willoughby 2002.

Wolfson, Susan J, Princeton Univerity – *Boxing Emma; or the Reader's Dilemma at the Box Hill Games* – *Romantic Circles Praxis Series* (www.rc.umd.edu/praxis/boxhill/wolfson/wolfson.html

Woolf, Virginia – *The Common Reader* – First Series. New York: Harcourt, 1925

Index